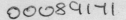

ABOUT FRIEL: The Playwright

Tony Coult is a teacher and playwright.

Series Editor: Philip Roberts is Professor of Drama and Theatre Studies, and Director of the Workshop Theatre, at the University of Leeds. Educated at Oxford and Edinburgh, he held posts in the Universities of Newcastle and Sheffield before arriving in Leeds in 1998. His publications include: *Absalom and Achitophel and Other Poems* (Collins, 1973), *The Diary of Sir David Hamilton, 1709–1714* (Clarendon Press, 1975), *Edward Bond: A Companion to the Plays* (Theatre Quarterly Pubs., 1978), *Edward Bond: Theatre Poems and Songs* (Methuen, 1978), *Bond on File* (Methuen, 1985), *The Royal Court Theatre, 1965–1972* (Routledge, 1986), *Plays without Wires* (Sheffield Academic Press, 1989), *The Royal Court Theatre and the Modern Stage* (CUP, 1999).

Associate Editor: Richard Boon is Professor of Performance Studies at the University of Leeds. He is the author of a number of studies of modern British political theatre, including *Brenton the Playwright* (Methuen, 1991), and is also co-editor of *Theatre Matters: Performance and Culture on the World Stage* (CUP, 1998).

ABOUT FRIEL

The Playwright and the Work

Tony Coult

faber and faber

First published in 2003
by Faber and Faber Limited
3 Queen Square London WC1N 3AU
Published in the United States by Faber and Faber Inc.
an affiliate of Farrar, Straus and Giroux LLC, New York

Typeset by Faber and Faber Limited
Printed in England by Bookmarque Ltd, Croydon

A CIP record for this book
is available from the British Library

ISBN 0–571–20164–4

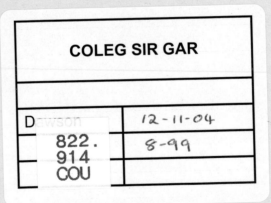
2 4 6 8 10 9 7 5 3 1

This book is dedicated to:
Sue Colgrave, Jonathan Martin, Annie Tyson –
'The Rose Bruford Three'.

Contents

Editors' Note

There are few theatre books which allow direct access to the playwright or to those whose business it is to translate the script into performance. These volumes aim to deal directly with the writer and with other theatre workers (directors, actors, designers and similar figures) who realize in performance the words on the page.

The subjects of the series are some of the most important and influential writers from post-war British and Irish theatre. Each volume contains an introduction which sets the work of the writer in the relevant historical, social and political context, followed by a digest of interviews and other material which allows the writer, in his own words, to trace his evolution as a dramatist. Some of this material is new, as is, in large part, the material especially gathered from the writers' collaborators and fellow theatre workers. The volumes conclude with annotated bibliographies. In all, we hope the books will provide a wealth of information in accessible form, and real insight into some of the major dramatists of our day.

Chronology

1950   Brian Friel begins writing short stories.

1958   First radio plays produced by BBC Belfast.

1959   Regular contributor to *The New Yorker*.

  –   *A Doubtful Paradise*, first stage-play, at the Ulster Group Theatre, Belfast.

1962   *The Enemy Within*, Abbey Theatre (then at the Queen's), Dublin.

  –   First collection of short stories, *The Saucer of Larks*.

1963   Spends six months with Tyrone Guthrie at the new Guthrie Theater, Minneapolis.

1964   *Philadelphia, Here I Come!*, Gaiety Theatre, Dublin; Helen Hayes Theater, New York, 1965; Lyric Theatre, London, 1967.

1966   Second collection of short stories, *The Gold in the Sea*.

  –   *The Loves of Cass McGuire*, Helen Hayes Theater, New York; Abbey Theatre, Dublin, 1967.

1967   *Lovers*, Gate Theatre, Dublin; Lincoln Center, New York, 1968; Fortune Theatre, London, 1968.

1968   *Crystal and Fox*, Gaiety Theatre, Dublin; Mark Taper Forum, Los Angeles.

1969   *The Mundy Scheme*, Olympia Theatre, Dublin; Royale Theater, New York.

1971   *The Gentle Island*, Olympia Theatre, Dublin; Peacock Theatre, Dublin, 1989.

1973   *The Freedom of the City*, Royal Court Theatre, London; Abbey Theatre, Dublin; Alvin Theater, New York, 1974.

1975   *Volunteers*, Abbey Theatre, Dublin.

1977   *Living Quarters*, Abbey Theatre, Dublin.

1979   *Aristocrats*, Abbey Theatre, Dublin; Hampstead
          Theatre, London, 1988; Manhattan Theater Club,
          New York; Abbey Theatre, Dublin.

   –   *Faith Healer*, Longacre Theater, New York; Abbey
          Theater, Dublin, 1980; Royal Court Theatre,
          London, 1981.

1980   Co-founder of Field Day Theatre Company.

   –   *Translations* opens in Derry; Hampstead Theatre
          and the National Theatre, London, 1981; Manhattan
          Theater Club, New York, 1981.

1981   His translation of Chekhov's *Three Sisters* opens in
          Derry; Chichester, 2000.

   –   Ewart-Biggs Prize.

   –   American-Irish Foundation Literary Award.

1982   *The Communication Cord* opens in Derry;
          Hampstead Theatre, London, 1983.

1983   Doctor of Letters, National University of Ireland.

1986   Editor of *The Last of the Name*.

1987   Adaptation of Turgenev's novel *Fathers and Sons*,
          Royal National Theatre, London; Long Wharf
          Theater, USA; Gate Theatre, Dublin, 1988.

1988   *Making History* opens in Derry; Royal National
          Theatre, London; Gaiety Theatre, Dublin.

   –   Doctor of Letters, University of Ulster.

1989   BBC Radio devotes a six-play season to Friel.

   –   *Sunday Independent* / Irish Life Arts Award for
          Theatre.

1990   *Dancing at Lughnasa*, Abbey Theatre, Dublin; Royal
          National Theatre, London.

1991   *Dancing at Lughnasa*, Phoenix Theatre, London, and
          Plymouth Theater, New York, wins Tony Awards for
          Best Play, Best Director and Best Supporting Actress.

1992   *A Month in the Country*, Gate Theatre, Dublin.

1993   *Wonderful Tennessee*, Abbey Theatre, Dublin;
          Plymouth Theatre, New York.

- *Dancing at Lughnasa*, Abbey Theatre national tour, Australian tour.
1994 *Molly Sweeney*, Gate Theatre, Dublin; Almeida Theatre, London; Roundabout Theater, New York, 1996.
1997 *Give Me Your Answer, Do!*, Abbey Theatre, Dublin.
1998 *Give Me Your Answer, Do!*, Hampstead Theatre, London; Roundabout Theater, New York, 1996.
- Friel's version of Chekhov's *Uncle Vanya*, Gate Theatre, Dublin; revived Donmar Warehouse, London, 2002; transferred BAM, New York, 2003.
- Film of *Dancing at Lughnasa*, screenplay by Frank McGuinness, is released.
1999 Lifetime Achievement Arts Award on the occasion of his seventieth birthday.
- Friel Festival: including *The Freedom of the City* and *Dancing at Lughnasa* at the Abbey Theatre, *Living Quarters* and *Making History* at the Peacock Theatre (all National Theatre productions), *Aristocrats* at the Gate Theatre, the Royal Shakespeare Company's production of *A Month in the Country* at the Gaiety Theatre and *Lovers*, *Winners and Losers* at Andrew's Lane Theatre, all in Dublin; and *Give Me Your Answer, Do!* at the Lyric Theatre, Belfast. Other events included *Brian Friel – A Celebration* at the National Library, Dublin, an exhibition of letters, playscripts, photographs and posters presented by the National Theatre Literary Department and Archive in association with the National Library of Ireland.
2002 *Two Plays After* (*The Bear* and *Afterplay*), Gate Theatre, Dublin; *The Yalta Game* (as part of *Three Plays*), Gate Theatre, Dublin. *Afterplay*, Gielgud Theatre, London.

Introduction

Dancing with Brian Friel! by Paul Durcan
To Brian Friel on his 70th birthday

Dancing with Brian Friel!
Who lives in that part of the South of Ireland
Which is more northerly than the North;
Who lives far away up in the South –
In the South that's far north of the North;
In County Donegal;
On the Inishowen Peninsula;
Who knows every millimetre of the road between
    Muff and Aught:
'The North Road to the deep South'
By Brian Friel
Life begins at seventy!
The all-clear of death
Being sounded far out to sea
Beyond Tory and beyond
On a single key of black ivory with one blind young
    lady's pink little finger.

A writer whose work is as rich in resonances and ideas as Friel's justifiably attracts a sometimes daunting scaffolding of critical and academic commentary. This book sets out to distil some of this excellent work into more manageable form. What has been fascinating to me has been how much of the best commentary on Friel has been from other artists – actors, directors, poets and playwrights. This may be because Irish culture still retains traces of the old scholar-poet, the bardic Man of Art, who, centuries before Christ, folded together the analytic and the creative.

Friel is a properly rigorous artist who scorns the idea that personality is relevant to understanding his work, and views mere biography as vulgarity. If this book sometimes appears to stray from that piety (one of his favourite barbs), it is because I have tried to show how the historical stream in which he has lived his life both feeds his work and is changed by his work. Like the bards of old, he speaks to and from his community.

An important emphasis of this book has been to give voice to some of Friel's artistic collaborators in the necessarily shared activity of theatre-making. Here, actors, designers, directors and other enablers of his work offer their insights and recollections. Of course, there is one grouping of collaborators largely absent from this book: the audience. Any play's meanings and feelings are embryonic in scripts and are given birth in rehearsals; but it is in performance that they mature and fully justify their existence. I hope, therefore, that readers never imagine that reading scripts (worse still, reading books about them) can ever substitute for experiencing the plays in performance. Happily, Friel's work is rapidly gaining a wider and wider audience as these words are processed and opportunities to see it are growing.

Friel's Roots

No play – and no writer, collaborator or audience – exists outside the complex web of dynamic connections that make up a society's history. Art tends to function like a seismograph, sensitive to the huge shifts in social and political life that are daily in motion beneath our feet. The political and cultural entity of Ireland, in all its configurations, has felt these tremors more acutely than many, and Brian Friel has acted as an artist must by transforming the vaguely felt and partly understood into the felt images and actions of theatre.

Early Gaelic culture

Gaelic society, the soil that has nurtured so much of Ireland's culture and writing, effectively begins several centuries before Christ when the Gaels, a European branch of the Celts, arrived in Ireland. For all the stereotype of the warlike and fractious Celt, this newfounded society was relatively stable. One of its defining characteristics was the absolute importance of the Artist in the way that society was governed and functioned. In the hierarchy of each tribe, the King was leader, supported by a warrior caste – the Military. Next came a stratum of society known collectively as Men of Art – what we might call an intelligentsia – lawmakers, healers, skilled makers and story-tellers. It was this latter group that acted as both the custodians of the myths and legends of the tribe, and also as elaborators and inventors of new stories. Their task was to fix the achievements of the leadership in popular imagination and thereby to create a stable society. On the other hand, they would attack the tribe's enemies with scorn and satire and were even credited with the ability to kill their enemies with well-turned curses. Assassination by poetry . . .

What also distinguished the story-tellers was their cross-border acceptability. Whereas ordinary members of the opposing tribes' armies would be attacked at border crossings, the story-teller was invariably allowed free passage. There seems to have been an instinctive sense that the artist, as both educator and entertainer, had a necessary role in preserving the past and creating the future. Centuries later, the subject of this book, Brian Friel, was to reactivate precisely this free-ranging and cohering political role for the story-teller in his creation, with other artists and scholars, of the collective Field Day, in the midst of the tension and insecurity of late twentieth-century Ireland.

Though this world of tribal kings, warriors and respected artist-administrators was not to last for ever, it managed to absorb the challenge of Christianity for a while when, in the fifth century AD, missionaries arrived from across the Irish Sea and from across the Channel. The monks brought with them a revolutionary new tool, destined to shift Irish culture into a new dimension – the habit and craft of writing. Not only could the stories and orally transmitted history-myths of old be recorded now, but subtly infused with the didactic purposes of the new Christian ideology. By the twelfth century AD the monks had established themselves so well – and the Kings of Ireland had adopted Christianity so well – that the roles of story-teller, historian, place- lore- and genealogy-preserver, were handed back to the court bards of old. Now, though, they had to undergo a rigorous fifteen-year training. Over the centuries the Irish art of narrative – oral and written – grew into a powerful and complex grounding for Irish social and cultural life.

The colonial relationship begins

That relatively ordered political situation came to a sudden end in the late fifteenth century. Ireland had suffered its invaders before. The original Gaels were themselves incomers, as were the Christian missionaries. In the ninth and tenth centuries the more warlike Scandinavians had left their mark by establishing 'towns', a new institution at this time – in particular Dublin, Wexford and Cork. By the twelfth century Scandinavian power from the north rolled back, to be replaced from the east by the Anglo-Normans, in the wake of William the Conqueror. They, too, became effectively absorbed, in spite of efforts (not least the death penalty for inter-racial marriage) to resist new influences. The area of influence colonized by England alone amounted to an area around the port of Dublin called The Pale ('The Fence' – hence the expression 'beyond the pale', meaning something out of the question, offensive, dangerous – the supposed characteristics of those beyond the Pale).

The bloody arrival on the English throne of the Tudor family in 1485 sowed the seeds of a poisonous relationship between Ireland and England that is still being worked out at the turn of the twenty-first century. The consequences of what happened in the late fifteenth century have influenced so much of Irish art afterwards, and all of Brian Friel's work shows its imprint. (Indeed, in plays like *The Freedom of the City*, *Making History* and *Translations*, he tackles the political consequences of the Ireland–England relationship head on.) The Tudor Henry VIII asserted total control over the governance of Ireland, largely by bribing the Irish kings with English titles. A dangerous precedent for English interference in Irish affairs was being consolidated.

Though this interference was first done in the name of English Protestantism, even the Catholic Queen Mary had begun a policy of 'plantation' – shipping over English and Scots people to provide a cultural and ethnic counterbalance to the native Irish. A pattern of the old-established 'Gael' and the imposed 'Planter' was instituted, a division that many feel exists still today, partly as a social fact, partly as an imprisoning myth. The Queen's archbishop in Armagh even suggested that the native Irish should be 'eliminated' and wholly replaced by English colonists. The fundamentally racist attitude of the 'civilized' mainland to the old Irish tribes was confirmed, and served to corrupt the attitudes of even those who thought of themselves as cultured. The great English poet Edmund Spenser, contemporary of Shakespeare and author of *The Faerie Queene*, took some, albeit patronizing, pleasure in Irish cultural achievements: '. . . and surely they savoured of sweet wit and good invention but skilled not of the goodly ornaments of poetry.' More disturbingly, he also functioned as secretary to the Lord Deputy of Ireland, tasked by Queen Elizabeth to smash rebellion in the southerly Irish province of Munster. Spenser's description of the victims of this mission carries echoes of defeated and refugee people down the centuries, but it surely reads as a description of a job, for him, well done: 'Out of every corner of the woods and glens they came creeping forth upon their hands, for their legs could not bear them. They looked anatomies of death, they spake like ghosts crying out of their graves, they did eat of the dead carrions, happy were they could find them . . .'

If poets were at the heart of Irish politics in pre-Christian times, by 1583 this English poet exemplifies all too harshly a new state of politics. By 1601 a notable revolt of the Irish against the English collapsed in the Battle of Kinsale. Spanish military power was supposed to reinforce the Gaelic chieftains in their revolt against English Protestant domination. In the event it proved too little and too compromised politically, and the tenuous unity of the chieftains too unreliable to defeat aggressive and self-confident English power. This hugely significant moment of Irish history was to become the pivot for Friel's 1988 dramatic meditation on the nature of history writing and the historical imagination, *Making History*. Centred on Hugh O'Neill, the most influential and thoughtful of Irish chieftains, the play dramatizes the choices available to O'Neill as effective Irish leader and, by extension, to Ireland as a whole. (Typically for Friel, he uses an historical pivotal point to allow a modern audience to reflect on contemporary positions.) From now on, the plantation of Ulster with (overwhelmingly Protestant) English and Scots became a feature of Tudor rule, later continued by Oliver Cromwell and William of Orange. A culture of anti-Irish, usually anti-Catholic, racism had taken root and was carefully nurtured.

Seventeenth-century reckonings

The Great Rebellion of 1641 pitched Ireland and England into a yet more profound crisis. The Ulster Gaelic Irish, many of whom had had their land confiscated to be handed over to the new settlers from the mainland, formed an alliance with Catholic landowners deeply unsettled about what would happen to their land titles. This was also the year in which Cromwell's London Parliament had decreed the absolute suppression of Catholicism. Cromwell, of course, had abolished monarchy and violently abolished an actual monarch, Charles I. The Irish rebel lords were thus victims of a terrible irony. In earlier years, many had pragmatically pledged allegiance to an English monarch in order to survive. Now the regicide Cromwell, self-styled defender of justice and democracy, turned on the rebellious Irish with a double fury. They were rebels against England and, so it seemed, rebels against Cromwell's republican ideal. His ruthless political logic found its bloodiest symbol in the siege and massacre at Drogheda: 'I believe we put to the sword the whole number of the defendants. [c.3,000]. I do not think Thirty of the whole number escaped with their lives. Those that did, are in safe custody for the Barbadoes' (*Cromwell's letter to the President of the Council of State, Dublin, 16 September 1649*).

The Restoration of the Catholic King Charles II in England seemed to relieve the pressure on Irish Catholics for a short while, but in turn increased the anxiety of the Protestant plantation Irish, who feared that it would be *their* turn to lose favour with England. English politics, however, moved on, dragging Ireland with it. In 1688, in search of a suitable monarch, Parliament invited the Protestant William of the

Dutch House of Orange to be King of England, and he it was whose army finally defeated the Catholic James II at the Battle of the Boyne in 1690. 'The Boyne' and the 'Orangeman' were firmly embedded in Protestant mythology as powerful symbols of Catholicism's defeat, and they remain so today. Ireland effectively became a fully fledged colony of England.

Paranoia about invasion from Europe through Ireland gave a pseudo-strategic justification for the unequal and potentially unstable relationship now established (and continued to do so until the end of the Second World War). Ireland was increasingly dividing into an ascendant, mainly Protestant, minority with wealth and political power and a discontented and politically disenfranchised Catholic majority. The fundamental pattern of politics and social living so disastrously established in this period still characterized the world into which Friel was born in 1929.

Republicanism rising

If the Republican Cromwell behaved little differently from assorted monarchs in the sixteenth and seventeenth centuries, it was the idea of an Irish Republic, separate from England–Scotland both in governance and in religion, that laid the final ground for the twentieth-century 'Irish Question'. Two revolutions – the French and the American – provided models for this new set of dissident ideas. Many of Friel's plays face westward to America – his first 'breakthrough' play is called *Philadelphia, Here I Come!* – in a way that his English contemporaries' plays do not. This neatly symbolizes a pattern of relationships between Ireland and the United States that recurs throughout the centuries. It is appropriate, therefore, that the shifts to a republican, anti-monarchist vision enters Irish history largely because of events in America. If the French Revolution of 1789 scared the English ruling class, nervousness turned to fear when the Americans – in a British colony – declared their intention to become independent. This American Revolution, begun in

1775, affected Irish politics in two ways: it offered a model of how a newly established population could create a set of ideas and ideals about self-government, and then carry through that vision into practical action; more particularly, it demanded the use of British troops that would otherwise have been available for service in Ireland. France and, more particularly, America thus became both lure and model for dissent and rebellion.

Nineteenth- and twentieth-century diaspora

One consequence of this tendency for the Irish – both settlers and the 'native' Gaelic – to look to America was that, as life got more desperate for the poor (which meant in particular the predominantly Catholic Irish living in the west of the country), the prospect of moving to a new world, out of domination by England, loomed all the more invitingly. The horrific potato famine of the mid-nineteenth century hardened this pattern out of sheer necessity. The flight of the educated Catholic Irish (another narrative pivot of *Making History*) from English Protestant domination to continental Europe had already characterized the first phase of England's colonization of the country. Now the economic serfdom to which thousands of the Irish had been reduced meant that survival could only be guaranteed abroad. (Friel was to write a TV drama-documentary, *The Next Parish*, on the great famine and emigration to the United States.) The famine, caused by potato blight, destroyed the staple diet of most poor Irish peasant farmers. To this day there is controversy about how culpable Britain was in allowing laissez-faire market forces to turn an agricultural disaster into a human tragedy.

As in more recent political disasters such as the anti-Semitic pogroms of Russia and, later, Germany, or the Balkans of the 1990s, the ports of the country filled with asylum seekers, refugees, emigrants. The Irish character began to take on a face of enforced internationalism. The missionary zeal of Irish Catholic priests had already made itself known in their God-appointed task to take the gospel to unbelievers in Africa and the Far East. (There is a distinct echo of this Irish internationalism – unlike British internationalism, not conventionally imperialist – in Friel's 1977 play *Living Quarters*. About the return to his home town of an Irish army general who has served with the United Nations abroad, the play is a reminder that Irish soldiery – perhaps because of a perceived neutrality and historical culture of opposition to imperialism – has frequently played important roles in United Nations actions.) Both his first 'success', *Philadelphia, Here I Come!*, and his next play, *The Loves of Cass McGuire*, are thoroughly involved in the relationship of Ireland with the United States. There is a consistency, therefore, in the discovery that Friel's early writing career owes much to his early success as a short-story writer for the *New Yorker* magazine, whose readership had an appetite for stories about 'the auld country', as well as to the encouragement of a great Monaghan-descended theatre director, Sir Tyrone Guthrie, who went on to establish a new theatre in the North American state of Minneapolis.

Irish literature and Irish identity

By the nineteenth century Irish society was heaving with the opposing interests of two broad groupings. One wanted independence from England, and was largely Catholic in religion and nationalist (desiring an Irish homeland) in politics. The other interest was dependent on England, where lay its roots and culture, and it was largely Protestant in religion and Unionist (supportive of the Union with England, Scotland and Wales) in politics. The complex interrelationship between colonized Ireland and the different classes and religious affiliations within it created a cauldron of debate and political action that always threatened civil peace in the country.

By the late 1800s the built-in Anglo-Irish power base known as the Protestant Ascendancy was being slowly eroded. Agitation by poor tenants over unjust rents and general poverty threatened the comfortable life of the Anglo-Irish with angry rebellion and sullen resentment. Blatant class antagonism was fuelled by the harsh economic climate for a peasant agriculture that was outmoded in the increasingly industrialized, technology-driven world of the nineteenth century. Ironically it was an English Protestant prime minister, William Gladstone, who finally did for the Irish Protestant Ascendancy. Determined to hold on to Ireland, and conscious that blatant injustice could only create social chaos and increase support for nationalism, he introduced into Parliament a Land Act based on three 'F's – Fixity of tenure, Fair rent, and Freedom to sell holdings. The Anglo-Irish landowners were reduced to little more than rent collectors. The British Parliament continued to undermine the Ascendancy by providing financial support to landlords who simply wanted to sell up and get out. In a short space of time, the picture of land ownership was transformed. Yet the fires of Irish independence would not be extinguished. Home Rule was a constant aspiration and a Home Rule party spoke for all but the most militant nationalists. Unfortunately for that aspiration, Gladstone and his Liberal Party lost the 1886 election and his proposals for Irish Home Rule went with him. In the face of a Conservative Party determination to maintain the Union at all costs, the Home Rulers began to fracture into more political groupings, ranging from the constitutional to the openly insurrectionary.

The cult of Celtism

In this new climate of nationalist excitement, Irish (and some sympathetic English) artists and scholars began to generate a new source of imagery and ideas to fuel the nationalist struggle. Beginning as the 'Celtic Renaissance', the movement's main impetus was first to discover, then to protect, then to elevate to mythical status the language and art of the old Gaelic culture. Histories – of the chieftains, and of the old pre-plantation feudal world – proliferated. The warrior-ballads, with their all-Irish heroes – Cuchulain, Queen Maebh and others – from the great Ulster cycle of myths, were rediscovered and translated into English (a paradoxical necessity given how dominant the language had become). An equivalent tendency in English culture amongst Pre-Raphaelites and others revived myths like that of King Arthur, and similarly expressed a distaste for industrialism and the emergence of mass society. The English movement represented an escape from engagement with the contemporary world in an effort to find some countercultural alternative. While this may have been partly true of the Celtic revival, it was far more important as a resource for national self-esteem, as if to say, 'Look, we have myths and legends as potent, if not more so, than yours; why then don't *we* have a homeland?'

Traditional sports, such as hurley and Gaelic football, enjoyed a turn-of-the-century renaissance, but most important of all, the Gaelic language itself was the focus of an intense effort of revival. Spoken overwhelmingly by poorer people in the west of the nation, it took on a symbolic significance for the metropolitan nationalists for whom the old language's greatest attraction was that it was *not* English, language of the invader and colonizer. At the turn of the century, Irish language was the single strongest signifier of Irish nationalism, and placed at the heart of the web of ideas, passions and social realities that made up an Irish identity.

It has been almost impossible during the twentieth century for Irish writers *not* to be writing about Irish identity. Brian Friel is no exception. Even when he deals with other aspects of his own experience, he finds himself dealing, at some level, with Irish identity. In *Philadelphia, Here I Come!* and *Dancing at Lughnasa* he questions the nature of memory and exile, and in particular the way that language hugely influences personality and culture. Inevitably, he finds himself returning to the web of connections between language, national identity and personal identity. For a writer, concern with language is also concern with his or her own medium, and each encounter with it brings him/her face to face with his/her own identity as an Irishman/woman. As Paul Durcan's seventieth-birthday present to him states, he is the man 'Who lives in that part of the South of Ireland / Which is more northerly than the North . . .' The landscape in which he grows up is transformed metaphorically (and, inasmuch as industrialized technology can be stimulated by political change, literally) by the political divisions and allegiances of society. The language he speaks and in which he writes is transformed, too, by politics. Yet Friel also knows, with the sophistication of a man very aware of twentieth-century scholarship about linguistics, semantics and culture, that language, in its turn, can transform politics – that language and politics participate in an endless dance, where one leads then the other, each transforming the other, sometimes to humanity's benefit, often not.

Issues of social justice, of parental relationships, of the partiality of memory, of the temptations of self-deception – all Friel themes, all 'universal' – are still refracted through his own concern with what it means to be a north Irish citizen and playwright, and also what it means to work in the powerful tradition of other Irish writers.

Irish drama – 'The Revival'

Most people know that Oscar Wilde and George Bernard Shaw were Irish. We sometimes need reminding that many of the most quintessentially 'English' playwrights of preceding centuries were actually Irish – Sheridan, Farquhar, Goldsmith, the actor-dramatist Charles Macklin – and that perhaps the greatest satirist of England and the emerging modern world was Jonathan Swift, a Dublin man. That most made their names as comic writers may have had to do with their ability to look at England and the English with a wry outsider's eye, both comfortable in and critical of English society. However, in a famously provocative piece of journalism called 'Plays Peasant and Unpeasant' (the title a sly parody of one of Shaw's collections of plays), Friel urged us to reject these men as having anything to do with *Irish* drama. Instead he proposed a definition of Irish drama as: 'Plays written in Irish or English on Irish subjects and performed by Irishmen'. For Friel, the moment Irish drama revived was the evening of 8 May 1899. A group of enthusiasts called the Irish Literary Theatre put on *The Countess Cathleen* by the then current leader of Irish literature, poet and playwright William Butler Yeats.

The significance of that night was both immediate and long-term. Immediately, the play dealt with a quintessential Irish theme: famine. The Countess sells her soul to the devil in order to save her starving peasants. The theme was attacked in the Dublin papers as blasphemous and an air of scandal immediately developed around the playwright. In his next play, *Cathleen ni Houlihan*, Yeats addressed the colonial relationship with England in a play set in the 1798 rebellion, expressing support for violent action against the British, as well as invoking that mythical personification of the Irish nation, Cathleen.

The longer-term and far more important result of Yeats's work was to establish a focus for ideas and debate about Ireland and Irish identity through drama. Collaborating with other theatre professionals and supporters, Yeats moved on to establish the Irish National Theatre Society, performing plays largely at the Abbey Theatre in Dublin but also committed to touring in other parts of Ireland. Thereafter, for a period of about twenty years, the 'Abbey' became a powerful nursery of writing and acting talent. Its first great discovery was John Millington Synge, an Irish Protestant playwright who had a strong awareness of the latest artistic developments on mainland Europe, but who also discovered an affinity with the peasant culture and language of the Western Isles of Ireland. He wrote his masterpiece, *The Playboy of the Western World*, about that peasant culture. In 1998, Brian Friel, John Arden and other writers with Irish connections marked the enormous influence that his writing had on Irish culture by attending the opening of Synge's cottage as a cultural centre. In his opening address, Friel said: 'He's the man who made Irish theatre and he's a man before whom we all genuflect.'

Artistic differences eventually pushed the Irish National Theatre founders apart, and Yeats's plans for a more heroic dramatic style rooted in mythology gave way to smaller writers' comedies and melodramas about rural Ireland – the 'peasant plays' that were to become characteristic of the Abbey's output. In Synge, however, they had nurtured a writer who managed to use the 'peasant play' formula to create drama of real tragicomic greatness. Inevitably, some of the characteristic flavours of his work became clichés in the hands of later, lesser writers and, as if to balance that tendency to a smallness of vision, a rival theatre, The Gate, opened in 1928 with an enthusiasm for the more avant-garde developments in staging, lighting and play-writing from Europe. If the Abbey looked into the rural heartland of Ireland, the Gate looked to Paris and Vienna. When Brian Friel writes his 1972 piece, he once again addresses those polarities of introverted vision, the 'plays peasant', and more ambitious work, 'plays unpeasant'. Contrasting the triviality, as he sees it, of the Dublin theatre scene in the early 1970s, he looks with a degree of envy to Europe and America:

> Meanwhile, in Germany Hochhuth writes surrealistic documentaries about human responsibility. In England Edward Bond writes about the violent self-destruction of mankind. In France Planchon celebrates change in all its forms. In America Edward Albee writes of the impossibility of human communication. And in Ireland, as I write this, in the capital's three largest theatres, Boucicault capers on the Abbey stage, *Cinderella* on the Olympia, *Robin Hood* on the Gaiety. Some entertaining impresario should book Nero and his fiddle for a long Irish season.

This piece also speaks of Friel's characteristic debate with himself about how drama should engage with the community; how to avoid writing propaganda – 'I do not believe that art is a servant of any movement' – at the same time as responding to the convulsions his own country, like the rest of the world, was then going through. By invoking the Abbey and criticizing it for its triviality at that moment (1972 was the year of Bloody Sunday and a year away from the reimposition of Direct Rule from London) Friel implicitly invokes that exciting turn-of-the-century period of the Abbey's leadership of Irish ideas. Here was a theatre, led by important artists and enthusiasts for drama who were prepared to deal with the big questions of nationalism and power and prepared to kick up a stink. Twice in his time with the Abbey Yeats himself stalked onstage to heckle back at outraged audiences who didn't like the ideas being presented to them.

That the energy in that early flowering of Irish theatre eventually drained away amidst disagreements on artistic policy was unfortunate, but the Abbey Theatre experienced another revival in the 1920s with the Dublin plays of another great writer, Sean O'Casey, who combined nationalism with a clear sense of injustice that he expressed in his membership of republican and socialist groupings. (O'Casey also quarrelled with the Abbey, as he had quarrelled with Ireland, and took up residence in England.) For Friel, characteristically more wary about political movements than O'Casey, it was the meeting with the young Belfast actor Stephen Rea that was to give him, in Field Day Theatre Company, a real political purchase on his culture in a way that had not seemed possible in Ireland since that first decade at the Abbey from 1899.

Barricade to border: the die is cast

Ireland during this period was undergoing the final stages of that transforming wave that had been gathering force throughout the nineteenth century. The 1916 Easter Rising, a tactical failure but a profound mythological triumph (and the reference point for O'Casey's *Juno and the Paycock* and *The Plough and the Stars*), resulted in the execution of many of its surviving leaders by British soldiers, thus ensuring an overwhelming tide of nationalist feeling in all but the north-eastern province of Ulster. By 1919 Ireland was riven by civil war over control of the independence struggle. In 1922 Britain finally accepted the reality of Irish nationalism and agreed to the creation of the Irish Free State. However, the Anglo-Irish Treaty decreed an enclave of six counties in part of the old north-eastern province of Ulster that were to remain within the United Kingdom. Historically, Ulster had always been a rebellious region of Ireland, and had given successive centuries of English government a headache. Now the region was predominantly Protestant and also industrially the most developed part of Ireland. The possibility for a poisoned or a potent political future rested very much on how the minority Catholic/Nationalist community were to be treated in the Protestant/Unionist-dominated province. Sadly, jobs, political power and freedom of expression tended to flow inexorably towards Unionists and away from Nationalists. The Irish Question remained unanswered and in 1929 the newborn Friel found himself a child of a divided society.

2

Friel's Life and Work

Brian Friel was born in 1929 in Killyclogher, near the town of Omagh, County Tyrone, in the newly established province of Northern Ireland. His father's father and his mother's mother couldn't read, and all his grandparents were Irish-speakers. Compared to many of his contemporaries, he is very closely connected to a much older, pre-literate peasant culture. On the other hand, his father Patrick – 'a quiet and reserved man', according to Friel – was a teacher and headmaster, full of the respect for learning and education commonly found in subordinated cultures. Young Brian attended Culmore Primary – his father's school – and fondly remembers his father teaching the school choir a song: 'Oft in the Stilly Night', by Tom Moore: '. . . we won a cup at the Omagh Feis [festival] and he was inordinately proud of us – and of himself. And for months afterwards he would line us up and start us off singing that Moore song. Then he would leave the classroom and cross the school yard and go to the far side of the country road and just stand there – listening to us singing in harmony in the distance. And although I couldn't see him standing there, I knew that we transported him.'

In 1964 he recalled for the BBC, being reduced to tears by his teacher-father's rage over his son's problems with algebra. It was the sound of Presbyterian chapel hymn-singing from the church next door that seems to have consoled him in his misery: '. . . although it may not have been the height of mystical experience, I can heartily recommend hymn-singing to all those who labour and are burdened.' His mother's influence was no less strong – 'a dominant vivacious presence'. Her family came from Glenties, in County Donegal, in what, in 1920, had become the Irish Republic. Moreover, he had six aunties, whom he knew well, women who clearly influenced both man and writer. Just before the Second World War, two of them had suddenly moved away from the family home in County Donegal, and later died in poverty-stricken exile in London. This sad fact became the seed from which grew perhaps his most famous play *Dancing at Lughnasa*.

The Friels were Catholics, which now placed them on the fringes of Northern Ireland society. In the south, in the Irish Free State, for all the felt mistrust of Protestantism, there was still a degree of respect for that minority belief. The Free State, for instance, supported both Catholic and Protestant schools. Not so in Northern Ireland, where to be Catholic was to be excluded, either by direct ostracism or by structural means such as vote rigging. The suspicion in which the Catholic community was held was extreme – 'traitors', either actual or potential. As a child, Friel remembers:

> there were certain areas one didn't go into. I remember
> bringing shoes to the shoemaker's shop at the end of the
> street. This was a terrifying experience, because if the
> Protestant boys caught you in this kind of no-man's-land,
> they'd kill you. I have vivid memories when I was twelve or
> so of standing at my own front door and hoping the coast
> would be clear so I could dive over to the shop; and then,
> when I'd left the shoes in, waiting to see was the coast clear
> again. If you were caught you were finished. It was abso-
> lutely terrifying. That sort of thing leaves scars for the rest
> of one's life.

Friel also recalled stealing red glass reflectors from air-raid shelters: 'I think we were vandals. I know we had no civic sense whatever . . . we were just thieving little street urchins, and the only therapy we needed was a kick in the pants.'

In his 1972 *Self-Portrait* Friel reflected on what he described as the 'bizarre' process of his education:

For about fifteen years I was taught by a succession of men who force-fed me with information, who cajoled me, beat me, threatened me, coaxed me to swallow their puny little pies of knowledge and attitudes . . . the little grudge I bear is directed against those men who taught me the literature of Rome and Greece and England and Ireland as if they were intricate pieces of machinery, created for no reason and designed for no purpose. They were called out of the air, these contrivances, and planked in front of us, and for years we tinkered with them, pulling them apart, putting them together again, translating, scanning, conjugating, never once suspecting that these texts were the testimony of sad, happy, assured, confused people like ourselves.

Perhaps it is unsurprising that when he himself takes up his father's profession, Friel chooses to teach Maths rather than English! Yet it is also true that Friel's whole writing career can be seen as a project precisely to speak for and through the 'sad, happy, assured, confused people' amongst whom he has lived. So much of Brian Friel's childhood experience seems to ripple out into his art – the strong, beloved authoritarian father, the imminent danger posed by sectarian division, the quietly rebellious refusal to conform to a 'nice' stereotype, the consoling powers of music . . .

Inevitably, the sectarian atmosphere served to increase the Catholic community's flight towards nationalism and allegiance to the Free State, later the Republic of Ireland. Friel's father was a committed nationalist, member of the Nationalist Party and a councillor for the Catholic Bogside and Creggan districts of Derry City, where the family had moved in 1939. Known to the Protestant Northern Irish as *London*derry, this piece of politically inspired city-renaming clearly sensitized Friel early to the way Irish names reflect history as much as geography. Indeed, his own name poignantly symbolizes the issue. His birth certificate has him as *Bernard* Friel because the Protestant authorities in the newly established Northern

Ireland province were not-so-subtly keen to eradicate traditional Irish names. *Brian* Friel, however, went on to St
Columb's school in Derry. (The school also educated Seamus
Heaney, perhaps the best-known Irish poet of the post-war
world, and John Hume, a leading activist in the later Civil
Rights movement in Ulster, and later a prominent Nationalist
politician.)

From his Derry life there seems to have grown a strong sense of
local attachment that also sings on in his work. Speaking of
Derry, Friel recalls that 'every going away was a wrench and every
return a fulfilment', but goes on to pinpoint the contradictions
that in some senses he identifies for all Ireland and on whose
horns the whole nation sits: 'The inquisitiveness of villagers; the
complacency of a market town. In one sense it's an easy atmosphere to live in, and in another sense it imposes its own rigid
rules of conduct because respectability here is equated with
virtue, and the trouble is that respectability is not an absolute
standard, but dependent on what people respect here and now.'

It is a sign of the absolute centrality of Catholic religious culture that so many young men of Friel's generation and earlier
seemed almost automatically to train for the priesthood. For
the vast majority of these young men, St Patrick's seminary at
Maynooth outside Dublin was the training ground and, aged
sixteen, it was here that Brian Friel came. The experience was
not a happy one – 'an awful experience, it nearly drove me
cracked. It is one thing I want to forget.' Friel does not speak
publicly about this time. Whatever the precise triggers that
brought about disillusion, it is reasonable to speculate that a
mind as questing and as willing to entertain uncertainties
would not have found a regime of unquestioning faith either
easy or congenial. At the very least the warmth and female
companionship of his aunts and sisters would have seemed
achingly absent in the austerity of the all-male priest college.
He told one interviewer: 'It's a very disturbing thing to happen
to anyone. I don't know if one ever recovers totally from an
immense experience of this nature . . . I wasn't very happy at

the time, but I was sixteen or seventeen and these are carefree years. If one has to have a "tragedy" in one's life, they are the best years to have it in.'

His education now continued, following in his father's footsteps to St Joseph's and St Mary's Teacher Training College, to do a one-year course: '. . . another blunt instrument. It was a crude place.'

Whatever the difficulties, Friel's path was conventional enough for the academic child of a teacher and a civil servant. He began teaching in schools run by an influential religious order called the Christian Brothers, originally set up to educate talented boys of limited means. Their educational philosophy was always conservative and traditional. In the *Self-Portrait* he reflects on his teaching years with some regret: '. . . what I was doing was putting boys in for maths exams and getting them through. In fact I fancied myself as a teacher because I worked hard at teaching the tricks and the poodle dogs became excellent performers. And I regret, too, that I used a strap. Indeed, I regret this most of all.' Later, Friel moved on to more congenial work in a primary school: 'It was a kind of epiphany, you know. It was something different. It wasn't the kind of Christian Brothers stuff.' It was during this ten-year period that Brian Friel began to produce creative writing.

Some writers feed voraciously from their own biography and experience. Others follow the American writer Gore Vidal's advice to 'write what you *imagine*, not what you know about . . .' Usually the best writers strike a balance between the two, taking the raw material of experience and transforming it through imagination into art; this seems particularly true for Friel. Dramatists also act like magnets for the ideas and passions that are vibrant in any moment in history. They focus them and give them tangible form so that audiences can better understand and work with them in their own lives. In Friel's case, as he begins his creative life in the late 1940s, he symbolizes and expresses a range of historical, political and social matters – largely to do with Ireland.

Geographically, he starts adult life living in a county and a city that are contradictory – more Catholic than Protestant, but ruled by Protestants. At the stroke of a pen on a treaty in London, he finds himself 'British', while his mother's family and friends a few miles away are now, constitutionally, 'Irish'. His family has Nationalist affiliations and his father takes them into public life as a town councillor. Like so many Irish people, Northern or Southern, Brian Friel is aware of the two great national forces to the east and west of his country, stretching and pulling him away from his roots: America, the most potent pole of attraction down the centuries for Irish citizens determined to survive, or to drag themselves from poverty to prosperity; Britain, the other economic safe haven but also, until the twentieth century, the political master, the cultural big brother, imposing its language and world view.

Personally, this Brian Friel is an intelligent, creative young man who begins to see the contradictions between Irish society's innate conservatism and the first intimations of a rapidly changing world. He is also aware of the damage in these. He teaches to earn a living, and though he enjoys it well enough, his real creativity is poured into the writing of short stories. A career begins.

Writing on the border

Friel's work began and blossomed in a country and a culture that often seemed rigid, undynamic and futureless. The fraught colonial relationship with England had left a complex legacy for the 1950s. In the Republic, a peasant, largely agrarian culture combined with the Catholic Church's dominant position in public life to maintain a stifling conservatism. Writing in 1972, Friel characterized 'the two allegiances that have bound the Irish imagination – loyalty to the most authoritarian church in the world and devotion to a romantic ideal we call Kathleen . . . Faith and fatherland.' Yet this was now the world of nuclear weapons, accelerating technology and a resurgent

Europe. In Friel's Northern Ireland/Ulster, its dominant Protestant religious culture differed largely in that industrialisation had taken a firmer hold than in the agrarian South. It was certainly as culturally conservative, perhaps more so, than the South. The communication channels between England and Northern Ireland should have ensured a quicker transition into post-war society. In practice, the defensiveness of that culture in regard to the South meant that change was not on the social agenda, from whatever source it came. In the South the gaze of writers and artists, anticipators and seismographers of cultural change, was habitually more focused on Europe than in the notionally more 'modern', industrialized North. Writers like Friel found themselves trapped in a kind of cultural no-man's-land – exiled from both communities by their creativity and their sensitivity to the profound psychological and social damage caused by patterns of living and feeling that failed to match up to the contemporary world.

Born in Omagh, raised in Derry, hemmed in by Northern Irish political realities, the writer Friel invented a location as the setting for much of his imaginative writing. However, Ballybeg, as he named it, is nominally in County Donegal, the part of the Irish Republic that is due west of Northern Ireland and therefore as much a part of 'the North' as, say, Belfast. Ballybeg is the anglicized form of the Irish 'Baile Beag', or Small Town. (He also occasionally refers to Ballymore – 'Baile Mor', or Big Town – when he needs to write about a larger community.) For Brian Friel, the border has always been more of a tripwire nuisance than a reality. Yet its presence in the personal and political mythologies of the Irish nations could hardly be ignored. The Catholic, nationalist writer who grew up in a Protestant, Unionist state embodied, even as he became an adult, all the contradictions of his country.

Fortunately, Friel was a talented writer and the 1950s were a period in which the short-story readership flourished, particularly in America. Two magazines, the *New Yorker* and the *Saturday Evening Post*, solicited material from a range of writers.

From 1952 Friel was under contract to the *New Yorker* to write stories. Not all were accepted. Rapidly learning professional writers' guile, he managed to sell much of the rejected work on to the rival *Saturday Evening Post*. Looking back on this period in 1964, Friel states: 'If it weren't for the *New Yorker* I couldn't live. Couldn't live at all. And they're so – I hate to use the word – they're so respectful. It sounds a pompous thing to say, but you know what I mean in the context. They have such respect for work and for their contributors.'

Introducing some of Friel's collected interviews, Christopher Murray evocatively outlines the tradition of Irish story writing in which Friel first worked: '. . . a world where authority was taken for granted; a patriarchal and religiously conservative society, dependent on mild eccentricity and occasional bouts of passionate revolt for its repertoire of stories . . . a world peopled by well-fed, ruminative priests, schoolteachers sporting immortal longings, copious inadequate fathers, wistful mothers and a seemingly endless succession of adolescent children poised on the threshold of disillusion'.

Speaking in 1982, Friel spoke of one overwhelming reason for his stopping short-story writing: 'It was at the point when I recognized how difficult they were. It would have meant a whole reappraisal. I mean, I was very much under the influence, as everybody at the time was, of [Sean] O'Faolain and [Frank] O'Connor, particularly . . . I think at some point round about that period [came] the recognition of the difficulty of the thing, you know, that maybe there was the need for the discovery of a voice and that I was just echoing somebody else.'

His first serious playwriting was for radio. Between 1958 and 1962 BBC Northern Ireland produced four of his plays, directed by one of the stalwarts of BBC Radio drama, Ronald Mason. (Mason told the critic Richard Pine that he considered most of Friel's work to be connected to his early exposure to radio, citing in particular *Lovers*, *Faith Healer* and *Making History*.) Radio has always been a drama medium that lies close to the short story. It can give very quick access to the interior world of characters. Many playwrights who grew up listening to radio in the 1950s found it a resource of great technical and imaginative freedom. For the first time, powerful interior monologues beamed their way into parlours and bedrooms in geographically and socially isolated regions. You no longer had to have access to metropolitan Dublin – or London – trendiness to be touched by this new way of seeing the world. In England, writers such as Tom Stoppard and Harold Pinter listened to and wrote for radio, and it began to attract its own drama specialists. Writers such as Giles Cooper and Henry Reed and producers such as Ronald Mason, Val Gielgud and Charles Parker developed a particular set of standards and techniques for radio drama. By happy coincidence, one of the pioneers of radio drama was the man who, in 1962, kick-started Friel's theatre career, Tyrone Guthrie. Guthrie was in every sense a big man, an English public schoolboy whose boyhood ambition to join the tail end of the First World War had been happily thwarted by a minor disability of the foot. As his name suggests, he had strong Irish roots. His family had a country house in County Monaghan, just south of what, in 1922, became the border. When Guthrie had applied to the BBC, it had been happy coincidence again that sent him back in 1924 to Ireland, to Radio 2BE, the British Broadcasting Company's outpost in Belfast. Guthrie's radio drama work bore fruit in what he described later as 'the microphone play'. Guthrie has his continuity announcer begin his play *Matrimonial News* like this: 'What follows is supposed to be happening in the mind of Miss Florence Kipling – who is sitting alone in a cheap restaurant in the Strand, in London. The time is about a quarter to twelve, midday. She has ordered a cup of coffee . . . Remember you are overhearing her thoughts. She is alone . . .'

This kind of elaborate setting out of the rules of the game was probably necessary for listeners-in to the new medium, but it is easy to see how close we are to the intimate, button-holing style of the opening of *Dancing at Lughnasa*, or the public confessional of *Faith Healer*. Friel was born in the year Guthrie's play was transmitted, so he couldn't have listened to it, but he most certainly benefited from it and its descendants. If you can hear a person's inner thought spoken, you can hear the distance between that thought and what he or she says in public. You are thus well set up to explore the distance between Private and Public, the very heart technically and emotionally of Friel's breakthrough play *Philadelphia, Here I Come!* Already in his radio plays, he is beginning to work with the obsessions and interests that surface later – the cracks and contradictions in family life and the ever-present theme of the insularity of rural Ireland. The critic Richard Pine sees these plays as transitional between short-story writing and drama. In particular he notes that Friel tends to end the plays anticlimactically. Lines that on paper can sit on the page and pulse quietly, that can be re-read and pondered upon, lose their impact if they are not written to be heard once only – in other words, if speech needs to be created as action rather than as thought.

In 1962 what Friel himself describes as 'pale' success with his short stories, radio plays and some early contact with the stage was about to be transformed by his fellow Ulsterman Guthrie.

1963–4: *A Doubtful Paradise* to *Philadelphia, Here I Come!*

Although Friel had two apprentice plays produced (*The Blind Mice* at the Eblana Theatre in Dublin (1963) and *A Doubtful Paradise* at the Group Theatre in Belfast), the earliest play that he will acknowledge is *The Enemy Within*, performed in 1962 at the Abbey in Dublin. A 'history play' about Ireland, it contributes to an ongoing pattern of two sorts of Brian Friel play, the other being the 'family play', based loosely on some aspects of the author's own life. In reality, of course, such distinctions are far too crude, and all the history plays turn out to be family plays and vice versa. Clearly the experience of training for the priesthood and his Catholic upbringing were working in his mind alongside the new creative energies of a young writer.

The contradictory demands of the public and the private person were worked out in the narrative of one of Ireland's great figures, St Columba, who exiled himself from political battles in order to cleanse his soul. Friel talked of wanting to investigate the idea of sanctity and the personal courage and commitment it required. In part, the play pits the demands of family against those of the public man. With Friel at the time being a young father who had chosen the risky life of the professional artist, this must have been potent material, and Friel himself had been reflecting on the exile that Irish writers like Joyce, Beckett and O'Casey had embraced in order to fulfil their artistic integrity. The play is also about the call of Ireland on the articulator of the country's soul (Columba the Priest/Friel the Artist): Friel has his Columba rage with frustration at the thing he both loves and hates: 'You soaked my sweat! You sucked my blood! You stole my manhood, my best years! What more do you demand of me, damned Ireland? My soul? My immortal soul? Damned, damned damned Ireland! – (*His voice breaks.*) Soft green Ireland – beautiful green Ireland. My lovely green Ireland. O my Ireland –'

The tone of that impassioned love-hate is a world away from the gentler, regretful, quietly nihilistic tone of the Irish short-story tradition. It shows that Friel was prepared to rage against the problematic aspects of his country's culture where necessary. The experience of having the play performed (and at the Abbey, too, with all the prestige and historical significance of that stage) clearly stimulated him to embrace the public art of theatre. The year after the play's production, Friel's stories had so impressed Tyrone Guthrie that he offered the young dramatist the chance to immerse himself in a learning experience that would transform him into an internationally known and loved playwright.

Friel's Career: '*Yeah. I know this guy. He's an Irishman. He's an observer here.*'

Since his radio days in Belfast with Station 2BE, Tyrone Guthrie's career had taken a path of ever-widening reputation and success that embraced the Old Vic in London, and the Shakespeare Festival Theatre at Stratford, Ontario in Canada. He had become a pioneer in the staging of classical theatre, particularly Shakespeare and the Greek dramatists, and had become closely involved in new stage–audience relationships at the new Canadian theatre. This international activity culminated in a plan that echoed some of the wave of new theatre building throughout Britain in the late fifties and early sixties. Guthrie wanted to create, in the United States where his reputation was well established, a brand-new theatre based upon modern approaches to the classics and constituted as a full-blown, professional repertory system. The unlikely winner of the auction to receive Guthrie and his ambitious plans was Minneapolis, in the Midwestern state of Minnesota. With the energetic enthusiasm created by a blank canvas and serious local support from business and community, Guthrie created a theatre and, more importantly, a company named after him.

Guthrie invited the young man to come and observe the theatre work in the first season in Minneapolis. Friel took up the offer and flew to America with his wife and two young children. The old relationship between Ireland and America, with all its overtones of escape and liberation, now became concrete in Friel's life. Admittedly he had been receiving dollar pay cheques for his short-story writing, and the 'exile' was only for a clearly understood six-month period, but the physical uprooting clearly held symbolic weight.

During the period that Friel was in Minneapolis, Guthrie was rehearsing Shakespeare's *Hamlet* and Chekhov's *Three Sisters*, and his assistant Douglas Campbell was doing Molière's *The Miser*. These embraced Guthrie's range from the classical to the more recent enthusiasm for family plays. By this term he meant those dramas that used the family as a holding form for substantial and profound truths about all of human society. Clearly this is true of Chekhov's work, but Guthrie saw *Oedipus Rex* and *Hamlet*, too, as family plays. Given that Friel was already working a vein of personal interest and literary tradition to do with family, it is reasonable to see one result of Friel's American education as being an awareness of the wider possibilities of the family play. Friel at that time felt it to be a powerful and significant experience. Later, he assessed its effect on him more reflectively: '. . . those months in America gave me a sense of liberation – remember, this was my first parole from inbred claustrophobic Ireland – and that sense of liberation conferred on me a valuable self-confidence and a necessary perspective . . .'

Friel's contemporaries in England – playwrights such as John Arden, Edward Bond and Ann Jellicoe – experienced a similar education in practical theatre in the Royal Court's Writers' Group, though their experience was more 'hands-on' than Friel's. He basically looked and learned, 'literally skulking about in the gloom of the back seats'. After a while he became a familiar face: 'People began to nod to me. I got a pencil and paper and occasionally pretended to jot down some profound observations. Some of the less than secure actors even began to ask my advice about their performance, God help them. It was all very gratifying.'

He was pleased to be described by an actor as 'The Observer'. It seemed to fit his own image of himself as an artist. The Minneapolis experience seems to have opened up to him theatre's apparently contradictory qualities of pleasure and discipline, sensuality and craft, imagination and dedication. In what is perhaps a revealing image for a man who trained as a priest, Friel talks about 'the iron discipline of theatre . . . I discovered a dedication and a nobility and a selflessness that one associates with a theoretical priesthood.' It also clearly offered Friel something of an immersion in the art and craft of theatre. Prior to this trip, he had been, by his own assessment, 'almost totally ignorant of the mechanics of play-writing and play-production apart from an intuitive knowledge'. Now he was to learn about 'the physical elements of plays, how they are designed, built, landscaped. I learnt how actors thought, how they approached a text, their various ways of trying to realize it.' More importantly, he learnt a revitalizing approach to his whole art:

> I learned, in Guthrie's own words, that theatre is an attempt to create something which will, if only for a brief moment, transport a few fellow travellers on our strange, amusing, perilous journey – a lift, but not, I hope, an uplift. I learned that the playwright's first function is to entertain, to have audiences enjoy themselves, to move them emotionally, to make them laugh and cry and gasp and hold their breath and sit on the edge of their seats and – again to quote the great man himself – to 'participate in lavish and luxurious goings-on'.

During and after the American experience, Friel kept up a series of submissions to the Belfast *Irish Press*. These were light pieces of comic journalism, but some of them hint at deeper concerns, now thrown into sharper relief by the educational exile he had undertaken. As George O'Brien, an American writer on Friel, has it: 'The columns are carefully calculated exaggerations of the intractable and unstable properties of the daily round and of the inadequacy of our command of it, a command which inevitably but laughably relies on language.'

In America, Friel finds himself 'bereft of the familiar props and amenities of home, such as they are. Now he has nothing to go on but language, with the result that a heightened sensitivity is felt to the primacy of language – rather than, as at home, of action – as a means of revealing the unnerving gap between perception and reality.' Like many writers before, the literal exile – in Friel's case from his beloved Derry/Donegal, and its particular use of language – inspired him to revisit the place and the language through drama.

On the family's return from America in 1963, Friel quickly settled to complete the play that established his reputation with critics as Ireland's leading contemporary dramatist. Though Friel acknowledged Guthrie as mainly a 'levelling' rather than a 'sign-posting' influence, he went on to talk about Guthrie's risk-taking. 'He was the kind of man who gave you the courage to take formal gambles and technical gambles on the stage . . .'

1964: *Philadelphia, Here I Come!*

The director Hilton Edwards was one half of the influential team that had turned the Gate Theatre in Dublin into an alternative to the Abbey. Where, in the years after the death of Sean O'Casey, the Abbey had tended to rest on its Irish peasant play laurels, the Gate, under Edwards and his partner (in life as in art) Michael Macliammoir, created a theatre that embraced the European modernist movements in theatre. Certainly the formal adventurism of Friel's new play would not have fazed anyone associated with the Gate Theatre.

Staged at the Gaiety Theatre, in Dublin, as part of the Dublin Theatre Festival, *Philadephia, Here I Come!* was welcomed by critics and audiences as the hit of the Festival. A young playwright was at last articulating his and a younger generation's frustration in a play that seemed in tune with other developments in English-language theatre, particularly from the Royal Court. In England, Bond's *The Pope's Wedding* (1962) and Wesker's *Roots* (1959) had similarly tested their society's inadequacies from rural locations, though in contrast to Friel social class was a more clearly articulated problem for the English writers. Friel's closer contemporary Pinter produced, in *The Homecoming* (1964), a kind of reverse image of *Philadelphia Here I Come!*, with its returning academic, home from the bright, history-lite world of American academia to wallow in and be swallowed once more by threatening, messy old London, with its inarticulacies of violence and patriarchy.

The success of the play in the 1964 Dublin Theatre Festival
and in another production the following year, together with,
presumably, some combination of Friel's embryonic literary
reputation and the play's title and theme, led to the play's great
success on Broadway in 1966. Friel went with the cast on out-
of-town try-outs prior to hitting New York. One venue was
Philadelphia, where Friel reported hearing one 'corpulent, sil-
ver-haired lady' ask: 'So he's coming to Philadelphia! So what
the hell's he crying about!' When it arrived in New York and
generated good reviews and excellent box office, Friel was, of
course, delighted, particularly as he felt the recast production
actually was good. However, his dry scepticism managed to
keep the experience in proportion (and to prepare him for later
disappointments on American stages). As he was later to
observe: 'Broadway is a theatrical warehouse where theatrical
merchandise is bought and sold, and if you have a well-pack-
aged and slick piece of merchandise it will have some kind of a
run. New York has as much to do with what's happening here
as *Dallas* [hugely popular American TV melodrama] has.'

His earlier play *The Enemy Within* had no particular formal
gambles or risks, but it did have at its heart a character who
wrestled with the inner person, who tried to reconcile the
demands of the public man with his private needs. In
Philadelphia, Here I Come!, after the experience of Minneapolis,
Friel uses a theatre device to work with those ideas (and much
else besides). The play is set on the night before a young
Donegal man, Gar O'Donnell, is to leave the stultifying life of
provincial Donegal for the wide-open spaces (metaphorically)
of the American Midwest (where, of course, thanks to Irish history, he has relations). Philadelphia is the city of brotherly love,
where a young man can be free and rootless, and therein lies
its fatal attraction. Throughout the progress of the play, Gar
is faced with what it means to uproot himself from family,
from familiarity, from Columba's 'damned Ireland . . . beautiful green Ireland'. This is a play about exile; there had been
other Irish plays about that quintessential Irish experience,

but it is also a play about the different worlds that Gar is exiled from.

By 1964 the Western, industrialized world was moving faster and faster into a period of change. The post-war military/political standoff (the 'Cold War') between the Soviet bloc and the capitalist West (led by the United States) had dominated the previous decade and sharpened the profile of American individualist culture in the imaginations of many young people, particularly through mass media and pop culture. American movies, TV, pop songs, car design, fast food all stood for a vigorous, exciting modernity, embracing materialist pleasure, the very opposite of the deep-rooted culture of rural Ireland, with its history of dark and bloody struggles, its religious culture founded in guilt and redemption, and its people's reassuring identification with the landscape. But, as Friel was later to explore in other plays, deep roots can also be poisonous. At the very least they can bind rather than be sources of strength, and on that dilemma rests the play's basic situation.

Philadelphia, Here I Come! also comes at that idea by another route: Gar's relationship with his father. Friel's drama is peopled with father figures who have problematic relationships with sons. By his own account this was not a particular problem in Friel's own relationship with his father, but it seems clear that his father's strength of personality gave him a dramatic model from which to extrapolate all sons' ambiguous feelings about their fathers. Gar's moving memory of a childhood experience, out fishing with his father, so sensuously evoked in its details – '. . . the boat was blue and the paint was peeling and there was an empty cigarette packet floating in the water . . . and young as I was I felt, I knew, that this was precious, and your hat was soft on the top of my ears – I can feel it – and I shrank down into your coat – and then, then for no reason at all except that you were happy too, you began to sing . . .' – is plainly related to Friel's own childhood reminiscence in the *Self-Portrait* of 1972, written as much as a parody of the kind of encounter Friel resents as anything:

We are walking home from a lake with our fishing rods
across our shoulders. It has been raining all day long; it is
now late evening; and we are soaked to the skin. But for
some reason – perhaps the fishing was good – I don't
remember – my father was in great spirits and is singing a
song and I am singing with him. And there we are the two
of us, soaking wet, splashing along a muddy road that
comes in at right angles to Glenties' main street, singing
about how my boat can safely float through the teeth of
wind and weather. That's the memory. That's what happened. A trivial episode without importance to anyone but
me, just a moment of happiness caught in an album. But
wait. There's something wrong here. I'm conscious of a dis-
sonance, an unease. What is it? Yes, I know what it is: there
is no lake along that muddy road. And since there is no
lake my father and I never walked back from it in the rain
with our rods across our shoulders. The fact is a fiction . . .
For some reason the mind has shuffled the pieces of verifi-
able truth and composed a truth of its own.

Friel realizes 'its peculiar veracity' in a composed and mature
way, but his character Gar experiences a different, more
painful, version of the truth when he asks his father about *his*
fishing incident. A yawning gap opens up between Gar's happy
certainty, warmed by the nostalgia of childhood, and his
father's indifferent and ineffective memory of the fishing trip.
In the uncertainty of what the past contains, all kinds of other
anxieties about his present and future flood in. If he can't rely
on memory, what can he rely on? Gar finally has to face his
own question:

PRIVATE God, Boy, why do you have to leave? Why? Why?
PUBLIC I don't know. I – I – I don't know.

The play ends on that anguished note, a stuttering into silence
that is all the more poignant because it is uttered by the character *Public* Gar. This is the remarkable formal device that Friel

invents in *Philadephia, Here I Come!* to allow us access to the theatricalized inner life of the character. It is a device of the theatre, and in one sense is at least as old as the good and evil angels of the medieval mystery plays. On the other hand, it is a modernist ploy in that it embraces and gives form to the idea of the inner mind as a separate entity, operating by itself and able to comment on the actions of the 'outer' being that is the social and physical manifestation of personality. This is an approach that can only happen after Freud's dramatizing of personality into id, ego and superego, all visualized as battling for control over the person. It is also quintessentially theatrical in that it develops out of the stage monologue. If the psychology is necessarily somewhat schematic, Friel engineers a bittersweet comedy out of the differences between the two facets of the character.

Beneath the comedy there is a hard edge of angry despair that refocuses attention on the culture of contemporary (early 1960s) Ireland. It is there in the stunted emotional relationship with his father, who is plainly intended to represent a common trait or tendency. Private Gar rages at the unhearing Screwballs, his father: 'I'm leaving you for ever. I'm going to Philadelphia, to work in an hotel. And you know why I'm going, Screwballs, don't you? Because I'm twenty-five, and you treat me as if I'm five – I can't order even a dozen loaves without getting your permission. Because you pay me less than you pay Madge. But worse, far worse than that, Screwballs, because *we embarrass one another*.'

S.B.'s inarticulacy – his inability to put his paternal feelings into words and images – hurts Gar deeply, though he in turn is only so ragingly articulate in his Private incarnation. This emotional inarticulacy is not just a matter of personality. It extends by implication to the whole world of Ballybeg, with its boasting sexual braggarts and its small-minded priest and by implication further still, to Ireland as a whole. Finally, the play works because it transcends the parochialism of Irish society and speaks for all adolescents who yearn to escape from a dull, authoritarian historical legacy to find their freedom, at the same time as fearing to lose contact with roots, with security, with locality. Gar's anguished demand is that the two should not, in a mature society, be incompatible. In that sense, Gar is also Ireland. If Gar is Every(young)man, so Ballybeg is Everytown. The literal translation 'Small Town', speaks of a community of great particularity but also of a space in Friel's and our imagination flexible enough to be home to all his characters and concerns. The achievement of *Philadelphia Here I Come!* is to pinpoint a critical truth in a very detailed social picture – two days in a Donegal backwater – and touch a far more general nerve in the way any of us live our lives.

1966: *The Loves of Cass McGuire* to *The Freedom of the City*

The next play was to be Friel's own refracted look at the narrative of *Philadelphia, Here I Come!* Cass McGuire is an Irish-American emigrant who returns to Ireland in old age after fifty years in the jungle of an American city. When she returns to her Irish hearth, her language and manner superficially coarsened by brash Americanisms and alcohol, she finds that the money she has been sending to her brother Harry is unspent and her pious purpose in sending it undermined.

Cass is persuaded to enter an old people's home, the ironically titled Eden House, notable for a statue of Cupid 'frozen in an absurd and impossible contortion'. The play is partly about the power struggle between Cass and her brother over her life. It is demonstrated in typical Friel form by having the characters dispute the manner and content of the play in front of the audience, as if the play were written by Pirandello: 'The story begins where I say it begins, and I say it begins with me stuck in the gawdamn workhouse! So you can all get the hell outa here! . . . What's this goddam play called? *The Loves of Cass McGuire*. Who's Cass McGuire? Me! Me! And they'll see what happens in the order I want them to see it.'

Friel has said that the play is 'a concerto in which Cass McGuire is the soloist' and, as in a concerto, there are 'rhapsodies' from the residents of the home, recalling their lives with what is increasingly obviously a large degree of illusion and self-deception. As in a concerto too, the solo instrument – Cass – is also fighting for her identity in this new world of illusion, symbolized by that grotesque garden Cupid. At first she battles with the middle-class respectability of Harry's orchestral accompaniment, but finds herself gradually overwhelmed by it.

Friel characterizes the four plays *Philadelphia, Here I Come!*, *The Loves of Cass McGuire*, *Lovers* (1967) and *Crystal and Fox* (1968) as analyses of 'different kinds of love'. Certainly this play probes into family love and the twists and turns of its ambiguity, and it does so, often, through energetic comedy. It is very much a play about Cass's inner life, but it is firmly rooted in an implicit critique of that old but insistent theme of emigration and the psychological damage that it can wreak. For Cass, the journey from America to Ireland was supposed to be a coming home to die close to the reality of one's home, a return to organic values. In Friel's vision, it is a journey to illusion and disappointment, finally as inauthentic as the crass Cupid in the garden. There is an implied critique of the state of Irish culture here, for all the talk of love.

The play was broadcast on 9 August 1966 on the BBC Radio Third Programme, just as rehearsals started for the Broadway production. In America the play failed to reproduce the huge success of *Philadelphia, Here I Come!* Some American critics felt that Friel hadn't caught the American tone properly in his portrayal of Cass. Directed, as were all these analyses of 'different kinds of love', by Hilton Edwards, a director well versed in European modernism, the play's reflections on the nature of drama itself may have proved too European and self-conscious for American tastes. Friel's own analysis of the comparative failure was: 'American audiences are more attentive than in Ireland, but I think they're terribly influenced by what critics tell them.' He also felt that the American production process was damaging to the play's artistic success: 'The best theatre was always done, in history, with a writer working with a director and a resident company. This is, of course, what you don't have on Broadway, and indeed what you don't have in Ireland except in the Abbey Theatre.'

In *The Loves of Cass McGuire*, Friel is wrestling still with his love of Ireland and his intense irritation with it. Like a Sisyphean Gar O'Donnell, he was constantly 'emigrating' to America through this period as American productions demanded his attention. This served only to increase his home-sickness. He would have also been increasingly sensitive to the quietly ticking bomb of sectarian violence and the certainty of action for justice that was to explode a couple of years later in his native Ulster. As *The Loves of Cass McGuire* was in rehearsal, he told a journalist of his feelings of frustration and resentment at being a North of Ireland Catholic: 'I . . . some-times get very angry and can't think calmly about the country at all. But I am committed to it, for good or evil. Whatever you flee from in one place, you'll probably find the same things somewhere else.'

In 1967, Friel moved with his family a few miles out of Derry into a house in the County Donegal town of Muff. The Ulster-born playwright, whose greatest support and most loyal audi-ences had been found in Dublin and America, now lived in the Republic of Ireland. He was no longer subject to the govern-ment of a Unionist-dominated Stormont, but the move sig-nalled less a conscious rejection of Belfast and Stormont in favour of Dublin and the Dáil than a gesture of dismissive indifference for the border and all the irrationalities it repre-sented. Muff and Derry were part of the same Irish landscape, with the same Irish soul, as far as he was concerned. In 1982, still living in Muff, Friel regretted having moved at that histor-ical moment and so missed being at the centre of the political developments that were about to envelop Northern Ireland: 'Just to be part of the experience. Instead of driving into a civil rights march, coming out your front door and joining it might have been more real. It would have been less deliberate and less conscious than doing it from here.'

That year (1967) also saw a vastly more successful production of *The Loves of Cass McGuire* at the Abbey, and the arrival in London of *Philadelphia, Here I Come!* He gave a talk in Chicago called 'The Theatre of Hope and Despair', which showed him taking in his contemporaries in Britain and Europe, and thinking about the broader role of the artist, perhaps stung by the more polemical, focused aesthetics of British and European counterparts. He makes gentle mock of those (unnamed) European dramatists – 'less indirect, less devious, less cautious' – that he believes are abandoning the family audience in favour of mutually back-slapping, presumably 'lefty', propaganda. If, sometimes, there is in Friel's position a schoolmasterly Blimpishness, he does finally work his way into a clear endorsement of the centrality of the artist's – particularly the dramatist's – position in society. At first, he rejects any crude cause-and-effect relationship between the way the arts develop and the way society develops:

> they are what they are at any given time and in any given place because of the condition and climate of thought that prevail at that time and in that place. And if the condition and climate are not right, the arts lift their tents and drift off to a new place.
>
> Flux is their only constant; the crossroads their only home; impermanence their only yardstick . . . This is the only pattern of their existence: the persistence of the search; the discovery of a new concept; the analysis, exploration, exposition of that concept, the preaching of that gospel to reluctant ears; and then, when the first converts are made, the inevitable disillusion and dissatisfaction because the theory is already out of date or was simply a false dawn. And then the moving on; the continuing of the search; the flux.

Impermanence, flux, a sense that there is so much that is unknowable and unpredictable in the world, is very much a theme of Friel's drama. It may be that the dogmatic culture of Catholicism creates just this flight from certainty if it is not embraced wholeheartedly. However, Friel has faith in his art as a tool for apprehending a fluid, complex world. At the heart of his talk is the idea that much of Western drama expresses despair and anger at the state of the world, whether from a materialist position such as Brecht's or an idealist one such as Beckett's, and he addresses the question of whether a 'theatre of hope' is possible. His conclusion is that the artist can indeed prefigure hope in an unsentimental and practical way. Perhaps surprisingly, or with typically Frielian sly humour, given that he was addressing a gathering of Catholics, he even invokes the atheist Marx to set out his own personal artistic position:

> '*Mankind takes up only such problems as it can solve;
> since, looking at the matter more closely, we will always
> find that the problem itself arises only when the material
> conditions necessary for its solution already exist or are at
> least in the process of formation.*' That quotation is from
> Karl Marx. And although he was talking of social revolu-
> tion, it applies equally well to art. It could well be that
> many of the problems the Christian of today faces arise at
> this point in history because the solutions are at hand or in
> the process of formation. Camus said: 'At the end of this
> darkness there will be a light which we have already con-
> ceived and for which we must fight in order to bring it into
> existence. In the middle of the ruins on the other side of
> nihilism we are preparing a renaissance. But few know it.'
> I am convinced that the dramatists are among the few.

1967: *Lovers*

His next play, *Lovers* (in fact two linked plays, *Winners* and *Losers*), for that year of brooding calm before the storm, began with the assembling on paper of reams of biographical materi-al about his character, seventeen-year-old schoolboy Joe. He described the first stage of his writing method at this time as writing everything he could about the character and his circumstances. For *Winners* he worked out the structure diagrammatically:

> I did sort of geometrical drawings of the play, of the form of this play. In the case of *Winners*, for example, I knew that this was going to be the shape of a rectangle. This was going to be the total shape of the play and half of it was going to be Mag, the girl, with Joe contributing occasional bits of conversation. The other part of the play was going to be the boy. That was simply the geometric shape of that play . . . I've never done this before. I did it with this play, though.

The double bill of plays that makes up *Lovers* inhabits a world of haunted disappointment and incipient tragedy, sometimes shot through with a grim humour. They are plays that fall into an established tradition of ironic Irish melancholy, but shading into tragedy.

In the first play, *Winners*, Mag and Joe are schoolkids in love and about to be married. They enjoy an idyllic few hours together revising for exams in the sunny hills above their town. The conventional, soap-operatic elements of the play involve the pleasures and pains of their relationship, Mag's pregnancy and the problems this gives her conventionally offended parents. What jolts the play out of easy melancholy is the use of two narrating 'Commentators', coldly dispassionate lecturers who comment on the action from the extremes of the stage, and make it clear from early on that something fatal has already happened to the two sweet-natured adolescents whose quarrels and tendernesses we watch. Through this characteristic reshaping of the conventions of 'what-happened-next?' narrative, Friel allows us, through the Commentators, to see their lives in context as well as in emotional detail. The Commentators, with their ring files full of information about the characters and the ambient weather conditions, aren't there to fill in detail that the dramatist is too lazy to dramatize – much of their information is bizarrely inconsequential, such as the water-level figures for the loch in which they drown, and the rise in population of their home town. Their somewhat obtrusive presence makes us reflect on what is truthful and what is simply factual. They tell us a sad story but frame it in such a way that we have to think about what 'sad' is, what is a 'story', what is a *newspaper* story, and how we deal with such a terrible event as the death of two young lovers by surrounding it with an armour of ultra-rationality. The Commentators turn the audience's attention back on itself and its/our reaction to the story: 'Life there goes on as usual . . . as if nothing had ever happened,' the play finishes, crystallizing the everyday mystery of how terrible events are absorbed by mundanity. Yet Meg and Joe are 'winners', because, dead, like an Irish Tristan and Isolde, they can never grow into older 'losers' like those in the companion play.

Losers has something of the comic gloom of *The Loves of Cass McGuire*, focusing on the lives of an older pair of lovers whose love is forced into stagnation. Adapted from one of his own short stories, 'The Highwayman and the Saint', it tells of Hannah and Andy's cramped life in Hannah's mother's house. Bedridden, she has turned her room into a shrine to a Catholic saint and rules the house with her guilt-inducing handbell. When the lovers try to make love, she interrupts them until they are forced to recite Gray's *Elegy in a Country Churchyard* out loud in order to mute mother-in-law's suspicions. It is a farcical sequence, but the play's pessimism suggests some of that old anger towards his own Church and its sexual puritanism that stemmed from his adolescent encounter with the priesthood. There are no expressionistic experiments like the Commentators, but the play does allow its main character, Andy, to address the audience, and it opens and closes with a powerful image of farcical nihilism: Andy, the fifty-ish builder staring through binoculars at a blank wall. Mrs Wilson and her pious companion Cissy Cassidy embody so much that Friel dislikes in 'Auld Ireland' that it is possible simply to see them as symbols of the country itself. Yet they are also prescient of something new, for the angelic little old lady Mrs Wilson and Cissy (her 'understudy' Friel calls her, using a consciously stagy term) are on the way out. The sadness is that Hannah and Andy are too old to break away from them and are fated to be dragged down with them. If they had been more like Mag and Joe, the winners who died, perhaps they would not have ended up in futility, losers who lived.

1968: *Crystal and Fox*

Now producing new work at a prolific play a year, in 1968 Friel finished work on *Crystal and Fox*. Some of his work so far had featured self-dramatizing characters, such as Gar O'Donnell, and he had learned to use his plays to explore the connections between lived reality and the reality of art in plays like *Lovers* and the *The Loves of Cass McGuire*. Now he was to conclude his group of plays about love with an exploration of betrayal and failure by a father who is also an artist of sorts.

Fox is a travelling showman whose lack of self-worth leads him to seek a kind of redemption in dismantling, one by one, all the relationships that have supported him in his rickety show business. He sacks and antagonizes his fellow artistes, trying to get back to an illusory innocence and the purity of his early love and life with Crystal. Because he addresses his problems negatively, he condemns himself to further self-hatred. Most poignantly he drives Crystal away by claiming that he has betrayed to the police their son Gabriel, who has attacked and killed a woman in possible self-defence. Friel is warning about a personal human tendency to destroy the thing that one loves most in the face of the felt tawdriness of life, but there is also a sense that, yet again, his characters have an Irish dimension to them. To seek to find personal salvation in a mythical past will never create meaning or redeem failure.

Ireland – Northern Ireland in particular – was about to undergo the first renewed political convulsions that had been latent for some decades, and the mythical past with its unresolved tensions was about to take its own revenge on the present. In September of 1968, speaking in America, Friel was backing away from the idea that he might write directly about his society's troubles:

> If I were an American man of thirty-nine years of age, I'd think I must be writing about this particular time and the people of my time. But why must I be so obsessed with writing about this morning's newspaper headlines? This seems to be their concern. You know, Selma [Black American protest march against Civil Rights violations] is as far back in American history as the Gettysburg Address, isn't it? And that was only a few years ago. An obsession with this morning's headlines is really what it is, and there's nothing as dated as this morning's headline.

Ironically, it was these Black Americans who offered the model for the Irish Civil Rights movement in the North of Ireland. As Northern Ireland Protestants reacted with increasing violence to what they saw as a challenge by the Civil Rights campaign to their power and privilege, Friel, who had been a Nationalist Party member in the early 1960s, was clearly going to reassess his own work. A month after his distancing himself in New York, from 'morning headlines' drama, Ireland took a significant turning. Speaking in 1970, Friel explained the extraordinary impact of that one day on him: 'Until October 5 1968, which was a red-letter day, I thought that society was absolutely dead. Then suddenly five young men, who had nothing to gain in temporal terms, organized a very shabby rally. The parallel is not accurate, but suddenly the whole thing was dignified, as in 1916. The police beat hell out of these fellows. And suddenly the conscience of Derry was aroused.'

1969 began ominously, with a Civil Rights march from Belfast to Derry that was attacked en route by Protestant mobs. The two cultures, Protestant/Unionist and Catholic/Republican, were on a frightening collision course, propelled by their distinct histories and the inequality of justice between them. As a Nationalist with his roots in the Six Counties, Friel must have asked himself what exactly he stood for in championing the Republic against the Union. If his next dramatic response to that question was not exactly writing about that morning's headlines, it was certainly an engagement with public questions.

1969: *The Mundy Scheme*

The Mundy Scheme is a farce about the political nature of the South of Ireland, based on the mordant idea that a crisis-beleaguered Irish government would sell its western regions (so loaded with mythology in literary and dramatic terms) to the United States as a mass burial ground. (Other schemes to rescue the disintegrating state, such as siting a US nuclear weapons base in Cork, have been rejected, the latter on the grounds that decent Cork girls might be seduced by American sailor-boys . . .) At this period, in part because of its historical links with the the New World through the diaspora of the poor, Ireland was acutely conscious of its possible status as little more than a cute colony of American cultural imperialism – the current, more European, orientation of the South was not to begin until its membership of the European Economic Community in 1972. Friel's farce is an expression of this anxiety, one that he shared: 'Ireland is becoming a shabby imitation of a third-rate American state. This is what *The Mundy Scheme* is about. We are rapidly losing our identity as a people and because of this that special quality an Irish writer should have will be lost . . . We are no longer even West Britons; we are East Americans.'

He submitted the play with, in his own words, 'the gravest misgivings and little enthusiasm', to the Abbey Theatre, with the unbending stipulation that it should be directed by Donal Donnelly (his first Private Gar), and should feature the actor Godfrey Quigley as the Taoiseach, F. X. Ryan. The Abbey management rejected the play by three votes to one and Donnelly angrily took it to the Olympia Theatre in Dublin, though Friel affected not to be surprised or worried by the verdict: 'I was not disillusioned. I have never seen myself writing for any particular theatre group or any particular actor or director. When I have written a play I look for the best possible interpretation from a director and actors, and after that my responsibility ends.'

The play was not particularly liked and the consensus is that it remains too one-dimensional a piece, its ideas insufficiently worked into the kind of rich dramatic tapestry Friel normally achieved. However, some of the ideas about the nature of Ireland and its ambiguous relationship to both a mythical past and a place in the modern world were about to re-emerge in the more powerful, more complex form of his next play, *The Gentle Island*.

1971: *The Gentle Island*

Friel's friend and fellow playwright Frank McGuiness spoke in 1988 about the impact of seeing *The Gentle Island*: 'When it was first presented in 1971, I think it was ahead of its time and perhaps deliberately ahead of its time, because then it was a prophetic play, prophetic in that it diagnosed the problems that were going to afflict Ireland over the last twenty years – the hypocrisy of the South, the violence of the North, and he brings the two together on this Gentle Island and exposes them mercilessly.'

The play opened at Dublin's Olympia Theatre in November 1971. Politically the situation in Northern Ireland had deteriorated by the play's first performance. Inter-cultural fighting was increasingly commonplace as two working classes fought each other on the ground for hegemony. Critically, the UK government had introduced internment without trial for terrorist suspects, a move that simply served further to alienate Nationalists, driving them into support of the IRA and other armed Republican groups. The British army, once welcomed into Derry's Bogside as protectors against Unionist attacks, was increasingly recognized as that of an occupying power. The weekend before the play's opening saw violent rioting throughout the province.

The Gentle Island is not a play about the North, but its evocation of an Irish society deeply riven by anger, frustration and intolerance perhaps coincidentally locked into the immediate civil war situation stirring in the North. The title is ironic, of course, playing on the romantic pastoralism of Ireland as perceived by Bord Failte (the Irish Tourist Board) and the cultural tourism of city(Dublin)-based cosmopolitans. It also holds in its associations the matrix of ideas surrounding the old western island culture so significantly discovered and given dramatic expression by Synge and the Abbey Theatre.

What is offered here, though, is a play about the clash between old and new, symbolized by the expended ejector seat from some sea-swallowed military aircraft washed up on the shore and now sat in like a throne by Ireland's de facto 'King', Manus Sweeney. It is also a play about East and West, rural and urban. Friel even draws on the mythological potency of the movie western to emphasize this. One of the characters is called Shane, an engineer from the East. He and Peter, a musician and teacher who seems to be Shane's lover, think they have found a peasant paradise, but its beautiful emptiness is the result of economic conditions that have depopulated the region. Their heavenly Eden turns to hostility and eventual violence. That they are gay in a homophobic culture is one reason for this ugly turn of events, but there are other problems that Shane and Peter catalyse rather than cause. When he hears that Manus wants the two Dubliners to come back to the island at Christmas, Shane says: 'Of course he does. Because we give support to his illusion that the place isn't a cemetery. But it is. And he knows it. The place and his way of life and everything he believes in and all he touches – dead, finished, spent.' And so it is, except in the romanticized imaginations of admiring outsiders. The unresolvable dilemma (in conventional economic terms, anyway) for the islanders is laid on the line in this exchange between Manus and Joe:

MANUS Fifty years ago there were two hundred people on
   this island, our own school, our own church, our own doctor. No one ever wanted.
JOE Scrabbing a mouthful of spuds from the sand, d'you call
   that a living?

When Frank McGuiness characterized *The Gentle Island* as
prophetic, it was in the sense that unjust and uncreative living
situations will breed despair and violence. On Sunday, 30
January 1972 the second great seal of Northern Ireland's fate
after Internment came with the killing by British paratroops of
seventeen unarmed civilians in Derry, demonstrating, yet again,
for Civil Rights. Amongst the demonstrators marching that
day was Brian Friel. Bloody Sunday resonates nearly thirty
years later even as this book is written, with another inquiry to
come into the truth of what happened. What is certainly true is
that the event understandably created a huge disturbance in
Friel – the Derry man, the Nationalist, the decent teacher, the
playwright with a powerful access to the potentials for despair
and betrayal in Ireland's culture.
   Above all, Friel was the playwright who in 1968 had fought
shy of dealing with contemporary issues head-on, rejecting,
from his New York bedroom, the morning's headlines as subject matter, and having burned his fingers over *The Mundy
Scheme*. Bloody Sunday, however, was unavoidable, a different
order of headline altogether, and by the following year he had
written one of his most important plays, *The Freedom of the
City*.

1973: *The Freedom of the City*

In 1970 Friel told a radio interviewer that 'the Troubles' were
a possible theme to write about. Yet he was very wary of the
overtly political: '. . . it's in many ways an obvious theme. And
it does have a kind of international relevance because of the
drift to the left over the world, because of the student distur-

bances [Friel refers here to protests and uprisings largely around America's Vietnam War], and for all these good reasons. But in some strange way I shy away from it; I don't understand this.'

Friel's fruitful quandary as a writer is that his instinct is frequently to explore personal dilemmas, the consequences of personal choices, and the degree to which men and women frequently fail to know their own weaknesses. On the other hand, he lives in a society whose past and present history insist, often bloodily, more frequently poignantly, on his sense of justice. The playwright as artist and the playwright as citizen have to find common ground. For English contemporaries of Friel, such as Arden, Bond and Wesker, these divisions are less painfully felt. There is a sense with Friel that the reconciliation is always a struggle but that his best work is spun out of that struggle, and *The Freedom of the City* provides just such an illustration.

Although unquestionably based on Bloody Sunday's events, in this play Friel had learned the lessons of *The Mundy Scheme*. He took the documentary material of 1972 and put it through a transformation process so that he could widen the thematic resources with which he could work. His take on the narrative symbols of Bloody Sunday is set two years earlier. Now that he is dealing with fiction and not documentary fact, the play becomes an exploration of Irish poverty – both material and spiritual – and a revisiting of all the old themes of despair, self-deception, and a doomed quest for freedom.

Speaking during rehearsals for the première at the Abbey, Friel was characteristically wary of his play being stereotyped:

The trouble about this particular play in many ways is that people are going to find something immediate in it, some kind of reportage. And I don't think that's in it at all. Very often an accident in history will bring about a meeting-point, a kind of fusion for you. And this is what happened. This is a play which is about poverty. But because we're all involved in the present situation people are going to say 'this is a very unfair play'. And of necessity it has got to be unfair in this public kind of way.

The huge sensitivity of the subject was made clear the following year when the New York production folded after only nine performances. This wasn't only the normal Broadway critics' response to a play deemed to be uncommercial, but a response to the fact that the play took seriously the claims for justice and freedom of the Catholic/Republican minority. The reaction was similar even in the supposedly more sophisticated London press. Reports of bomb scares at the Royal Court Theatre in London contributed to an atmosphere of danger and unease around the play. Friel himself was surprised by the amount of instant judgement characterizing the play as terrorist propaganda. On Irish television, he said:

> If you're working in the arts you're always astonished at that kind of response because you always think that what you've been saying is read by two friends and nobody else and when you get the British Army moving into your agent's office asking questions, ringing back to Belfast asking questions, when you get threatening letters, you are really astonished! . . . I was kind of alarmed at it. Suddenly I was being threatened by all kinds of people and institutions.

Most of Friel's mature plays deal with struggles for freedom. Escaping – to America, from America, from Dublin to the western isles, from the western isles to Glasgow, from life to death – his characters are forever wrestling with what freedom is and where it might be found. Invariably they fail either to understand or to achieve freedom. Sometimes it is because of their own inadequacy, but always their failure is compounded by the condition of Irish culture. It is that social dimension that seems to well up from Friel's own feelings of anger and frustration with his homeland. It is appropriate, then, that this play

with 'Freedom' in its title opens with an image that is a nega-
tion of freedom: '*Three bodies lie grotesquely across the front
of the stage –*' Two young men and a middle-aged woman have
escaped from the tear gas and rubber bullets fired on them during a demonstration by sheltering in the Mayor's Parlour of
Derry's Guildhall. This place is the heart of Protestant power in
Derry, and the rooms around it would have been familiar to
Friel's councillor father. As they hide up there, they talk about
their reason for being on the march, about what they can do
(very little) and about their own unfulfilled and difficult lives.
Skinner, a typically garrulous Friel character, capable of eloquently articulating others' problems but not of addressing his
own, tells Lily why, in his opinion, she is marching. As he does
so, he probes beneath the layer of ideals and abstractions that
Lily has expressed to what he sees as a deeper and more mundane truth:

> Because you live with eleven kids and a sick husband in two
> rooms that aren't fit for animals. Because you exist on a
> state subsistence that's about enough to keep you alive but
> too small to fire your guts. Because you know your children
> are caught in the same morass. Because for the first time in
> your life you grumbled and someone else grumbled and
> someone else, and you heard each other, and became aware
> there were hundreds, thousands, millions of us all over the
> world, and in a vague groping way you were outraged.

Woven into the texture of the introspective events inside the
Guildhall are contributions from characters – more accurately
roles – who are part of the pattern of events. Amongst others
there are a Judge, a Sociologist, a British Army Brigadier, a
Pathologist. They are official voices, authoritative but partial
and therefore demonstrably unreliable. There is a satirical edge
to their pronouncements and Friel is engaging with another
profound concern: that of language – its power to define, contain and distort. The play concludes with a Judge issuing a
summary based on the actual Widgery Tribunal into the events

of Bloody Sunday. Its gist is that the army and security forces were provoked into firing and that Lily, Michael and Skinner were armed. Neither in life nor in the play are the protesters armed. The final stage picture unequivocally defines the dead three as victims of injustice: '(*The entire stage is now black, except for a battery of spotlights beaming on the faces of the three. Pause. Then the air is filled with a fifteen-second burst of automatic fire. It stops. The three stand as before, staring out, their hands above their heads.*) Black-out.'

Yet the opportunity Friel has given them to speak to each other and be heard by the audience has widened and deepened their tragedy. They are not faceless victims, and their tragedy is caused by factors greater than the sharp edge of a neo-colonial army. It is woven deep into the fabric of a society that blunts their humanity and creativity. Often in Friel authority figures (fathers mainly) betray their offspring, and the greatest of these is the State, the ultimate father figure (though Ireland's national muse is conventionally always female). Friel's anger at the waste of lives, a compassionate anger, rumbles through his plays, its target the Ireland he will not leave but cannot wholly endorse.

The year that began with Bloody Sunday continued with the overturning of an experimental power-sharing executive by a summertime general strike of Protestant workers. For Friel's community the outlook was grim, as it was for the community at the other end of the sectarian spectrum. British attempts to manage the crisis militarily were highly counterproductive, and strains in British political life were hindering any clear view of the crisis. Friel had obviously come to a watershed of sorts with *The Freedom of the City*. He was later (1982) to say of the play:

I think one of the problems with that play was that the experience of Bloody Sunday wasn't adequately distilled in me. I wrote it out of some kind of heat and some kind of immediate passion that I would want to have quieted a bit before I did it. It was really – do you remember that time? – it was a very emotive time. It was really a shattering experience that the British army, this disciplined instrument, would go in as they did that time and shoot thirteen people. To be there on that occasion and – I didn't actually see people get shot – but I mean, to have to throw yourself on the ground because people are firing at you is a very terrifying experience. Then the whole cover-up afterwards was shattering too. I still had some kind of belief that the law is above reproach!

This passage clearly demonstrates the massive effect those events had on Friel as well as the familiar struggle to keep his aesthetic guard up against dramatic oversimplification. Although his next three plays were to revert more characteristically to that blend of individual tragic melancholy and sometimes savage humour at the expense of his nation and its history, all three plays resonate with political ideas more strongly than those written before the events of the seventies.

1975–7: *Volunteers* to *Living Quarters*

One aspect of Friel's skill as a playwright was his developing ability to create richly symbolic narrative settings within which to explore his obsessions. Irish history, and its contemporary resonances, had been part of Friel's playwriting toolbox since *The Enemy Within* in 1962. In *Volunteers*, the new play that premièred at the Abbey in 1975, history is made palpable in the set design. The basic holding form for the play is an archaeological dig in 'a city', almost certainly Dublin, whose rapid development at this time had uncovered archaeological remains. At this period, Dublin Corporation was involved in building an office block on an old Viking site at Wood Quay, described as 'one of the major archaeological discoveries of the century'. Towns themselves were a legacy of the Scandinavian wave of the ninth and tenth centuries and the bony evidence of that contribution to Irish history is a skeleton whose discovery has temporarily halted the building of a new hotel complex. 'Leif' lies visible to the audience. The setting, elaborately described by a writer determined to be in full control of the meanings his play can generate, is a visual metaphor that presents history as quite literally underlying present-day Ireland. The workers on the site are mainly volunteers – Desmond, a student, and a group of IRA prisoners who have volunteered to do the work (the title 'volunteer' is also one given to all ordinary IRA members). This potent mix of Ireland's violent past – Leif appears to have been ritually murdered – and violent present – the IRA men know that their act of betrayal in volunteering for the dig will be fatally punished by their imprisoned colleagues – allows Friel to uncover ideas and perceptions about Ireland and bounce them around the walls of the dig. (It is as if the theatre 'fourth wall' itself is already part of the shored-up structure, a 'pit' temporarily opened in the world of business and bland modernity for the excavation of awkward perceptions and necessary questions.) In a lecture called 'Digging for the Truth: The Detective Process in Brian Friel's Theatre', the theatre scholar Katherine Worth put this play in a tradition ranging from Beckett to crime fiction – 'a fascination with mysteries, searches and hidden places of the self'. Once again Friel sees political history through the anguished psyches of men who are trapped by their own fates – fates that are themselves seen as products of a flawed and unresolved Irish history.

Volunteers was not a critical success at the Abbey, in the way that superficially 'warmer' plays like *Philadelphia, Here I Come!* or *Lovers* had been. Friel observed at the time: '. . . more than its effect on audiences is the fact that a barrage of bad notices can very often submerge a play for three or four years. It often takes that long for a real opinion to emerge. And it also means that foreign theatres will be slow to put on a work which has been poorly received by the critics in Ireland.'

54

Poor reviews kept audiences away. Friel's own bitterness with his country's civic life, wittily articulated by IRA man Keeney (a typically Frielian character, fatalistic but gabby), and the lack of an obvious 'love story', may have alienated audiences. *Volunteers* is nevertheless an important play in Friel's output precisely because it eschews sentimentality and offers a real opportunity to deal with themes of power and authority in the context of Irish history.

Irish history and its hold on the present, never far from Friel's concerns, seem particularly close to the surface in the clutch of plays of the seventies, from *The Freedom of the City* in 1973, to *Translations* in 1980. (*Faith Healer*, in 1979, is exceptional in every sense.) In 1976 he wrote two short dramas for BBC TV Education: *Farewell to Ardstraw* and *The Next Parish*, about the Great Famine and emigration to America.

Brian Friel is often described as a 'Chekhovian' writer, and there is a sense in which an old-fashioned literary craftsmanship based in naturalism does partly describe his work. Yet his output is shot through with non-naturalistic devices. Temperamentally not an 'experimental' writer who explores form for its own sake, he nonetheless introduces technical devices that perhaps derive from the authorial control he became used to having in his prose fiction. (Without doubt also, he has always kept himself well informed about developments in European and American theatre form, and has appropriated what he feels he needs.) We have seen how, in plays like *The Freedom of the City* and *Lovers*, time can be manipulated and the deaths of characters announced without losing them from the stage. This has the effect that Brecht sought of taking away the conventional gratification of surprise and substituting curiosity – as if to say: 'Now that I know that character will die soon, I can focus on what has led her to death.' (Unlike Brecht, Friel has no problem with generating a mystery that may not be solvable, nor does he worry that some tragic events in life are simply 'fated'.)

In his next play, *Living Quarters*, he invites comparison with another twentieth-century innovator, Luigi Pirandello, who also worked from a basis of naturalism but asked the audience to incorporate into their experience awareness of the artifice of what they were watching. In *Six Characters in Search of an Author* Pirandello created characters who were aware of their own status as playthings of the author. Friel, similarly, in *Lovers: Winners* gives dramatic form to the outside world's influences on, and perceptions of, his characters through the impassive Observers on either side of the stage, holding clipboards of information. In *Living Quarters* another variant of this technique is used as 'Sir', another Recording Angel-like figure with a ledger of biographical facts, narrates the story of Commandant Frank Butler of the Irish army, returning to Ballybeg to be honoured after service with UN forces in the Middle East. The difference now is that Sir interacts with his characters, who treat him partly as stage director in rehearsal – 'Are we all set? Good. Now – you've all been over this hundreds, thousands of times before. So on this occasion – with your co-operation, of course – what I would like to do is organize those recollections for you, impose a structure on them, just to give them a form of sorts' – and partly as playwright, as when the alcoholic army chaplain Tom Carty protests about the way he is written up in the ledger:

SIR 'As the tale unfolds they may go to him for advice, not because they respect him, consider him wise –'
TOM (*Sudden revolt*) Because they love me, that's why! They love me!
SIR '– but because he is the outsider who represents the society they'll begin to feel alienated from, slipping away from them.'
TOM (*Beaten*) Outsider?
(ANNA *goes to* TOM *and puts her arm around him.*)

The central metaphor of the play derives from the practice of theatre but its underlying themes have to do with our capacity to deceive ourselves about the control we have over our lives. Typical also for Friel's concerns at this time is his probing at the institution of the family. Family reunions are staples of drama, and the conflicting needs of rival siblings, their challenge to (usually paternal) authority, and the lurking presence of sexual betrayal are all there in *Living Quarters*, with the added context that the form of the play – Sir's assembly of them in a kind of ritualized picking at the scabs of their lives – involves the audience as necessary participants in the event rather than being mere voyeuristic spectators.

1978: *Aristocrats*

Friel has sanctioned publication of some of his work diaries that give valuable insights into the mental and emotional processes of his writing. Writing about a later batch of extracts, Friel observes: 'I do not keep a diary. But occasionally, usually when the work has hit a bad patch, I make sporadic notes, partly as a discipline to keep me at the desk, partly in the wan hope that the casual jottings will induce something better.'

Amongst the many richnesses in these 'casual jottings' is an ongoing anxiety about finding an exciting new idea for a play. His next play, *Aristocrats*, follows up many of the themes of family life in an Irish social context explored in *Living Quarters*, but he is concerned about 'an odour of musk – incipient decay' (1 September entry). He develops the anxiety into thought about the necessity for the artist not to pander to superficialities, to 'drop in for the crack (*sic*)'. In his commentary on the making of *Aristocrats*, we can feel this struggle with the temptations of easy solutions worked out. Characteristically the first phase of the writing process is about a process of listening for 'faint signals' (31 August), or about getting 'a scent of the new play' (7 November). It is as if the play exists already fully grown and the writer's job is to search for it, stalk it and make it his own.

31 August 1976
Back from holidays and now stancing myself towards winter

and work. Throughout the summer there were faint signals of a very long, very slow-moving, very verbose play; a family saga of three generations; articulate people wondering about themselves and ferreting into concepts of Irishness. Religion, politics, money, position, marriages, revolts, affairs, love, loyalty, disaffection.

Would it be a method of writing to induce a flatness, a quiet, an emptiness, and then to work like a farm-labourer out of that dull passivity?

1 September 1976
A. B. describes C. B.'s new play to me as 'a romp'. A curious phrase, attempting to disarm. This is merely to make you laugh, it suggests; the artist is on Sabbatical; the man like yourselves is At Home to you; drop in for the crack.

This is precisely what we can't do. We cannot split ourselves in this way. We must synthesize in ourselves all those uneasy elements – father, lover, breadwinner, public man, private man – so that they constitute the determining artist. But if we attempt to give one element its head, what we do is bleed the artist in us of a necessary constituent, pander to an erratic appetite within us. The play that is visiting me brings with it each time an odour of musk – incipient decay, an era wilted, people confused and nervous. If there are politics they are underground.

10 September 1976
Somehow relevant to the play – Mailer on his daughters: 'If he did something wrong, they being women would grow up around the mistake and somehow, convert it to knowledge. But his sons! He had the feeling that because they were men their egos were more fragile – a serious error might hurt them for ever.'

17 September 1976
A dozen false starts. And the trouble with false starts is that once they are attempted, written down, they tend to become

actual, blood-related to the whole. So that finally each false start will have to be dealt with, adjusted, absorbed. Like life.

30 September 1976
Coming back to the idea of the saga-drama, maybe even a trilogy with the Clydesdale pace and rhythm of O'Neill. Possibly. Intimidating.

3 November 1976
For some months now there is a single, recurring image: a very plain-looking girl of about thirty-eight – perhaps slightly masculine in her mannerisms – wheels on to the stage her mother in a wheelchair. Her father follows docilely, like a tinker's pony.

7 November 1976
I think I've got a scent of the new play. Scarcely any idea of character, plot, movement, scene; but a definite whiff of the atmosphere the play will exude. Something stirring in the undergrowth. At the moment I don't want to stalk what may be stirring there. No. I will sit still and wait. It will move again. And then again. And each time its smell will become more distinct. And then finally when that atmosphere is confident and distinctive, I and the play will move towards one another and inhabit that atmosphere.

27 November 1976
'You have chosen to be what you are' – Sartre.

[Now, as the play-creature is stalked and its outlines and manners more clearly understood, Friel spins off occasional thoughts about the wider picture. Two of the most interesting of these concern Chekhov (2 June) and the nature of the dramatic experience (16 December). About Chekhov, Friel's perception about the melancholy being a way to avoid tragic closure is clearly part of his own attempt to understand what he wants to get from his own, Chekhovian, work forming itself in his mind. On the nature of drama itself, he makes a very Frielian distinction between 'meaning' and 'perceptions of new adjustments and new arrangements'. Though this phrase might itself be thought an excellent definition of 'meaning', the distinction underlines his characteristic wish for meaning not to be pinned down reductively, but to be understood as a dynamic process rather than a fixed construct. Before that, Friel's next entry is significant because it is about a moment when a characteristic Friel choice – about form – seems to be presenting itself.]

7 December 1976
The crux with the new play arises – as usual with me – with its form. Whether to reveal slowly and painstakingly and with almost realized tedium the workings of the family; or with some kind of supra-realism, epiphanies, in some way to make real the essences of these men and women by sidestepping or leaping across the boredom of their small talk, their trivial chatterings, etc. etc. But I suppose the answer to this will reveal itself when I know/possess the play. Now I am only laying siege to it.

10 December 1976
THE CANARY IN THE MINE SHAFT. Title? (It is important when its song hesitates and stops.)

15 December 1976
A persistent sense that the play is about three aging sisters. And a suspicion that its true direction is being thwarted by irrelevant politics, social issues, class. And an intuition that implicit in their language, attitudes, style, will be all the 'politics' I need. Concentrate on the three girls. Maybe another married sister who visits with her husband. Maybe set some years back – just pre-war?

17 December 1976
Endless and disturbed wanderings in various directions, with considerations of masks, verse, expressions, etc. etc. But the one constant is Judith who is holding on to late young-womanhood, who has brothers and sisters, and who misses/has nursed an old father. THE JUDAS HOLE?

O'Neill: '. . . but O'Casey is an artist and the soapbox is no place for his great talent. The hell of it seems to be, when an artist starts saving the world, he starts losing himself. I know, having been bitten by the salvationist bug myself at times. But only momentarily . . .'

28 December 1976
Judith–Alice–Claire; and Father.

7 January 1977
Making no headway with the new play; apart, perhaps, from the suitability of the word 'consternation' to our lives. I feel – again – that the intrusion of active politics is foreign to the hopes and sensibilities of the people who populate this play.

8 January 1977
The play – this must be remembered, reiterated, constantly pushed into the centre of the stage – is about family life, its quality, its cohesion, its stultifying effects, its affording of opportunities for what we designate 'love' and 'affection' and 'loyalty'. Class, politics, social aspiration are the qualifying decor but not the core.

10 January 1977
Going back over four months of notes for the new play and find that the only residue left by dozens of strained excursions is: an aging, single woman; a large house for which she acts as medium; a baby-alarm; the word 'consternation'; and perhaps various house furnishings that are coyly referred to as Yeats, O'Casey, Chesterton, etc. Cryptic symbols that may contain rich and comprehensive revelations – or disparate words that have no common sympathy? So all I can do is handle and feel them. Talk with them.

25 January 1977
Every day I visit the site where the materials of the new play lie covered under Cellophane sheets. I have no idea of its shape from those outlines. I can envisage what the final structure may

be. But I have no plans, no drawings – only tempting and illusory 'artist's impressions'.

31 January 1977
Is there an anti-art element in theatre in that it doesn't speak to the individual in his absolute privacy and isolation but addresses him as an audience? And if it is possible to receive the dramatist and apprehend him as an individual, is the art being confronted on a level that wasn't intended?

2 May 1977
Mark time. Mark time. Pursue the commonplace. Tag on to the end of the ritualistic procession.

24 May 1977
The play has become elaborate, like a presentation Easter egg.
  Has it a centre?

25 May 1977
A persistent feeling that I should leave the play aside until it finds its own body and substance. Stop hounding it. Crouch down. Wait. Listen. In its own time it may call out.

26 May 1977
To see the thing exactly as it is and then to create it anew.

2 June 1977
What makes Chekhov accessible to so many different people for 180 years is his suggestion of sadness, of familiar melancholy, despite his false/cunning designation 'Comedies'. Because sadness and melancholy are finally reassuring. Tragedy is not reassuring. Tragedy demands completion. Chekhov was afraid to face completion.

21 June 1977
My attitude to the new play alternates between modest hope and total despair. What I seem to be unable to do is isolate its essence from the faltering existence I keep trying to impose on it. I keep shaping characters, looking for i-nodes of realisation,

investing forms – when what I need to do is determine what the core of the play is and where it lies.

10 September 1977
I have a sense that everyone (i.e. all the characters) is ready in the wings, waiting to move on stage; but somehow something isn't quite right on the set. So they drift about, smoking, scarcely talking to one another, encased in privacy. A sense, too, that that slight adjustment, if only I knew what it was, could endow them all with articulacy. Maybe that's the essence of the play: the burden of the incommunicable.

17 September 1977
Six days at THE JUDAS HOLE, when it seemed to take off, not with a dramatic lift, but resolutely, efficiently. And now at a standstill – that total immobility when it is not a question of a scene stuttering and dying but when the entire play Swansea specious, forced, concocted. Trying to inflate and make buoyant something that is riddled with holes.

19 September 1977
Moving, inching forward again. But whole areas – central characters, integral situations – about which I know nothing. And my ignorance and their magnitude looming and threatening.

26 September 1977
The play has stopped; has thwarted me. I still work at it. But it sulks. And yet – and yet I sense its power. If only I could seduce it past its/my blockage.

17 October 1977
The imagination is the only conscience.

11 November 1977
On a day (days? weeks! months!) like this when I come upstairs at a fixed time and sit at this desk for a certain number of hours, without a hope of writing a line, without a creative thought in my head, I tell myself that what I am doing is

making myself obediently available – patient, deferential, humble. A conceit? Whether or not, it's all I can do.

13 December 1977
'*Sometimes, however, to be a "ruined" man is itself a vocation*'
– Eliot on Coleridge.

16 December 1977
The dramatist has to recycle his experience through the pressure-chamber of his imagination. He has then to present this new reality to a public – 300 diverse imaginations come together with no more serious intent than the casual wish to be 'entertained'. And he has got to forge those 300 imaginations into one perceiving faculty, dominate and condition them so that they become attuned to the tonality of the transmission and consequently to its meaning, Because if a common keynote isn't struck and agreed on, the receiving institutions remain dissipated and unreceptive. But to talk of 'meaning' is inaccurate. We say 'What is the play about?' with more accuracy than 'What does the play mean?' Because we don't go to art for meaning. We go to it for perceptions of new adjustments and new arrangements.

1 February 1978
Yesterday I finally browbeat the material into Act 1. There may be value in it. I don't know. Occasionally I get excited by little portions. Do they add up to anything?

19 May 1978
The play completed and christened ARISTOCRATS.

Performed at the Abbey in the spring of 1979, *Aristocrats* is the play of Friel's most readily characterized as 'Chekhovian' because of its constant echoes of the three great Russian plays – like *Three Sisters* it is about frustrated sisters in a dull provincial town; like *Uncle Vanya* it is about the flawed authority of a patriarch, and like *The Cherry Orchard* it assembles a family in an old country house as both are about to succumb to the social changes of the modern world. As the diary suggests, Friel is keen to subsume the political hinterland into the characters' lives, rather than foreground them. Nonetheless the play's setting is full of political resonance. The large house outside Ballybeg is home to the Catholic O'Donnell family who have for generations been involved in the law and governance of Ireland. Now, with the impending death of District Justice O'Donnell, patriarch of Ballybeg Hall, things are about to change. The capacity for fruitful change amongst the family is diminished by their character flaws (Friel's diary borrowed Sartre's 'You have chosen to be what you are' to express that idea), but their own ability to deal with change is also the result of their father's decayed authority. Like Lear he has created a vacuum of authority that, in *Aristocrats*, generates a genteel havoc of despair and decay in his family. Other Friel themes are present as well – there is a hovering academic, the American Tom Hoffnung (ironically, the German for 'hope'), who seeks, like the sociologist (Dr Dodds) of *The Freedom of the City*, to see a dry, impersonal pattern in the history of the house.

By contrast its inhabitants and owner experience their various personal crises viscerally. The corrosive effects of class are explored in the engagement of Claire to the local greengrocer. This accomplished pianist is also an impoverished daughter of the faded aristocracy and marrying 'down' to trade is her last hope for a decent standard of living. The politics in *Aristocrats* are about decay and despair rather than passionate change. The 'big house' culture, last remnant of a feudal past that has limped into the first half of the twentieth century, is on its way out and new shifts have to be made in society to accommodate the changes. In its way *Aristocrats* is no less a political play than *The Freedom of the City*, because it is rooted in a pattern of Irish social life that profoundly affects people's lives. This is true in spite of Friel's unease with the idea of a political play as expressed in his diary entry: 'The play is about family life, its quality, its cohesion, its stultifying effects, its affording of opportunities for what we designate "love", "affection" and "loyalty", Class politics, social aspiration are the qualifying decor but not the core.'

In the character of Eamon, Friel brings to a pitch a particular character type that is a staple of his own and Irish writing in general – the loud-mouthed truth-teller who lives out a pattern of failure, yet ends by transcending failure because of his ability to speak truth where others equivocate or resort to violence. (The part was first performed by the Belfast-born actor Stephen Rea, soon to partner Friel in the Field Day project.) In his next play (actually written before *Aristocrats* but performed at about the same time), Friel takes up the idea of the failed truth-teller and offers him, for large parts of the play, sole occupation of the stage.

1979: *Faith Healer*

The 'exceptional' play that sits apart from the seventies plays on public themes and public men was in rehearsal in New York while *Aristocrats* was opening in Dublin. *Faith Healer* is one of Friel's most remarkable plays. Its basic form is four monologues, delivered direct to the audience by three characters, about the life and times of Frank Hardy, a travelling faith healer from Ireland. In his intimate sharing of his life history, Frank tells stories and anecdotes that are also referred to in the second and third sections, monologues by his wife and his agent, but they are remembered differently, with different emphases and in order to communicate different meanings. Clearly Friel's old theme of the unreliability of memory is part of his concern here, but the technical daring is achieved by means of apparent artlessness – in Eliot's phrase from *Four Quartets*, 'A condition of complete simplicity /(Costing not less than everything)'. In its form *Faith Healer* reiterates the world of the bardic story-tellers who spoke for the community in medieval and pre-Christian Ireland but it now speaks, as it were, for the community of story-tellers and those who engage with stories, for whom the faith-healing metaphor is a powerful symbol.

Because of the centrality of the Frank Hardy role, the actor who plays him stamps a great deal of personal authority on the play. To date, there have been three significant productions, with lead performances by actors all now sadly dead – James Mason in New York, Patrick Magee in London, and Donal McCann in Dublin and London. It was a casting coup to have a noted though perhaps slightly unfashionable Hollywood actor to back the production with his own name and reputation (and there might even have been a useful frisson precisely in Mason's unfashionable status, befitting Frank's own slightly peripheral relationship to the two worlds of theatre and medicine). Certainly Friel himself was impressed with Mason: 'Mason did a kind of retrospective on his life . . . It was superb acting, and I enjoyed working with him. He's so hard-working . . . He's 73 or so now, but he takes great care of himself, diets, does an hour and a half of exercise every morning. The acting instrument is in marvellous condition.'

The play was briefly revived in 1981 at the Royal Court in London, with Mason replaced by the great Irish actor Patrick Magee. Magee had created a reputation for his acting in Beckett, as well as creating a chillingly memorable de Sade in Peter Brook's famous production of *The Marat-Sade* by Peter Weiss. Magee's physical state, sadly, was a world away from Mason's – albeit his acting instrument was still in marvellous condition – and the show lasted for only six nights. Partnered by Helen Mirren as Grace, his wife, the production was by all accounts a knife-edge experience because of Magee's drink problem. Friel's colleague, the playwright Thomas Kilroy, nevertheless singles out Magee's performance without denigrating the later, better-known one of Donal McCann:

The actor playing Frank Hardy, a great actor, as it happened, was displaying personal failure up on that stage and a chilling identity was forged between the role and the damaged man who was performing it . . . I have never been so frightened in the theatre. Most of those nights Magee was so drunk that he barely made it into the spot on stage. But as soon as that infernally seductive voice began, Frank Hardy was present, a Frank Hardy who was carrying failure on his back like a great bag, unable to straighten up and desperate to stagger back into the wings and away from this place of cruel witness. There will be other remarkable performances in this role because it will always attract great actors but I think no one will catch the stricken faith healer in quite the way that Magee did.

Donal McCann took the role twice – once in 1981 for the Abbey and twelve years later again for the Abbey and the Royal Court Theatre. He was directed by the new young director at the Abbey, Joe Dowling, and the chemistry of Frank Hardy, McCann, Dowling and Friel established a new and distinctive note in the dramatist's repertoire. In very few ways is this play obviously 'political'. Nevertheless, although an allusive and 'mysterious' play, it is based on closely observed social reality. The country towns of Scotland, Wales and Ireland that Frank Hardy tours are peopled by men and woman who need the faith healer not so much because medicine has let them down, but because they seek an edge to living that conventional religion and mundane rural life fails to offer. Healing is in some ways incidental:

FRANK . . . (*Moving through seats*) And the people who came – what is there to say about them? They were a despairing people. That they came to me, a mountebank, was a measure of their despair. They seldom spoke. Sometimes didn't even raise their eyes. They just sat there, very still, assuming that I divined their complaints. Abject. Abased. Tight. Longing to open themselves and at the same some fearfully herding the anguish they contained against disturbance. And they hated me – oh, yes, yes, yes, they hated me. Because by coming to me they exposed, publicly acknowledged, their desperation.

Frank Hardy is not a con man – at least, not in the sense that he manipulates his audiences out of greed or cynicism. Indeed, he is as much in fearful thrall to his gift as those who come to his village-hall meetings. His obsessive self-questioning is going to doom him because it will, perhaps fatally, undermine him. As the audience, we become part of that undermining because we are witness also to the slowly disintegrating Grace and to his long-suffering and remarkably unremarkable agent Teddy, both of whom experience Frank's experiences through the lenses of their own subjectivity. In the end, Frank returns to his home town and knowingly sacrifices himself to the primitive faith of his audience. Knowing that his healing won't always work, and that the penalty for failure is to be murdered by brutal local men drunk on ignorance and blind faith, he goes to his death with a terrible fatalism. At this point he is narrating in the past tense and we know that once more we are sitting in a theatre listening to a dead man speaking (as to Grace, too, the successful suicide. Only Teddy, the perennial fixer and bag-carrier, slogs on in the material world).

Faith Healer is such an astonishing and rich piece of work that it is dangerous to fillet out meanings aside from the total gesture that the play makes. However, the central metaphor is once again a theatrical one – Frank performs, he acts (in the sense of undergoing a transformation that gives him access to some kind of communicative power), he moves his strange little caravan from village hall to village hall like some old fit-up theatre company. His gift, as various commentators have noted, is analogous to the artistic gift, but analogy is what it remains. The play transcends its metaphorical associations because of the precision of characterization, not just in Frank but in Grace and Teddy too. It is unfortunate that these latter characters tend to be seen as secondary to Frank, but they too have their own lives tested and twisted by Frank's peculiar talent. Grace especially, driven to despair and alcoholism by the terrible things that have happened to her, in particular miscarrying on a remote roadside, is a great tragic figure. All three characters have illusions or play with illusions, in order to deal with their private fears. Their variously contradictory accounts of the sad events of their lives show illusion working both to soothe and to deceive.

In this play, Friel finds a well-nigh perfect balance of innovative (if also ancient) form, and his constant obsessions with memory, language, failure and his native land. The play, though, is firmly rooted in social reality. With his characteristic refusal to sentimentalize the rural peasantry, Friel submits his hero to their murderous craft tools – axe, crowbar, mallet, and hayfork. We are at the still point of a turning world, twentieth-century in its technology but ancient in its now rootless superstition. *Faith Healer* is, yet again, a play about Ireland in history.

Its initial poor reception, especially from two influential Broadway critics, must have tested Friel's faith a little, even though publicly he was always relaxed about failure on Broadway. 'Stagnant and tedious,' wrote Richard Eder in the *New York Times*. 'Pretentiousness carves its own tombstone,' wrote Clive Barnes in the *New York Post*. Whether these judgements would have been different had the main character not been played by the high-profile James Mason, it is impossible to say. What is highly probable is that the form of the play disconcerted reviewers because it did not conform to accepted views of dramatic 'action'; but very few Friel plays have conventional 'action', because very often the plays are about a failure to 'act' (in the sense of affecting the world). They are plays about indecision and failure to connect, either because of social inhibitions or, crucially for Friel, because of failures of language. Indeed, *Faith Healer* goes further than many plays in terms of conventional 'action' in that Frank Hardy chooses, at last, the release of a violent death rather than struggle with the uncertainties of his unreliable gift. At the end of the play, and of Frank's second monologue, he moves in to meet the ignorant and drunk farmers at a wedding party, knowing that he will fail to heal their crippled mate and die because of it: 'And as I moved across that yard towards them and offered myself to them, then for the first time I had a simple and genuine sense of home-coming. Then for the first time there was no atrophying terror; and the maddening questions were silent. At long last I was renouncing chance.' It is precisely because he embraces this certainty, renouncing chance, that death is all that is left to him. For Friel, chance and uncertainty are the nearest thing to a guarantee of fruitful life.

In a programme made for Radio Telefis Eireann, Friel agreed with interviewer Seamus Deane's ideas that Frank Hardy's death was inevitable 'because he can't bear the intolerable pressure of a gift that is no longer in his control', and that the play is a kind of parable for the writer's art. 'But I don't want a transference made from Francis Hardy to me living in Donegal or anything like that . . . I think when the possibility of being able to control what you must do is no longer in your hands and can no longer be summoned, Death occurs. Maybe not necessarily a physical death but a spiritual death occurs. And this is what happens to Francis Hardy.'

Characteristically, Friel then steers the conversation with Deane on to the idea that one of the abuses of the creative gift that would cause spiritual death would be to propagandize. Yet the creator of *The Freedom of the City* was already a survivor of that accusation and his next venture was about to take him further into the firing line of some ignorant critics.

'Friels on Wheels' – writing for the fifth province

By the end of the 1970s Friel's role as a powerful representative voice in the culture of Ireland was clearly established and, with tragic irony, perhaps even enhanced by the political and social disaster that was unfolding in Northern Ireland. Events that directly resulted from the whole long, problematic history between England and Ireland had forced him, as an artist, to confront the tensions that were now killing people in his province, in his home town and in the fields and streets that formed the mythical imaginative world of his work. Nevertheless, the artist Friel managed to combine the documentary political play with his ongoing feeling for ideas that had always fascinated him. As we've noted, the two plays that speak directly about political and military events in the seventies, the decade of their setting and their writing, wrap into their world many of the ideas of Irish identity and history, language, myth-making and deception that are present even in his earliest short stories. The critic Fintan O'Toole has argued that Friel's work is not fundamentally political, that a political play must show a kind of ultimate faith in the possibilities of political action to solve problems (or at least to manage them). By that rather narrow standard he is right. Friel continually questions the foundations of memory and evidence, and so could be said to undermine trust in material reality, the basis of political action. However, he must surely be accounted a political playwright in the sense that he responds to politicized situations all the time. Even in plays like *Philadelphia, Here I Come!* the political fact of Irish emigration dominates the plot even as it is shot through with themes of memory and father–son relationships. Friel has always fought shy of acknowledging any definition as a political writer, still more as a political activist, although he has plainly functioned as a political *citizen* from time to time, taking part in Civil Rights marches, including the one that fateful January in 1969 that turned into Bloody Sunday. His suspicion of political theatre – or his definition of it – was clearly set out in 1967 in a lecture he delivered in Chicago (that American connection again . . .):

> If I had a startling revolutionary idea to propagate and if I were a slick propagandist I could go down among you and, by talking to you individually, I could probably find four or five who would buy my idea or at least take it home on approbation. But if I were to preach that explosive idea from here, you collectively would be all so eager to prove how orthodox you are that I'd be lucky to escape without

violence . . . in the present commercial theatre set-up, the dramatist has got to be wary if he wishes his play produced and have people listen to him. He cannot *appear* to exhibit the same outrageous daring that the painter shows. It means that he must work more deviously than his fellow artist. It means that he must work more cautiously. And, therefore, because of his indirection and his necessary caution and his obligatory deviousness, he is never going to be as ultra-modern, he is never going to be as apparently revolutionary. But if he is of his time, his flux will be as integral but better camouflaged, his groping as earnest, his searching sincere.

This model of playwriting as 'devious' is perhaps compatible with the man who found the certainties of priesthood hard to handle, who grew up in a culture where issues of national identity and their rooting in language are always on boggy, treacherous ground, and who had first established a reputation in the commercial world of the short-story commission. As his Minneapolis stint taught him, finding and keeping an audience have always been part of the calculation, albeit he has been able to do this increasingly confidently and instinctively as his reputation has grown. In that 1967 piece he takes to task 'European' dramatists, by which he seems to mean a range of politically inspired dramatists such as Brecht, Peter Weiss, and English contemporaries of his such as Bond, Wesker and Arden, for losing the 'common touch' and 'preaching to the converted'. It could equally well be argued that, in the years immediately following 1967, political events around the world – in the Vietnam War, in the Soviet invasion of Czechoslovakia, in the student uprisings in many cities of the developed world, in anti-capitalist uprisings in many Third World countries, in the massive revitalization of the idea of both the domestic and the erotic imparted by the politics of feminism – a new audience was created for a radically politicized theatre. If the tide of audience numbers for that theatre has since gone out under a

later wave of individualist politics, it could be said that Friel
was, compared to some of his contemporaries, rooted in a
rather conventional idea of the playwright and his/her audience. If towards the end of the 1960s, he was, by his own
admission, out of touch with the broad movement of international politics, the tragic turn Irish politics took in the 1970s
drew from him as a citizen and as an artist a powerful response
in the two plays *The Freedom of the City* and *Volunteers*,
which were catalysed by contemporary political violence. For
all his scepticism about political playwrights (feeling it necessary to caricature them as propagandist), these two plays
clearly marked a turning point. Though far more subtle and
wide-ranging than Republican propaganda (which is what
Unionists and English newspaper critics ignorantly thought
them to be), audiences engaged with *The Freedom of the City*
in particular as a powerful indictment of the role of the
British and their army in Ireland. If he was not a political
writer in Fintan O'Toole's sense, he was plainly a political artist
in some sense. By the end of the 1970s culture and politics were
about to be locked together in a new project that, for a decade,
most obviously reconciled his artistic and civic impulses.
With the Belfast actor Stephen Rea, he set up Field Day
Theatre Company.

Field Day

The founding of the company in 1980 was as inseparable from
the political situation in Northern Ireland then as it was from
the interests and enthusiasms of the young actor and the older
dramatist. Stephen Rea, Belfast-born son of a Protestant bus
driver, auditioned for a BBC Children's Radio show called 'I
Want to be an Actor'. At Queen's University, in Belfast, in the
1960s he read English and French. However, it was the contact
with young Republican intellectuals that gave Rea a dissident,
forward-looking perspective on his education and his national
identity: '. . . these Border Catholics coming in and seeing the

whole thing as a sham. The austerity of Michael Farrell [Republican theorist] and the appropriate disrespect of Eamonn McCann [leading Sinn Fein activist] took the place and showed it to be a pile of shit.'

The real passion of Rea's study, however, was the development of the Irish literary renaissance and in particular the role the Abbey Theatre played. The model of theatre the Abbey offered was not just the guardianship of Irish/Gaelic identity that had flourished and, in some assessments, gone stale since the turn of the century; it was also the notion of touring to small venues, of 'taking-theatre-to-the-people' that was a part of the Abbey tradition Rea was attracted to. Little wonder, then, that after university he headed for Dublin and the Abbey. Yet here he was disappointed to find what he perceived to be a stale, apolitical regime. In 1971 he went to London, where he met up with an expatriate Abbey actor, Jack McGowran, who offered him a part in O'Casey's *The Shadow of a Gunman*. Rea's acting career bloomed in England, and he became a well-respected figure with a number of the new, experimental and political touring companies such as Freehold, People Show and 7:84. These companies were part of a wave of alternative (sometimes dismissively called 'fringe') theatre companies that gave voice to the left-leaning and/or anarchistic explosion of the late 1960s and 70s, particularly among students, often the movement's biggest supporters. Sometimes Arts Council funded, they provided a cutting edge of anti-authoritarian, youth-oriented political expression and an eclectic range of styles. Perhaps most significant for Rea was the fact that few companies had theatre buildings. What they did have, in various states of disrepair, was Ford Transits (Bedfords, if they were very hard up; Mercedes, if they were particularly favoured by the Arts Council). The possibility of combining radicalism and touring was being demonstrated month by month, mile by mile, in mainland Britain, in response to the political and social crises of the time (including the knock-on effects of massive oil-price rises, strikes and the spreading poisons of fascist and racist sentiment). Freed of the suffocating embrace of the repertory or, worse still, commercial theatre, these companies sought to create new audiences for theatre, as often as not in working-class communities. In England and Scotland, 7:84 Theatre Company offered a model that must surely have intrigued Rea. Formed by a group of actors and 'led' by a playwright, John McGrath, who had moved from the comparative respectability of mainstream television, 7:84 Scotland in particular produced work whose purpose was to redefine Scottish identity in a socialist/anti-capitalist context.

In 1975 Rea triumphed on the fixed stages of Richard Eyre's Nottingham Playhouse in Trevor Griffiths' *Comedians* (playing an Ulster milkman who aspires to become a club comedian), and at the National Theatre in Synge's *The Playboy of the Western World*. Almost inevitably, given his enthusiasms and the networking of actors, he fetched up at the Royal Court Theatre in London, where fixed stage and radical new work combined. One such production, directed in 1973 by the English actor Albert Finney, was of Brian Friel's *The Freedom of the City*.

'There was an instant rapport between us,' said Friel; 'we seemed to be thinking about the same kind of things. Then I hardly saw him for the next six years. In 1979 I gave him a call. We met and had a chat about things. It was purely instinctive. We both wanted the same things and we decided to work together to achieve them.' The rapport was entirely logical, given both men's critical, tangential relationship to the mainstream politics of their birthplaces. It was also plain good luck for both artists, offering a new and vital connection to their society and history. For Rea, it offered the possibility of reconnecting him with his homeland after the successful but not completely fulfilling years in England. For Friel, it offered a specific platform for a new play, *Translations*, that he was finishing. For both, it offered the possibility of speaking about the modern Ireland they wanted to live in, a borderless Ireland that was Irish in identity but free of the old models of the Irish 'peasant' play palely imitative of Synge or the myth-soaked fantasy of Yeats. These were Ulster artists setting out to create a post-Ulster theatre that would tour to local audiences, not conventionally theatre-going, on either side of the border. The name 'Field Day' hinted phonically at their own surnames and had echoes of celebration in a communal space, as well as suggesting something military. If in some respects the inspiring model was 7:84 Scotland, central to the beginnings of Field Day was the ancient and, by 1980, bloodied city of Derry.

Derry in Field Day; Field Day in Derry

Marilynn Richtarik, a chronicler of Field Day's beginnings, suggests that a good starting point from which to appreciate the huge significance of this city for which Friel feels so much affection is the 1944 Education Act passed in wartime London. Thanks to its transformation of post-war state education in Great Britain and Northern Ireland, by the mid-to-late sixties there had emerged a new class of educated Catholics, often from working-class backgrounds, who identified more with their English, European and American peers than with the old priest and peasant castes of southern Catholicism. In Northern Ireland, the sense of injustice over housing, voting and jobs began to be articulated in a nascent Civil Rights movement. Clearly echoing the slightly earlier but ongoing struggle for Black Civil Rights in the USA, the movement in Northern Ireland had to deal with the same core issues of discrimination and prejudice. Derry, with a Catholic majority, was governed by Protestant Unionists, thanks to a rigged voting system. The vast majority of its unemployed (the highest in Western Europe) were Catholic. In a succession of symbolically important actions, the government in Stormont seemed to be penalizing and marginalizing this ancient centre of Northern Catholicism throughout the 1960s, as its railway connections were wound up, RAF and Navy establishments pulled out and factories closed. Most significant and, for some, the real fuse that detonated the Civil Rights campaign, was the issue of a new university for Ulster – necessary, as Queen's in Belfast was already overcrowded. Derry was an obvious choice, with an existing institution – Magee University College – in place and ripe for upgrading. Geographically, Derry was a natural western counterweight to Belfast in the east. Politically, of course, Derry was Catholic and Nationalist, though the Unionist-ruled City Council threw in their lot with Catholics to fight for the university. The Unionist Lord Mayor argued that a new university would encourage new industries and so reinforce an atmosphere of unity in the city. In 1964, however, the Stormont government of Northern Ireland chose the relatively small and overwhelmingly Unionist town of Coleraine for the new university. Derry's Unionist MPs were reluctantly obliged to stab their own city and its interests in the back as their party imposed a vote of confidence on the party's rule. A majority against Derry as the new university town was thus guaranteed.

The young Civil Rights leader John Hume, now a Nationalist MP, saw this decision as marking the point where the chance of orderly change in Northern Ireland probably disappeared, although he also believed that the campaign itself was a model for cross-sectarian unity. As the clamour for Civil Rights grew, so groups formed to generate pressure, particularly among students. Future Field Day director, the poet Seamus Heaney, wrote in 1966 of the possibility of an explosion: '. . . something is rotten, but maybe if we wait it will fester to death.'

On 4 January 1969 a Civil Rights march from Belfast to Derry was ambushed near Derry by loyalists supported by off-duty policemen, the marchers beaten up and scattered. That night, the extremist Protestant leader Ian Paisley found himself surrounded in the city's administrative building, the Guildhall, by a large, angry crowd. After dispersing them and freeing Paisley, Unionist police attacked the Catholic Bogside area of the city, insulting and assaulting residents. On 12 August the loyalist Apprentice Boys' parade around Derry triggered retaliatory rioting that ended in petrol-bombing from Catholic areas and CS gas volleys from the RUC. Soon afterwards, British troops were called into Derry and Belfast by the Stormont government to restore peace. Many Catholic residents and Republican activists welcomed them as protectors.

Any possibility of a positive political outcome finally disappeared in 1972 on Bloody Sunday. Amongst the sweet ironies surrounding Friel's 1972 play *The Freedom of the City* was that (although set two years earlier) it was clearly inspired by Bloody Sunday, and its main setting was Derry's Guildhall. What's more, Skinner, the character who articulates the building's symbolic weight with his '. . . this is theirs boy, and your very presence here is a sacrilege' was played by Stephen Rea. Few spaces can have been more charged with political meaning than this, both in drama and the wider public theatre of political struggle. By 1980 it was to acquire a still stronger, though altogether more positive, charge because of Friel and Rea's cultural intervention with Field Day.

By the 1970s Friel's beloved Derry City, which might have become a focus of peaceful change, had become a byword for violent struggle. Its nationalist population, increasingly frightened and intimidated, was a major recruiting ground for the Irish Republican Army. The Guildhall in Derry, once attended by Brian Friel's father, took on a symbolic character as the focus first for protest and then increasingly for violent attack as the symbol of Unionist political domination. Over the years, however, Derry City Council threw off the old naked corruption of vote-rigging. By 1980 a power-sharing executive was led by the Nationalist Social Democratic and Labour Party, representative of the majority in Derry.

Economically these were bleak times. On top of the isolation of Derry by Stormont, the one-year-old Conservative administration under Margaret Thatcher in London had begun a series of economic policies that plunged many traditional industrial areas into severe recession. The resulting unemployment and poverty were continuing recruiting sergeants for militant republicanism. The arts could be seen as something of a palliative to material harshness and on the mainland this was certainly a view that was beginning to be canvassed in arts funding circles.

It was the SDLP ruling group that made the hugely significant offer to Friel and Rea of the Guildhall for the first Field Day show, even while the building itself was held up by scaffolding after recent IRA bombing. In some ways this offer reopened the old wound of the new university. There was no civic theatre in Derry and a university campus would have offered one. In the absence of a theatre, the Guildhall was used from time to time for amateur productions, although its interior was far from ideal acoustically or in terms of its flexibility. However, the City Council supported Field Day with a grant of £13,000 and substantial administrative support. They also promised lighting and a new, temporary stage for the show.

For Friel there was a wider sense that Derry was the right place to be – not just his own feeling for the place or because it had offered him money and space to work, but because of its very status as overlooked, marginalized city:

> I believe in a spiritual energy deriving from Derry which could be a reviving breath throughout the North. I think there is more creative energy here than anywhere else. Derry doesn't look to either Belfast or Dublin, but to itself, that's why I want to work here . . . a dispossessed people living in a state they never subscribed to, with Donegal lying just across the bay . . . Now, however, *the dispossessed are coming into their own* and if this island is to be redefined the essence of redefinition could come from here [my italics].

Derry's Guildhall was a charged space. Its carved wooden staircase has busts of Queen Victoria, Edward VII and George V. William of Orange's victories are commemorated in glowing stained glass. English names of councillors are engraved in the stone walls. Not only was the space charged with symbolism, but the production itself bore the weight of the hopes and expectations of a community desperate for a resolution to the often bloody contradictions within it. These Ulster artists, with their play about the renaming of Northern Ireland by a colonizing British force, in a building scarred by Republican bombs, acted like a magnifying lens to light up the political landscape.

By opening night on 22 September every available ticket had been sold. As the *Irish Press* reported, the opening night of *Translations* was 'a unique occasion, with loyalists and nationalists, Unionists and SDLP, Northerners and Southerners laying aside their differences to join together in applauding a play by a fellow Derryman'. That Thursday night has gone down in Irish theatre and political folklore in a way that risks sentimentalization. Yet sentiment was certainly understandable. Famously, the company received a standing ovation, led by the Mayor of Derry, Mrs Marlene Jefferson, a Unionist. In the audience, applauding alongside her, were Sinn Fein councillor and Republican community activist Eamonn McCann, Mary Holland, another senior journalist on the Irish question, and John Hume, later to win the Nobel Prize for his mediating skills in the service of the 1998 Good Friday Agreement. In the stage manager's show report for the night, the number of curtain calls, against procedure, went unrecorded as they rolled on and on. His only comment on the report was a curt but expressive 'What can I say?!'

After Derry

If the opening night of *Translations* was a landmark in Irish cultural history, the tour that followed was the real justification for the setting-up of Field Day. Although it went to big theatres in both Belfast and Dublin, the company took its skilful blend of meditations on the nature of language and historical epic, and poignant love story to Newry, Dungannon, Armagh and Enniskillen – names potent with troubled associations in the

North – as well as to venues in the South. The last venue in Ireland was Cork Opera House on 15 November and by then Field Day had clearly established a cultural bridgehead in the whole of Ireland. Where that bridgehead should now lead was a matter not only for Brian Friel and Stephen Rea but also for a new group of directors who were brought on to the board to progress the work. Friel and Rea's initial impulse had been to set up an ad hoc company to produce *Translations*. It was an intuitive gesture based on the practicalities of making theatre. However, the huge groundswell of appreciation for the play, from new audiences in out-of-the-way places to metropolitan intellectual elites, suggested that more was possible. The Northern Ireland poet Seamus Heaney in particular wanted Friel to 'keep the energy rolling because my sense of that moment and that play was that this was what theatre was supposed to do'. Accordingly Heaney, together with the poet and critic Tom Paulin, broadcaster and musician David Hammond and academic and poet Seamus Deane were co-opted on to the Field Day board. Now that a company was established with some work under its belt, a policy – or at least a sense of direction – began to emerge. For Friel, never a man for clearcut manifestos, this was always going to be a groping, testing, intuitive process. It somehow matched his own sense of rootlessness and impermanence as part of the Northern minority. He expressed this paradoxical position to Fintan O'Toole in 1982: 'That could be one of the reasons, where you are certainly at home but in some sense exile is imposed on you . . . In some kind of way I think Field Day has grown out of that sense of impermanence, of people who feel themselves native to a province or certainly to an island but in some way feel that a disinheritance is offered to them.'

1979–80: *Translations*

This period was an exceptionally productive one for Friel. *Aristocrats* and *Faith Healer* had been worked up to production, *Translations* was on the stocks in his study, and so was a translation of Chekhov's *Three Sisters*. This last project was critical in many ways. As with some contemporary English playwrights – Trevor Griffiths had recast *The Cherry Orchard* in the 1970s, Edward Bond had translated *Three Sisters* in the 1960s, and Michael Frayn had made his *Uncle Vanya* ubiquitous – with Friel the act of translating this writer seemed to offer a way of focusing his own ideas and technique. (Friel director Patrick Mason observes that with Chekhov, for the first time in the history of drama, language is stripped of rhetoric without damaging its ability to be profound and expressive.) For Friel it was the wish to tackle the old Irish paradox that writers must almost inevitably work in the language of the colonial power (England historically, but more and more America culturally). In particular, Friel was impatient with what he heard as a prissy 'Bloomsbury-ite' tone in the classic English translations commonly in use. His wish was to find an Irish idiom of speech that would accept the English language but colour it with the expressivity and sense of locality of Irish. Around this time he had come into contact with the Austrian scholar George Steiner's book *After Babel – Aspects of Language and Translation*. Steiner was one of the most influential literary and social critics of the post-war world, a German Jewish intellectual and refugee from Hitler who had written about the role language plays in defining political reality. His ideas about language and the act of translating were extremely influential upon the understanding of the relationship between literature and political power at exactly the point when multicultural perspectives on art were beginning to be properly appreciated. Two amongst many key ideas in the book fed Friel's imagination at this point:

i) Instead of acting as a living membrane, grammar and vocabulary become a barrier to new feeling. A civilization is imprisoned in a linguistic contour which no longer matches, or matches only at certain ritual, arbitrary points, the changing landscape of fact.

ii) Eros and language mesh at every point. Intercourse and discourse, copula and copulation, are sub-clauses of the dominant fact of communication. They arise from the life-need of the ego to reach out and comprehend, in the two vital senses of 'understanding' and 'containment', another human being. Sex is a profoundly semantic act.

Steiner's landscape imagery in i) clearly fitted into Friel's reading about the first English Ordnance Survey of the Irish colony, which was begun in the early nineteenth century, close to where Friel was born and still lives. The basis of that exercise was the renaming of places to make them more comprehensible to English-speakers, a process of apparently pragmatic translation that had profound effects: hastening the irrelevance of Gaelic as a language and therefore the end of Gaelic culture. The modern world – itself transforming from a simple into a commercial imperialism – was changing the very nature of Irish identity with pens and rulers; but always over the horizon, if commerce and culture faltered, was the English military. Yolland, the 'reluctant soldier' and map-maker who falls in love with old Ireland and a young Irishwoman, is an agent of change as powerful as the soldiers sent in to punish the natives at the play's end for their apparent act of violence against British rule. His love for Maire in defiance of protocol and language barriers – neither speaks the other's language – gives poignant and moving expression to Steiner's second idea: that sex is a profoundly semantic act (that is, sex always happens in a context of meanings).

The success of *Translations* with audiences is largely to do with Friel's brilliant instinct to embed within the symbolic resonances of languages, maps, imperial ambitions, a love story that in lesser hands would merely sugar the pill of abstract ideas. Friel's achievement is to use the erotic relationship to speak for the whole colonial relationship. The fact that the relationship is doomed is a reflection of the trap that colonialism always springs – that however well-meaning the individual agents of change, it is a fundamentally unjust relationship; and the reaction to it will always be cruel in some sense. Yolland's disappearance echoes the abduction and killing of English soldiers in the twentieth-century Troubles.

The play is also shot through with good jokes about the way assumed English cultural superiority is shown up. Lancey, Yolland's superior, hears Jimmy Jack reciting Homer in Greek and assumes, in his ignorance of both languages, that it is Gaelic. In the powerful relationship between the two local men, Doalty – outgoing passionate defender of the old and local identity – and Manus – Dublin-educated modernizer and compromiser with the new world – foreshadow the political divisions in Irish nationalism that characterized the country's twentieth-century history. When *Translations* opened in Derry and later toured the North, exactly these tensions were current in audiences, who would have recognized the human dimension to political struggle as entirely contemporary. That, as much as the love story and the recognition of local history, is what made this first Field Day project so widely respected by all its audiences.

The notes Friel was making on *Translations* throughout 1979 again show how wary he was about finding himself in the role of 'political playwright'. His dilemma always seems to be that his artistic impulse to engage with society and give its turbulence and pain human images comes up against his mistrust of certainties, expressed as anxiety at being thought 'political', as the entry for 22 May attests: 'The thought occurred to me that what I was circling around was a political play and that thought panicked me.' As usual, there is evidence of struggle and self-doubt, but in contrast to some diary entries there is a concreteness of detail in this writing process, perhaps deriving from the great importance of historical and political research.

Extracts from a Sporadic Diary: *Translations*

(These notes were made throughout 1979. I was working on a play that came to be called *Translations*. *Translations* is set in a hedge-school in Ballybeg, County Donegal. The year is 1833. The British army is engaged in mapping the whole of Ireland, a process which involves the renaming of every place name in the country. It is a time of great upheaval for the people of Ballybeg: their hedge-school is to be replaced by one of the new national schools; there is recurring potato blight; they have to acquire a new language (English); and because their own land is being renamed, everything that was familiar is becoming strange.)

1 May 1979
Mayday. Snowing. Still circling around the notion of the hedge-school/ordnance survey play. Reluctant to touch down, to make the commitment of beginning.

11 May 1979
Bits and pieces of the new play are coming together. Characters are acquiring form and voice. Attitudes are finding shape and tongue. But only on this very basic level are there the first stirrings. The bigger issues – what the image of map-making evokes, what the play was born of and where it hopes to go to – none of these is acquiring definition. But at this point one still hopes for the numinous.

14 May 1979
Went to Urris today, the setting of the hedge-school in the play-in-the-head. No response to the place apart from some sense of how the ordinary British sappers might have reacted to this remote, bleak, desolate strip of land attenuated between mountain and sea. And perhaps in an attempt to commit myself to the material I bought a first edition of Colonel Colby's *Memoir of the City and North Western Liberties of Londonderry*.

The people from Urris/Ballybeg would have been Irish-speaking in 1833 – so a theatrical conceit will have to be devised by which even though the actors speak English – the audience will assume or accept that they are speaking Irish. Could that work?

15 May 1979
I keep returning to the same texts: the letters of John O'Donovan, Colby's Memoir, *A Paper Landscape* by John Andrews, 'The Hedge-Schools of Ireland by Dowling', Steiner's *After Babel*. And at each rereading I get interested in some trivial detail or subside beneath the tedium of the whole idea. For some reason the material resists the intense and necessary fusion of its disparate parts into one whole, and the intense and necessary mental heat that accomplishes that. One aspect that keeps eluding me: the wholeness, the integrity, of that Gaelic past. Maybe because I don't believe in it.

16 May 1979
I can envisage a few scenes, the hedge-school classroom; the love scene between lovers who have no common language; the actual task of places being named. Nothing more. The play is not extending its influence into unrealized territories. Stopping short at what it says and shows only.

22 May 1979
The thought occurred to me that what I was circling around was a political play and that thought panicked me. But it is a political play – how can that be avoided? If it is not political, what is it? Inaccurate history? Social drama?

23 May 1979
I believe that I am reluctant even to name the characters, maybe because the naming-taming process is what the play is about.

[Having, above, used a metaphor from the forge – 'the material resists the intense and necessary fusion of its disparate parts into one whole, and the intense and necessary mental heat that accomplishes that' – Friel now seems confident of the heat but continues to agonize over his materials. In this next entry he externalizes the remarkable balance of elements that character-ize the end product by telling himself what he does not want to write. As with a sculptor, the creative process for the writer is often about whittling away the unnecessary in order to reveal the creation that, in a way, already exists.]

29 May 1979
Reading and rereading Colby and Andrews and O'Donovan and Steiner and Dowling. Over the same territories again and again and again. I am now at the point when the play must be begun and yet all I know about it is this:

I don't want to write a play about Irish peasants being sup-pressed by English sappers.

I don't want to write a threnody on the death of the Irish lan-guage, I don't want to write a play about land-surveying.

Indeed I don't want to write a play about naming places. And yet portions of all these are relevant. Each is part of the atmosphere in which the real play lurks.

1 June 1979
What worries me about the play – if there is a play – are the necessary peculiarities, especially the political elements. Because the play has to do with language and only language. And if it becomes overwhelmed by that political element, it is lost.

18 June 1979
In Ballybeg, at the point when the play begins, the cultural cli-mate is a dying climate – no longer quickened by its past, about to be lunged almost overnight into an alien future. The victims in this situation are the transitional generation. The old can retreat into and find immunity in the past. The young acquire some facility with the new cultural implements. The in-between ages become lost, wandering around in a strange land. Strays.

22 June 1979

Something finally on paper. But what is on paper is far removed from what I thought the play would deal with. For some time there will be this duality – the actual thing and the ideal thing, neither acknowledging the other. Then at some point they must converge. Or one is lost – and then the play is lost.

25 June 1979

Work on the play at a standstill. A complete power failure. This is always accompanied by a lethargy so total that it seeps into everyday things; all activity collapses. And it is also accompanied by a complete loss of faith in the whole idea of the play.

I have never found an antidote to this lethargy, just drive the work on, mechanically, without belief, vaguely trusting in an instinctive automatic pilot.

2 July 1979

A busy week. The first thirteen pages rewritten a dozen times. To create the appropriate atmosphere. To create each voice and endow it with its appropriate pitch. To indicate the themes that will be inhabited and cultivated and to guide the play carefully towards them. Sheepdog trials.

And now standstill again. Because now that so much is on paper – the characters introduced, their voices distinctive, the direction of the play indicated – everything is so subtly wrong, just so slightly off-key, just so slightly out of focus, that the whole play is flawed. And the difficulty at this stage is to identify those small distortions. Because what the play and the characters and their voices and the themes ought to be – the ideal, the play-in-the-head, the model – can't be known until it is made real. The catch-22 situation. So you rework, go back over notes. And try to keep faith with that instinct. And at the same time you are aware that each day, as each page is forged, faith is being transferred from that nebulous concept in the head to the permanent and imperfect word on the page.

3 July 1979
Complete stop. Are the characters only mouthpieces for certain predetermined concepts? Is the play only an ideas play? And indeed are those ideas amenable to dramatic presentation?

4 July 1979
A persistent sense – the logic of the emotions? – that the character Manus is physically maimed.

6 July 1979
One of the mistakes of the direction in which the play is presently pulling is the almost wholly public concern of the theme: how does the eradication of the Irish language and the substitution of English affect this particular society? How long can a society live without its tongue? Public questions; issues for politicians; and that's what is wrong with the play now. The play must concern itself only with the exploration of the dark and private places of individual souls.

11 September 1979
What is so deceptive and so distressing is that the terrain looks so firm and that I think I know it intimately. But the moment I begin to move across it, the ground gives under me. There are a few solid stepping-stones – some characters fully realized – some scenes complete and efficient – but they exist without relationship to one another.

9 October 1979
Persistent, nose-to-the-desk, 9.30 a.m.–5.30 p.m., grinding work. Two acts completed. About to begin Act 3. Final acts are always less taxing because they are predetermined by what has already happened and at this point each character only completes himself, fulfils himself.

I'm not sure what has been achieved. I am more acutely aware of what has been lost, diluted, confused, perverted than of what has been caught and revealed. A sense, too, that on occasion I have lost faith in the fiction and shouted what should have been overheard. But there is still time.

5 November 1979
The play, named *Translations*, completed.

Talking during rehearsals of *Translations* in the barbed-wire-surrounded Guildhall, overlooked by British army barracks, Friel distanced himself from English writers like Howard Brenton, who, he felt, '. . . can indulge in the rhetoric of propagandist drama because it's safe there: they're secure in a continuing culture which has hardly changed in hundreds of years. But here we're continually thrust into a situation of confrontation. Politics are so obtrusive here. For people like ourselves, living close to such a fluid situation, definitions of identity have to be developed and analysed much more frequently.'

Whether it is just or accurate to characterize Brenton as a propagandist, or accurate to describe English political culture in the seventies and eighties as secure, this assessment by Friel of his political stance beams in on an essential of his and a great deal of other Irish writing: that politics is inextricably bound with national identity, and that the struggles around that idea are often bloody. As well as combining all the themes he dismisses in his work journal if seen in isolation, *Translations* is a powerful study of how present-day Irish identity came to be formed. It is one of a handful of English-language plays of this period that manage to express richness of ideas in a form that is both immediately accessible and uncompromised – Griffiths' *Comedians*, Bond's *The Sea* and Churchill's *Top Girls* achieve similar results by hitting on a particularly productive metaphorical holding form. *Translations* is one of Friel's greatest achievements.

Field Day director Seamus Heaney pinpointed the success of *Translations* and also hinted at the difficulties in following such an act: 'That play went intravenously into the consciousness of the audiences and the country . . . I suppose what we were searching for were other ways in which that kind of stirring and self-inspection could be extended beyond theatre.'

Much of Friel's time after *Translations* was given up to the nurturing and guiding of Field Day (and for a decade his plays were premièred by the company), but he regretted also having to spend time and energy doing interviews about the company.

1981: *Three Sisters*

The next Field Day project was Friel's Hibernian *Three Sisters*. His interest in the politics of translation, seeded in the research for *Translations*, could now become practice by engaging with Anton Chekhov, the writer who, of all great dramatists of the past (Synge excepted), offered the closest model for Friel. From Field Day's point of view, the project offered the chance to fulfil their ambition to perform the classics in ways that would appeal specifically to Irish audiences. The two great touchstones for this policy as far as Friel was concerned were clearly the Abbey at the turn of the century and Guthrie's Minneapolis venture from the early sixties. Friel's own favourite metaphor for his act of translating was musical: '. . . if you do use that one [Elizaveta Fen's translation] you must get your actors to assume English accents because it's English music. As English as Elgar. The officers say, "Jolly good. Wasn't it splendid?" . . . It's all a question of music. The audience will hear a different music to anything they've heard in Chekhov before.' His method was to sit with six English translations in front of him and work line by line: '. . . to see first of all what was the meaning of it, then what was the tone and then eventually what was the sound. It took nine months in all.'

The production once more rehearsed and opened in Derry, and inevitably there was less of the extraordinary buzz of expectation that had surrounded *Translations*. What there was on opening night was the buzz of a British army helicopter anachronistically intruding on Chekhov/Friel's dialogue. The dress rehearsal had already been abandoned after a car bomb exploded in the town, and the atmosphere was tense, with bomb threats on opening night. If there was any temptation to use Chekhov to escape immediate political realities, they were denied by the company's commitment both to Derry and to Irish English for Irish audiences. For Eileen Pollock, born in

North Belfast and a stalwart of the English alternative theatre movement: 'Brian's translation is much better than others at extracting the humanity of the situation, tragedy and all, with a ripple of humour. It is very hard work and while it is not an Irish play, it brings it into the understanding of the Irish actor.'

The play was directed by Stephen Rea and successfully consolidated the Field Day theatre work as well as making explicit a Friel/Chekhov connection that was to risk becoming a critical cliché, or, in one of Friel's favourite words, a piety. Rea's recall was that: 'In places of no theatrical sophistication, the audience loved it. They simply followed the story. In some cases they hadn't seen a play for 30 years.'

One very practical problem was that Friel's version was longer than other versions, and people were continually leaving before the end to catch the last bus home. The critics' reaction in Dublin, where it played the Gaiety, was sniffy, most feeling that Chekhov's text didn't need Friel's translating. Nevertheless *Three Sisters* did fulfil the core Field Day project in making classic theatre available to local Irish audiences, North and South.

The year of *Three Sisters* also saw Friel's international reputation consolidated with the Dowling/McCann *Faith Healer* at the Royal Court in London, and *Translations*, with Stephen Rea (until he left to direct *Three Sisters*) at the Hampstead Theatre, transferring to the National Theatre, and finally opening in New York. This bounding upward of his critical reputation and the accompanying journalistic circus (reinforced by his duties as a Field Day spokesman) all contributed in some measure to his next play for Field Day. In particular the praise lavished on *Translations* seems to have irked as much as gratified:

> I was being categorized in some sort of a way that I didn't
> feel easy about, and it seemed to me that a farce would dis-
> rupt that kind of categorizing . . . [*Translations*] was treated
> much too respectfully. You know when you get notices
> especially from outside the island, saying, 'If you want to
> know what happened in Cuba, if you want to know what

happened in Chile, if you want to know what happened in Vietnam, read *Translations*,' that's nonsense. And I just can't accept that sort of pious rubbish.

1982: *The Communication Cord*

Of course no Friel play would be created only as a perverse gesture against critical overreaction. What he does is to take nagging themes and concerns from one play and rework them in a different form. For Friel the challenge was also formal – farce was new technical territory to conquer. Publicly, he played the managerial game by announcing to a newspaper, perhaps a touch cynically: 'Unlike my other plays, I have written it primarily to give pleasure . . . There might be a chance you could take more out of it, but you wouldn't need to.'

Practically there was an urgency for Field Day to earn some money. *Three Sisters* had a large cast and a heavy set, and left the company out of pocket. Another popular success such as *Translations* would be distinctly welcome. *The Communication Cord*, a parodic counterweight to *Translations*, was more than just a comic potboiler, in spite of Friel's disingenuous reassurance. Its setting is very similar to that of *Translations*: a traditional Western Isles-style cottage (albeit a carefully restored heritage-industry version of one). There are elements of *The Gentle Island* here too: an apparently idyllic setting that literally, in this case, falls in on the sophisticated metropolitans who think they have found a kind of paradise. The restored cottage also functions like the archaeological dig of *Volunteers*. It is a stage metaphor for history, existing in three time zones – the 'past' time of the cottage's origins, the 'present' time of the story we are watching, and the time the play event itself occupies. Around the uses to which the cottage is put , mostly involving classic farce ingredients of greed, sex and social status, Friel spins a plot driven by miscommunication, the primary engine of all farce, and a main preoccupation of the writer's at this time. There is also, underneath the farcical manoeuvrings, something of the old Friel anger with Irish nationalist sentimentality, and impatience with middle-class exaggerated reverence for peasant life. To some extent this was also Friel's revenge on those who, after the manner of turn-of-the-century Celtic Revivalists, in his view saw the peasant characters in *Translations* over-piously. Indeed, the set looks at first glance like any number of post-Synge peasant plays from the Abbey's doldrums, and there is clear satirical intent in that. As the *Irish Times* reviewer noted, the play was '. . . a send-up of the sentiments so movingly expressed in its author's own *Translations*. In that fine play about the plunder by stealth of a community's cultural identity, both culture and identities were lovingly drawn and painfully clear. In *The Communication Cord* all is confusion as phonies fall over each other in their stampede to assert their mock cultural identities.'

Luckily for Friel and Field Day, the play was successful at the box office, doing approximately ninety per cent business wherever it played. Only Belfast, ominously, resisted the play, in spite of good reviews. Attitudes were hardening, and Stephen Rea's comment presaged a new problem for Field Day: 'Belfast seems scared of Field Day and what we stand for. There is something intrinsically political about what we are trying to do in that we stress our Northern but also our Irish, identity, and that bothers a lot of people.'

The problem was twofold: there was a critical backlash against the huge success of Field Day as an enterprise, and in the North (Six Counties) an apprehension that this was an anti-Unionist project. The first was perhaps inevitable given the huge expectations after *Translations*, but the claims made by Friel's associates for the cultural significance of Field Day struck some as pretentious. (One sceptical critic described programme notes by Seamus Deane and Tom Paulin for *The Communication Cord* as 'written in drunken euphoria on holiday from Academe (and common sense)'.) The second set of objections was harder to refute, inasmuch as most of the Field Day board were on record as being cross-border nationalists.

Friel in particular wrote of creating a cultural 'fifth province' via Field Day that might one day lead to a new political arrangement: 'Field Day is not about changing the North – I hate using grandiose terms like this – but in some way the very fact that it's located in the North and has its reservations about it, and that it works in the South and has its reservations about it, it's like, as somebody said, an artistic fifth province . . . I think out of that cultural state, a possibility of a political state follows.'

The difficulty of balancing the different demands and opportunities Field Day proposed was exemplified in the negotiation Friel undertook with the Ulster-born English playwright David Rudkin in 1982. Like Friel, Rudkin had grown up in Ulster, was a nationalist by temperament, dealing with political realities through powerfully personal analogies, and had a high critical reputation if certainly a lower public profile.

Friel's immediate concern, expressed to Rudkin, was that Field Day was becoming too reliant on his name – the 'Friels on Wheels' jibe. It had always been the plan to recruit other playwrights and Rudkin appeared to fit the bill perfectly. The fact that he was an Ulster-born playwright with a very high, if below-the-parapet, reputation was reason enough for Field Day to seize the day and commission Rudkin. Rudkin, in turn, had always wanted to address the problems of Ireland from the point of view of the Ulster Unionist culture with which he was familiar. The resulting play, *The Saxon Shore*, was an historical piece set in Britain at the end of the Roman Empire, with a tribe of Saxons 'planted' as defenders of the Empire's outposts against the northern Celts. It was a haunting and complex script whose basic analogy was with the transplanted Protestants of Ireland who were similarly used (and by implication abused) by the British Empire. It was a play that sought to increase understanding about the 'plantation' character of Protestant culture. With Ulster Protestants like Rea and Tom Paulin on the Field Day board there was no apparent ideological reason for the play's rejection by Field Day, which duly came some months later in a letter from Friel. It was unfortunate that the unanimous decision of the board should have been left to a fellow-playwright to communicate, but the consequential ill feeling and speculation about the reasons for the play's rejection were painful for all concerned. Rudkin believed he had been rejected because he had been too understanding of the plantation mind-set, offending what he saw as the nationalist agenda of Field Day. Rea spoke powerfully about his love of Rudkin's work but felt that the play simply didn't work in the way Field Day wished: '. . . his other plays always seemed intensely personal, and that's what I liked about his writing, loved about his writing.'

In *Ashes* Rudkin uses intense personal experience to open out wider political ideas, as Friel does at his best. In the end, *The Saxon Shore*, for all its brilliance, was probably not quite enough like a Friel play for Field Day to risk at that moment, lacking a certain audience-pleasing warmth and sense of place characteristic of Friel's work. Certainly it was a harsh lesson in the realpolitik of play commissioning for the inexperienced (in theatre administration) poets and academics on the board – Friel perhaps more than most.

The energy and time required to create, administer, and sometimes defend Field Day was obviously a burden for so creative a man as Friel. The organization itself was burgeoning into publishing and there was obviously a shift occurring, from the ad hoc mechanism to produce *Translations*, into something with a much wider brief – one that because of its political implications was bound to create controversy and debate. Not that he was less than enthusiastic about the idea: 'It's hard not to sound pretentious about the whole thing, but I find the experience wonderful and just want to keep it going year after year.'

Perhaps this exhilarating optimism was fated to change, as all artistic projects must naturally transform and reform. That it continued to function at all was at least in part due to a looseness of structure allied to passionate commitment from the founding guiding spirits, Friel and Rea. Board member

Davey Hammond said of the ad hoc spirit of the company: 'It'd be a bit like a Showband – it'd have the life of a Showband – last for three or four years and then we'd go off and join another band as well. But in fact it hasn't. It's lasted since 1979. Nine years already and it might go on even longer.' Nevertheless, after a period where at least one play a year, sometimes more, was coming out of Friel's study, between 1982 (*The Communication Cord*) and 1988 Friel produced only one script – the dramatization of Turgenev's novel *Fathers and Sons*.

1987: *Fathers and Sons*

It would be truer to see this time as fallow preparation rather than as sterility. Politically the period was fraught, as the Irish political problem rumbled on unsolved and apparently unsolvable. Like other playwrights before him, Friel looked outside his immediate experience in order to come at the problem of his own culture. The dramatization of Turgenev's novel, mooted by his wife as a device to unblock his creativity, was far more than a holding operation, because it refocused and gathered up energies for a new phase of work.

Specifically, as with Chekhov (whom Friel sees as living 'metabiotically' with Turgenev), he was able to examine a culture in which all manner of political disturbance was lurking and to do this through his strengths as a writer – mapping the complex emotional landscape of the family through the torments of a young man caught up in a changing society. Friel makes use of the significance of music as an organizer of experience in a way that clearly anticipates *Dancing at Lughnasa*. The script was offered to Field Day, but its casting demands ruled out anything but production by a large, well-resourced company. In the event, the National Theatre in London did the job and a National associate director Michael Rudman directed.

1988: *Making History*

The creative unblocking that followed *Fathers and Sons* also brought a new play for Field Day. Friel had been toying with plays about Hugh O'Neill for many years. In Ireland's history, O'Neill, the sixteenth-century Earl of Tyrone, is as iconic a figure as Henry VIII or Nelson in English history. Educated in England and sympathetic to European Renaissance culture, this Gaelic chieftain nevertheless became the focus for rebellion against English domination of Ireland. O'Neill also symbolizes a pivotal moment of failure of Irish independence in that he presided over defeat at the Battle of Kinsale in 1601. A Spanish-backed uprising of the Gaelic lords was defeated there and O'Neill was finally forced to flee to Catholic Europe, ending his days in Rome. Clearly Brian Friel recognizes something of himself and his contemporaries when he tells a BBC interviewer how he is attracted to '. . . [O'Neill's] capacity to dart into and out of his Gaelic consciousness and his English consciousness, his Gaelic experience and his English experience. He used them both but he allowed neither one to obsess him.'

For these reasons too, an O'Neill play from Friel was always going to be acceptable to Field Day, fulfilling its function of revivifying Irish history in the light of twentieth-century sensibilities, and dramatizing the dilemmas of someone transcending categories in the search for a new understanding. Like *Translations*, the new play could contribute to the Field Day project of establishing an Irish identity, free of England yet not bogged down in crude Gaelic nationalism.

As well as this iconic figure familiar to him from school history, Friel had before him two other important texts. The (Southern) Irish playwright Thomas Kilroy, much admired by Friel, had become a member of the Field Day board and had already written, in 1969, a play called *The O'Neill*. Kilroy's work uses the figure of O'Neill as a barometer of the changes that Ireland was going through at that time, as it began to face outward to Europe and to embrace a post-war world of technological and economic regeneration. O'Neill, educated in England and married to a Staffordshire nobleman's daughter, serves this purpose admirably, personifying Ireland's feudal past and its potential to move into the modern world. Both Friel's and Kilroy's plays dramatize this rich historical contradiction, and both were heavily influenced by Sean O'Faolain's pioneering 1942 study of O'Neill, which is already alert to the theme Friel was to pick up in the 1980s: 'If anyone wished to make a study of the manner in which historical myths are created he might well take O'Neill as an example . . . a talented dramatist might write an informative, entertaining, ironical play on the theme of the living man helplessly watching his translation into a star in the face of all the facts that had reduced him to poverty, exile and defeat.'

Working to this wartime template, Friel delivered to the Field Day Theatre Company a play that engages with another core Field Day activity: the writing and interpretation of Irish history. Throughout the 1980s, Field Day had evolved from an ad hoc organization for touring plays into a far more ambitious curatorial role in respect of Irish culture, producing literary anthologies and polemical pamphlets. In the process, the organization rubbed shoulders with the academic world, and friction was sometimes the result. Sean Connolly, an academic historian at the University of Ulster, has argued that part of the energizing spirit behind *Making History* is a desire on Friel's part to re-engage with the arguments over historical truth generated by *Translations*. The Faber anthology of Friel's writings contains 'Making A Reply to the Criticisms of *Translations* by J. H.Andrews', his response to academic criticism of that play's historical accuracy. According to Connolly, in *Making History* he is, in effect, killing two birds with one stone. He is dealing, as he did in *Translations*, with characteristic Frielian preoccupations about language and its role in creating national identity, using a narrative founded in a 'cross-border' love relationship to humanize the ideas. In place of the earlier play's imagery of map-making and naming, *Making History* focuses on the relationship of Hugh O'Neill with his biographer, Bishop Lombard of Omagh. O'Neill is making history in the straightforward sense that he is a political and military figure initiating great public events; but the real makers of history, Friel invites us to reflect, might be the historians. Lombard has identified a need for an Irish hero. In the great ideological struggles between the Catholic Church and Protestant reformism, O'Neill is a potential propaganda weapon for the Roman cause, and Lombard insists on moulding the interpretation of history to suit his church's ideological ends. In writing about O'Neill, he deliberately blurs the roles of recorder of information and creator of narrative, and he does so for partisan, ideological purposes. O'Neill is irked by this distortion both because it is offensive to his sense of honesty and also because it seeks to write his English wife out of history. Mabel Bagenal, a figure of energy, competence and brisk sweetness, is as central to O'Neill's (and Friel's) female-sympathied sensibility as she is inconvenient for Lombard. For him she is the wrong gender, the wrong nationality and the wrong religion, and he is the one literally making history by writing in his history book. Friel thereby questions the whole basis of the historian's calling, and by default acknowledges that the creative process is the best route to understanding. Already in *The Communication Cord* he had satirized the tendency of some Irish to believe a sentimentally idealized version of historical truth, and in *The Freedom of the City* he created memorable art out of a supposed search for objective truth – the Bloody Sunday inquiry under Lord Widgery – that plainly resulted in a fiction deemed acceptable to British public opinion of the time. At the time of *Making History*'s writing, the political situation in the North was as deadlocked as at any time in the post-1968 Troubles. Central to the intense propaganda war between the IRA and the British state was the creation of mythical figures as rallying points for recruitment. The greatest success (or disaster, for the British) of this period was the hunger strikes of the early 1980s, and in particular the death of Bobby Sands. Sands, a convicted IRA member, and nine of his comrades starved themselves to death in protest at the British government's refusal to grant them the status of political (as opposed to merely criminal) prisoners. Sands was even elected to the UK Parliament and his martyrdom focused Republican anger powerfully. The culture of self-sacrifice and subsequent secular canonization was already well woven into Irish historical experience by the executions of the 1916 Easter Rising leaders, and by the death of Michael Collins, most probably at the hands of opponents of his efforts to negotiate peace with the British. Friel was clearly responding to a sensitive and potent area of interest in looking at the creation of myths for political purposes.

In a BBC 'Arena' profile of the company coinciding with the tour of *Making History*, Friel completes the circle by addressing the future of the company in terms the play itself establishes:

> I'm not sure what history will say about Field Day. I imagine that history will accommodate Field Day into whatever narrative is appropriate for future people in certain circumstances. Which is one idea that I looked at in *Making History*. I don't think there's a single driving force behind Field Day any more than there's a single idea animating it or informing it. Maybe it's nothing more than the public expression of an affinity of interest between certain people, each of whom jealously pursues his own artistic life but who is happy to be expressed in this communal way. You may not fully agree with everything Field Day does or says – he certainly doesn't look to Field Day to represent him.

Perhaps there is a quietly prophetic strain of individualism audible in these remarks. Certainly as the tour progressed as usual from Derry Town Hall and wound its way round the Field Day circuit, Stephen Rea, playing O'Neill, was drawing strength from the whole enterprise, both theatrical and cultural. Tullyhogue Castle, near Dungannon, where they played, contains Hugh O'Neill's crowning-stone, which Rea visited on tour:

> I went there not knowing that anything existed of the old fort and of course it's there in all its perfection. It's a wonderful pure atmosphere. Its extraordinary to be somewhere you know that O'Neill definitely was. There's a line in *Making History*: 'The land is a goddess that every ruler in turn is married to. They come and they go but she remains the same.' I had a wonderful day that day. I remember we had a lot of children in the audience – it's very difficult to play for children. But they were quiet, incredibly well-behaved. I think it's to do with acknowledging that where you are is a centre. That it's important. In Dungannon that night, it was the centre of everything, you know? 10-year old boys, girls were sitting knowing that their place was the centre of history, you know? It's great! One of the important things we're about, I think, is that people aren't getting their ideas second-hand, on television. It isn't an RSC tour, it's not being delivered from headquarters, it's being delivered from within.

A space was opening up between the guarded individualism of the writer and the actor's commitment to community and in that gap a new piece of Irish theatrical history was about to be made.

1990: *Dancing at Lughnasa*

Friel's next theatrical venture is doubly significant as a new high point of critical and commercial success, but also because it marked the break with Field Day and, more sadly, with Stephen Rea. By the beginning of the 1990s Field Day had become a complex and sometimes controversial entity. Its role as a definer and evolver of Irish literary culture had been consolidated by the vast enterprise of the *Field Day Anthology of Irish Writing*, a labour of love, particularly for Seamus Deane, a very proactive Field Day director. Also feeding the controversies begun by *Translations* and its disputed historical accuracy (a positive outcome of the company's desire to engage with their society at profound and effective levels) were attacks on the male-centredness of the project from some feminist critics. These were unarguable, at least in the sense that women played no formal creative or executive role in the company at this point, and were conspicuous by their absence from the *Field Day Anthology*.

Since *Translations*, Field Day had produced other Friel plays as well as work by other Irish writers and poets. Friel's notorious unease with fixity, his stubborn individuality, was probably already irking beneath the surface of his success and reputation. The man who found training for the priesthood painful perhaps felt awkward in a potentially new priesthood of academics and archivists, however committed to creativity. His own drama work for the company, which he had co-founded for pragmatic reasons, was characterized by exploration of the public, social life of Ireland. (The exception might seem to be his 'translation' of Chekhov's *Three Sisters*, which seems, with its themes of frustration and slightly absurd melancholy, like a preparation for *Dancing at Lughnasa*; but even the Chekhov play is a public gesture in Friel's objective of finding an Irish English language, the better to reach his Irish audiences.) *Dancing at Lughnasa* didn't shun the public but was obviously closer to the writer's experience. Whether or not the Field Day project simply took up too much creative energy, the period between 1980 and 1990 was marked by stretches of what might crudely be termed 'writer's block'. The new play seems to have made its own claim for a new start in a new production setting. As Friel told John Lahr in 1991:

> Any life in the arts is delicate . . . you've got to forge rules for yourself, not for the sake of moral improvement but for the sake of survival. Rule number one would be to not be associated with institutions or directors. I don't want a

tandem to develop. Institutions are inclined to enforce characteristics, impose an attitude or a voice or a response. I think you're better to keep away from all of that. It's for that reason that I didn't give *Dancing at Lughnasa* to Field Day to produce.

The anarchist in Friel typically lumps directors, of whose calling he is sceptical, and institutions together. (As contributors to the third section of this book note, this is partly generational – a hangover from days when writers were very vulnerable to the whims of insensitive directors and indigent actors.) According to an *Irish Times* report, Stephen Rea was 'deeply annoyed and disappointed' that the Abbey and not Field Day was offered *Dancing at Lughnasa*. Not least of the benefits that would have accrued to the company would have been income, as the play went on to earn large amounts of money in productions in London and on Broadway (not that anyone could have predicted this on opening night.) Rea and others similarly taken by surprise would perhaps have done well to heed the stubborn individuality of Friel's 1969 declaration of authorial independence, quoted earlier, in relation to the rejection of *The Mundy Scheme* by, ironically, the Abbey Theatre.

In 1994, Friel quietly resigned from Field Day. From that point on, his work becomes, on the surface, more introspective and meditative, following the broad pattern of *Faith Healer* rather than *Translations*. However, the 1990 play was to be a Field Day enterprise in the sense that it combined that group's wish to work with Irish themes in a form that was accessible and familiar. Its creative roots were in Friel's own close family, but its catalyst was a conversation with a fellow playwright. Mel Gussow writes of this famous encounter:

Late on a summer's evening in London in 1987, Brian Friel walked along the Thames Embankment with Tom Kilroy. The two playwrights had just left Britain's National Theatre, where they had seen Friel's dramatization of

Turgenev's *Fathers and Sons*. As they passed homeless men and women curled up in doorways and trash-filled alleys, the writers speculated about the lives of these unfortunate people. Friel said he had two maiden aunts who ended up like that – destitute and abandoned in London. Just before World War II, they had suddenly left the family home in the tiny village of Glenties in Ireland, and never returned. Caught up by the story, Kilroy suggested Friel write a play about it.

Dancing at Lughnasa is undoubtedly Friel's 'greatest hit' of the 1990s – perhaps even of his whole career. It has a power to move audiences that transcends national barriers, or familiarity with theatre styles, or political preoccupations. Judges in Irish amateur drama festivals have their task vastly eased (or perhaps complicated) because so many groups offer the play. It seems that, when Friel connects his own biographical material to a potent social image (in this case the homeless rough sleepers of post-Thatcher London), he manages to speak to and for a receptive constituency in a way that occurs rarely in modern drama. It recalls a play like Arnold Wesker's *Roots*, which also grew from a meeting of deeply felt biographical material and the precise imagining of a social and political turning point. *Dancing at Lughnasa* and *Roots* are similar in other ways too: both plays chart the impact of a modern capitalist economy on rural culture, one in pre-war Ireland, the other in post-war England, but both on the cusp of change; and both use the power of music as a major signifier of the way human needs and modern technology briefly intersect. Wesker's Beattie Bryant brings a record player home and fruitlessly tries to enthuse her family – her mother in particular – with her new-found metropolitan enthusiasm for classical music. The unmarried sisters in Friel's play are transformed, if only for a few instants, by the new valve radio, beaming dance music into the rural silence of their cottage. Music liberates and disturbs in almost equal measure and comes to both groups of characters through new consumer technology. The plays finally have different preoccupations, of course. Wesker is interested in the growth of a new personality, someone who struggles to take on the new challenges of her world. It is, for all the pain involved, an optimistic play, ending in an ecstatic moment of articulacy. Friel's is so much darker, as he contemplates the death of a way of life that both supports and stifles the lives of his characters. If *Roots* is a celebration of humanity as it encounters the modern world, *Dancing at Lughnasa* is an elegy for it. The women experience their ecstasy only fitfully and bleakly. The play's dedication is: 'In memory of those five brave Glenties women' – meaning his own aunts on his mother's side. He has described the play as an act of piety, and that religious terminology embodies a kind of sad fatalism about his characters that is only slightly relieved by the narrator's – by implication Friel's own – meditation on memory, music and isolation with which the play concludes. It is one of the tricks that the piece plays (intentionally or not), that audiences experience the play as a wholly warm tribute to the 'five brave Glenties women' and a lament for their finally unfulfilled lives. The play is certainly both of these. Yet in the most remembered scene – the sisters dancing to the reel pouring into their kitchen from the Marconi radio set – Friel's directions are unequivocal:

the movements seem caricatured; *and the sound is too loud; and the beat is too fast; and the almost recognizable dance is made* grotesque ... *this too loud music, this pounding beat, this shouting – calling – singing, this* parodic *reel, there is a sense of order being consciously subverted, of the women consciously and crudely caricaturing themselves, indeed of* near-hysteria *being induced* [my emphases].

These really are bleak moments. Yet the sweetness of the music and the feeling of release we share with the sisters as their unarticulated anger is temporarily purged in this powerful piece of stage action adds strength to what might be a draining moment. We are taken back to a layer of the play – and to a theme – that runs like a constant, turbulent river through all of Friel's work: the insecurity about language and its power to define experience. Again, the play echoes Wesker. Beattie Bryant invokes her metropolitan boyfriend Ronnie Kahn:

> 'Well, language is words,' he'd say, as though he were telling me a secret. 'It's bridges, so that you can get safely from one place to another. And the more bridges you know about the more places you can see!' . . . So then he'd say: 'Bridges! bridges! bridges! Use your bridges, woman. It took thousands of years to build them, use them!' And that riled me. 'Blust your bridges,' I'd say. 'Blust you and your bridges – I want a row.' Then he'd grin at me – 'You want a row?' he'd ask. 'No bridges this time?' 'No bridges,' I'd say – and we'd row.

Michael's final speech takes this theme on. What might be misfelt in production as a celebration of melancholic memory is actually something harsher. Michael acknowledges that what he remembers is in many ways false – 'atmosphere is more real than incident . . .' The sisters danced 'as if language had surrendered to movement . . . Dancing as if language no longer existed because words were no longer necessary . . .' Now the sisters' sweet redemption in the music and the dancing is almost romanticized. The real strength of the play is in the gap between the warmth of feeling they share with each other and the audience, and the despair that their objective world inhabits. It is their inability to speak and talk effectively that means they are, and were, powerless – not without huge strengths and fine qualities and quirky individualism, but finally unable to hold together in the harsh realities of the new world. The only place where language does not exist and words are no longer necessary is not just in some autumnal glow of memory but in death itself.

Prior to its appearance on Broadway in 1991, the London cast of the play took it for a one-night stand in Glenties, home to Friel's mother and aunts, who were the models for the play's women. It was, inevitably, a sentimental journey, with a packed school hall heaving with people for whom the McLoones ('Mundy' is a local variation on the name) still live in some memories. In a resonant piece of quick-fix restaging necessitated by the small playing area, the elaborate trompe l'oeil cornfield of Joe Vanek's exquisite set was replaced by bales of real hay from fields surrounding Glenties.

1992: *The London Vertigo*

Friel now opened another play in Dublin, a characteristically quirky project, unlikely ever to make the same waves as *Dancing at Lughnasa*, then picking up awards and nominations on Broadway (including 'Best Play'). Cathal MacLochlainn was a Donegal-born actor who made the almost inevitable translation to London and an anglicized identity as Charles Macklin. His London career was hugely eventful and he exercised a lasting influence on acting styles both as a performer and as an acting tutor. Pope famously apostrophized his Shylock in the couplet: 'This is the Jew / That Shakespeare drew'; but Macklin was also a playwright and in his sixties he wrote a play called *The True-Born Irishman*. A satirical comedy about anglophile Irish society, it would have appealed to Friel on several levels. Like MacLochlainn/Macklin, Friel had experienced the tidal pull of London (and New York) on the Irish writer and had tackled in his own work the same themes of national identity and its vulnerability from overseas centres of success. *The True-Born Irishman* was well received in Dublin but perceived as parochial in London, where Macklin was based, and the play did not take off. Thereafter his plays were rooted in London experience and enjoyed greater commercial success. Friel had many times talked and written about the problem of balancing an international perspective with a commitment to local identity. In Macklin he finds a comrade-in-art facing similar problems and sets about re-presenting his eighteenth-century predecessor to the late twentieth century.

In an act somewhere between translation and editing the play, he transforms it into *The London Vertigo*, that condition of nauseating hyperactivity to which the exile is likely to succumb. Friel cuts Macklin's cast of fourteen down to five in order to give it a chance of commercial production in the constrained economics of modern theatre production. In the process he also focuses the themes of Irish nationality more clearly by excising some of Macklin's rhetorical attitudinizing and allowing a more sophisticated audience to draw its own conclusions. In the words of John McVeagh, an Irish academic, 'By laying down the mallet and taking up the rapier, he achieves a deeper penetration.'

1992: *A Month in the Country*

Five years after dramatizing a Turgenev novel for the National Theatre in London, Friel turned to Turgenev's one major play, a work that returned Friel to that parallel world of provincial ennui that nineteenth-century Russia offered him to set against his own country. Working on the play was, Friel admitted at the time, in lieu of anything original presenting itself from his own imagination, but he clearly found a revitalizing energy from the job. The constraints of the basic givens of plot, theme and character clearly allow him to write with a lighter burden of self-critical anxiety at the same time as exercising his craft in a satisfying way. Asked why he had returned to Turgenev, he said: 'Maybe because he is nineteenth-century Russian and I don't feel at all distant from that world. Because he is great but flawed; and the flaws allow in – maybe invite – the cheeky translation.'

The re-dramatization process (he worked from a literal translation by Christopher Heaney) enabled Friel to make direct contact with a writer whose own artistic journey and political situation he felt close to. Turgenev was writing in mid-nineteenth-century Paris, where radical ideas were cracking the facade of old Europe, just as old Ireland was being transformed in Friel's time. As with *Three Sisters*, a major concern was cracking the technical problems of translation. Typically, his working metaphor is musical: 'My first duty is to transpose the text into a key that is comfortably within the range of Irish actors . . . there are, of course, much larger issues at stake here. The practice of translation has to do with matters greater than pitch and range. But the Irish translator's dominant concern is a practical one: a play scored for Irish voices to sing.'

In his preface to the published script, Friel pins down one of those insights into other writers that clearly reflects back on himself: 'He [Turgenev] fashioned a new kind of dramatic situation and a new kind of dramatic character where for the first time psychological and poetic elements create a theatre of moods and where the action resides in internal emotion and secret turmoil and not in external events.' He writes of a 'metabiotic' relationship between Turgenev and Chekhov. Turgenev is the precursor and innovator who makes Chekhov's work possible, and once the younger man's work is established, *A Month in the Country* finds new acceptance as a consequence of Chekhov's success.

'And between them', writes Friel, 'they changed the face of European drama.'

1993: *Wonderful Tennessee*

Themes from *Dancing at Lughnasa* make appearances in Friel's next play, *Wonderful Tennessee*; however, they are wonderfully transformed into something as rich and rather stranger. The basic plot is very simple: three married couples arrive at a deserted pierhead on the west coast of Ireland to visit Oilean Draiochta ('Island of Otherness; Island of Mystery', as Berna translates it). Terry, the outgoing bookie and showbiz fixer, has set up the trip for his friends and partners ostensibly to celebrate a birthday; but the boatman that is to ferry them to the island never arrives (a fairly clear homage to Beckett, and also a nudging reference to Charon, ferryman to the Greek mythological Underworld). The six remain for a hot summer day and night, camped on the quayside, their characters slowly peeling open in all their flawed particularity. Yet it is the distant island shimmering in the heat haze, and the silent quayside whose peace their chattering and singing invade, that have as powerful a presence as any human. The island has a history of 'otherness'. It stands as a symbol of all their desires for transcendence and release from immediate reality. On the island, monks once experienced visions (even if they were largely the result of fasting and sleep-deprivation), and in the 1930s a group of Catholic youth, high on alcohol and spiritual fervour, are supposed to have succumbed to the island's pagan history and ritually killed one of their number. (The play invokes Friel's earlier play *The Gentle Island*, with something of the same sense of irony.) Just as the Lughnasa fires that fascinated Father Jack badly burned one of their devotees, so the island links the modern world via the Christian to an elemental, pagan life that can kill; but in the exposure to that ancient world, the superficially mundane concerns of some bourgeois Dubliners become refocused and readjusted. Like *Volunteers* the play creates an environment in the playing space that is profoundly symbolic. The pier is a special space, neither land nor sea, an essentially theatrical space, on which great personal transformations are possible because they are not tied to convention. Because the pier on which the characters sit and dance and sing and ponder their lives bridges land and sea, stage and audience, and because the audience is effectively looking at the characters from the island's mysterious point of view, it involves them as more than mere thrill-seeking spectators.It seems to give the audience a role as witnesses, like a Greek chorus, observing but also willing the slow evolutions and transformations that are taking place amongst the unheroic people from the mainland in an unheroic time. In Christopher Murray's potent introduction to the play he writes: 'Although they never get to the holy island there is a sense in which the island comes to them. When they all leave, "silence and complete stillness" descend again and overcome their departing noise. The pier recovers its divine presence.'

Wonderful Tennessee was too unusual a play to replicate the fantastic commercial and critical success of *Dancing at Lughnasa*. Its 'failure' on Broadway merely confirmed Friel's oft-repeated characterization of the Great White Way as some kind of glorified bazaar.

1994: *Molly Sweeney*

The new phase of more introspective writing post-*Lughnasa* continued in 1992 with the first thoughts on the play that was to become *Molly Sweeney*. The 'Sporadic Diary' records clearly that a major stimulus for the play was a problem Friel was having with his own eyesight. These problems and their treatment pushed him into contact with a clinical world that came to provide factual scaffolding for the deeper and wider concerns he was to explore (in the same way as colonial history had done in *Translations*, or archaeology in *Volunteers*). Eyesight and blindness have always been powerful dramatic symbols, and Friel uses the condition he writes about to explore relationships that have always interested him, not least the power negotiations and strategies in loving relationships, marital, sibling and parent–child. The difficulty of starting to work is eloquently expressed in these terse asides to himself. We are eavesdropping on a writer for whom all past achievement is irrelevant in getting new work off the blocks. As so often, Eliot's *Four Quartets* find their echo in Friel's life and work:

> Each venture
> Is a new beginning, a raid on the inarticulate
> With shabby equipment always deteriorating
> In the general mess of imprecision of feeling.

From the date in late August when the published diary begins, Friel's creative mood is one of anxious preparation, listening out for some echo in the air that will coalesce into a play idea. Most of his conversation with himself, when not about his hospital appointments, is about the Russian writers with whom he closely identifies, and Jung's philosophy.

Extracts from a Sporadic Diary: *Molly Sweeney*

28 August 1992
Went to an eye specialist in Letterkenny yesterday. He says I have incipient cataracts (just the aging process?) and perhaps glaucoma. He is to arrange a meeting with an ophthalmologist in Altnagelvin Hospital in Berry.

29 August 1992
The examination is set up – 10 a.m. in Altnagelvin next Monday. A young ophthalmologist with a good reputation.

10 November 1992
Still looking for something to fill the gap left by the completion of WONDERFUL TENNESSEE. I might look at an adaptation, Gogol, maybe? THE INSPECTOR CALLS? Why does THE LADY WITH THE DOG keep coming back to me?

12 November 1992
Doing nothing. A sense of emptiness. Too lethargic even to do this. Reading.

15 December 1992
Not working. Not even circling around anything. Reading fitfully and indiscriminately.

1 January 1993
A passing reference in a biography of Dostoievsky that Turgenev and Dostoievsky both took part in a production of Gogol's THE INSPECTOR GENERAL. Interesting – however unlikely. Who is the Irish Turgenev?

2 January 1993
Dostoievsky – anti-Semitic, anti-Protestant, anti-Catholic: 'You judge very rightly when you opine that I hold all evil to be grounded in disbelief, and maintain that he who abjures nation-

alism abjures faith also . . . A Russian who abjures nationalism is either an atheist or indifferent to religious questions . . .

4 *January 1993*
Four empty months stretch ahead until WONDERFUL TEN-NESSEE rehearsals. I feel I ought to have something in hand, planned. Another translation? A dramatised life of Dostoievsky? Something to do with Turgenev and Dostoievsky, those rivals and diametrically opposite, together doing Gogol's THE INSPECTOR GENERAL – with Gogol in the cast?

20 *January 1993*
Why is it that the (very badly translated) letters of Bulgakov and the diaries of his wife seemed vivid and irresistible in 1937 when the trials and the purges were at their most indiscriminate? Around that time Bulgakov wrote a play about Stalin (when Mandelstam was in prison – Akhmatova in despair – Pasternak, Prokofiev, Shostakovich all in deep trouble). Why does a life touch us at the point when it abandons the Great Virtues and scurries around in frantic despair? (The wife's letters/diaries with their distancing comments on their friends who have been arrested have disappeared: 'Nemesis has been visited on . . . 'I always detested that man . . .') Why do we then join in the official chorus? Self-protection only? But we believe what we say? Why is cowardice at the centre of our lives? Bulgakov wrote to Stalin (as Mandelstam did) again and again. And to Gorky, Gorky the hero, who had 'access'. And did Gorky himself believe?

26 *January 1993*
C. G. Jung: 'It is important to have a secret, a premonition of things unknown. It fills life with something impersonal, a numinosum. A man who has never experienced that has missed something important. He must sense that he lives in a world which in some respects is mysterious; that things happen and can be experienced which remain inexplicable; that not everything that happens can be anticipated. The unexpected and the

incredible belong in this world. Only then is life whole. For me the world has from the beginning been infinite and ungraspable.' WONDERFUL TENNESSEE?

[A little over six months later a low point of invention suddenly presages an idea about eyesight and blindness and a new hare is running for Friel. He circles round the idea, at one point using a metaphor of seduction – 'But it is necessary to be attentive to it. Later – courtship.' Clinical reading struggles, often painfully, with the need to humanize the pathology and find a point of contact with Friel's own interests. Then, in two stark sentences written on 22 September, over a year after the process was begun, the whole play that is to be appears.]

14 March 1993
Not working, Nothing simmering. The mad hope that miraculously a fully formed play will leap from the head. And why not?

15 July 1993
First stirrings of a possible play, A man/woman loses sight at five years of age. Blind for thirty-five years. Sight (partially) restored.
   Have ordered various books and papers on this subject.

27 July 1993
Wondering sporadically about the sight play. Vaporous notions that appear and disappear occasionally.
   I tell myself that I am waiting for the reading material and then the play will manifest itself with dizzying luminosity!

29 July 1993
   'I do not know which to prefer,
   The beauty of inflections
   Or the beauty of innuendoes,
   The blackbird whistling
   Or just after.' [from a poem by Wallace Stevens]
The sight-blind play?

30 July 1993

Sniffing around – more focused than sniffing – the blind-sight idea. (I lose interest and then come across a phrase like 'mentally blind' or 'agnosic' or 'blind-sight' – and the barb sinks into the side of the mouth. Or a word like 'gnosis', i.e. long periods of impaired vision, blurriness, which reaches out to gnosis, a knowledge of mystical things.)

And aware, too – indeed uneasy – that too much sniffing can induce addiction; a point of no return; a commitment to a journey that hasn't earned – doesn't inspire – belief.

Cave [Latin: Beware!]. (But sniff on!)

1 August 1993

Maybe a blind person functioning perfectly well in a familiar situation; the promise of sight; operation; consequences. If sight restored is used as a metaphor then it will be blunt and crude. But why not document – without extension, without hint of analogue – the story of a blind person? A medical story that is also offered as a love/spiritual story?

7 August 1993

The play seems to be gathering round three people. Is the blind person a man or woman? My instinct at this stage is a woman.

8 August 1993

Is it time to sit down at the blind play?

9 August 1993

The answer to the question above is No. But it is necessary to be attentive to it. Later – courtship.

12 August 1993

Making notes on the blind play. Constantly being diverted from the central issue which is: Who are these people and what is their story? – not How is their story told?

'She says, "I am content when wakened birds,
Before they fly, test the reality
Of misty fields, by their sweet questionings;

But when the birds are gone, and their warm fields
Return no more, where, then, is paradise?"' [Wallace
Stevens again]
Blackbirds – wakened birds – innuendoes – testing reality –
sight restored?

13 August 1993
Every day adding a few lines to the notes on the blind play.
Today I think the play is about seeking – and fabricating – par-
adise. (The result of reading W. S.'s poetry?)

24 August 1993
I have got a lot of blind material from my agent and have been
reading it closely – Valpo, Strampelli, Berkeley, Locke, Van
Sindeti, Sacks, etc. etc.
    No idea at all if there is a vein there.

25 August 1993
Working through the blind books with diminishing relish. My
instinct is to toss them aside and confront the play directly.

31 August 1993
Weary of reading about prostheses, nystagmus, visual and tac-
tile experience, etc. etc. Back to fundamentals:
    a person is restored to sight
    the experience is enormously difficult
    the new world is a disappointment – the old world was bet-
ter the person goes into a decline and dies

15 September 1993
Time to look again at the blind play. I haven't worked at the
material for some time but I have a sense that it is stirring in the
background. And the shape it seems to be claiming is a three-
hander – a woman, two men. Maybe not distinct monologues;
contrapuntal; overlapping.

22 September 1993
There are three voices – in fact the play is a trio for three voices: the blind/cured wife, her husband, the ophthalmologist. The

men force her to be sighted. The process kills her.

[The absolute clarity of that summary of *Molly Sweeney* seems to come about because it finally fuses Friel's immediate material circumstances – his eye problems – with his long interest in flawed, authoritative men who, Lear-like, create misery trying to do good. Now the work shifts into a second phase in which Friel worries at the basic premise to make it reveal itself more clearly. He has to make an organic third thing come out of the fusion and collisions between the clinical and the emotional. The entries move on, charting the slow process of defining what the play actually is, a process of questioning and probing for what the material might offer. Gradually the play reveals itself to the writer and by the start of 1994 questions of craft and form begin to take precedence over questions about the play's identity. Friel is even making comparisons with his own work, noting its relationship to *Faith Healer*.]

8 November 1993
If/when I go back to the blind play I must approach it more easily, more openly, not schematically. Allow it to flow easily through me. Don't try to control the erratic transiliences.

    You are the music
    While the music lasts.
Where in Eliot?
Freud: 'The final therapy is work and love.'

9 November 1993
The desk is cleared. The blind books are arrayed before me. The play is chronologically due – but maybe not spiritually? An innate sense of duty, the work ethic, years of discipline – all conspire to force a beginning. And why not?

22 November 1993
The blind play keeps getting snagged in complex medical explanations. The various eye books keep demanding attention. But the play is about people and the medical condition of one of these people mustn't be allowed to dominate.

23 November 1993
The play – the play – the play! Of course it won't begin to stir until I know everything about these people – first.

24 November 1993
Turgenev wrote A MONTH IN THE COUNTRY in 1850 – It was first successfully produced in 1879 (with Maria Savina). He doesn't seem to have cared; was astonished at the success then. The more I read about him the more convinced I am that he was an amateur. What attracted him was the idea of being a writer, a painter, a traveller, a linguist, a European, a Russian exile. And who loves Russia more than a Russian exile?

The idea of a metabiotic relationship between himself and Chekhov should be looked at. Turgenev's (failed) play created an atmosphere sympathetic to Chekhov's new drama. And the success of that new drama made possible the warm revival of Turgenev.

29 November 1993
The blind play is stationary; hasn't even the first stirrings of movement. I think because I don't know anything about Martha (?) apart from her condition. Is she even a woman?

30 November 1993
I have a sense that if I begin to put them (the characters) down on paper they will become – gradually – corporeal. It's a method, I suppose.

1 December 1993
A letter from the ophthalmologist in Altnagelvin Hospital: I am to have the eye operation there next Monday. I'll be in the hospital, I'm told, from 10 a.m. until 4 p.m. Or I may stay in overnight.

2 December 1993
The blind play is trammelled by basic questions. The characters (how many?) are acquiring some definition – not a lot. But their method of revealing themselves is nowhere near a solu-

tion. (And although I write that, I keep casting the play in monologues; or duets; or trios; but not in any kind of usual dramatic exchange.)

8 December 1993

Altnagelvin at 10 a.m. on Monday. Operation on the right eye – 1.15 p.m. to 2 p.m.

Left the hospital at 3.45 p.m.

Back yesterday to get the bandages off. 'Perfect!' said the ophthalmologist.

Due back next Monday.

Have written two longish first monologues – husband and wife. But looking at them both today I know that both are wrong – wrong in pitch and in tone but more importantly wrong in form.

9 December 1993

Since I've had the operation on the right eye this ink is quintessential blackness, the page blinding white. The new eye hasn't learned to discriminate – it is equally impressed by everything. So that reality has a surreality that alters, adjusts, distorts everything. But no more pain.

11 December 1993

The eye improves daily. Occasionally a sense that there is an eyelash in it. Or that a tiny, circular haze tags along just behind the line of vision. But the sight is immeasurably better. Now the left eye seems useless.

12 December 1993

The blind play is going nowhere. Nowhere near lift-off.

Getting irritable – worse, *weary* – with it all.

13 December 1993

Over the weekend I wrote the wife's first speech. A dozen times. And again this morning.

I'm not unhappy with it. The sound is real enough. The tone is right enough. A woman may materialize.

If I could get the ophthalmologist's first speech today . . .

14 December 1993
Called back to Altnagelvin for a check-up this morning. All's well.

The wife's first speech doesn't seem so accomplished today.

14 [sic] December 1993
Got an opening statement from the ophthalmologist. Nowhere near an individual voice; but a kind of Identikit picture of the man emerging.

Wrote the statement a second time. Now even the Identikit is gone.

18 December 1993
Attempting to move on to the husband's voice. Have got something on paper for the wife and ophthalmologist. Faltering. But at least marks on paper.

20 December 1993
I now have something down for all three and each piece instantly demands adjustments in the previous piece. So everything is fluid. And as I write each character it is clear that they can't be written but can only evolve, developing (and revealing) their characters and characteristics as they discover themselves, not as I add to them, compose them.

21 December 1993
On one of his trips back to Russia Turgenev, the sixty-year-old, fully Europeanized, foppishly dressed, altogether elegant artist, had dinner with Tolstoy and his family. They persuaded (maliciously?) Turgenev to demonstrate the latest dance craze – the can can. Turgenev in his vanity did. And in his diary that night Tolstoy wrote: 'Turgenev. Cancan. Sad.'

22 December 1993
Something wrong with the ophthalmologist. I'm not getting him. The elements are all there but they don't cohere. I've written his first speech eight times, I'm sure.

26 December 1993
Synge's intro. to PLAYBOY: '. . . Ibsen and Zola dealing with the reality of life in joyless and pallid words. On the stage one must have reality and one must have joy . . . In a good play every speech should be as fully flavoured as a nut or an apple . . .'

27 December 1993
Every day over the Christmas period I sat at the desk and read the first three speeches. They are the voices of three distinct people. And I think they are pitched right. (Of course they'll be rewritten a dozen more times.) But I'm not sure of two things: are they speaking at the appropriate time in their lives; and is this – now – the right time to feed the information. (So much of this is arbitrary. Timing is less important – at this stage – than tone.)

30 December 1993
Various interruptions. Comings and goings, Discomfort (at least) with the right eye. But every day obeisance has been made to the manuscript.

It is without joy. But what is there is there, waiting to be added to. And doing this entry is both a gesture to the discipline and an act of evasion. Because just now I'm writing this to avoid the big hurdle of Martha's second monologue.

7 January 1994
The new play – form, theme, characters – is so like FAITH HEALER. A second candlestick on the mantelpiece; a second china dog.

17 January 1994
The play stutters on, the Overall retreating further and further and each tiny section taking on a bloated and distorting importance.

I go back to Altnagelvin hospital tomorrow. I'm very uneasy with the new eye. I don't seem able to accommodate it. It flaunts its power.

23 January 1994

First act completed (sort of). Didn't go near the desk yesterday.

Anne [Friel] thinks it is too short. Maybe.

What is lost, so far, is the overreaching, perhaps excessive, notion that this could be a trio – all three voices speaking simultaneously, in immediate sequence, in counterpoint, in harmony, in discord. Instead I have a simple linear narrative in traditional form; with the language, sentiments and modest ambitions of FAITH HEALER – without FAITH HEALER's austerity.

Act 2 must be post-operation – with excursions back and forward.

24 January 1994

Should Act 1 be longer? Perhaps yes. Perhaps a Martha–Frank courtship sequence, then a Martha–Frank marriage sequence? They could be valuable as long as they are pre-operation.

25 January 1994

The play is at a standstill. Because Anne said Act 1 was too short?

26 January 1994

Difficulty: to balance the material in such a way that the medical element is essential but always subservient to the human. This means that the medical-technical processes and language have to be so thoroughly absorbed that all that is left is the watermark, the colouration.

Today just sitting at the desk . . . being available. It is probably more accurate to say that the author haunts the theme than to say that the theme haunts the author.

28 January 1994

Act 1 finished – again. All I can say is that it is longer.

31 January 1994

Act 1 – has its shape. I have a lot of work to do on it but I'm not unhappy with it.

The unease now is that Act 2 could easily and very rapidly

sink into a long whinge. To delicately draw the arc that carries us from the 'successful' operation, through disenchantment, to giving up.

1 February 1994
The right eye is bullying me. I think I'm sorry I had the operation. I will have to go back to the ophthalmologist. Wrestling with various kinds of glasses – driving, reading, TV.

8 February 1994
First two monologues (Martha, Frank) of Act 2 done. Now stuck (hence this) at Rice. I'm stuck with him because I don't know his story, I think.
   Titles: MARTHA. VISIONS.

14 February 1994
Back at the desk, trying to plug into the rhythms of the play. Still stuck with Rice.
   Title: VISION.

17 February 1994
Still haven't got Rice's monologue but something *is* on paper and I should get it. Part of the difficulty now is to keep firm control of the flow of 'facts' and 'information' on that whole rich period between Bandages Off and Despair – all that delight, all that terror for all of them – to reveal the complete range and the emotional transition.

24 February 1994
Into the final stretch of the play: a sequence (or two? or three?) of very short monologues, followed by three long, concluding (and difficult – no, tricky) monologues. Then start at the beginning again.

14 March 1994
Last night I wrote the final paragraph of the final monologue (Molly's). Her name and the title of the play changed once more – NOW MOLLY SWEENEY.

28 March 1994
Now, this morning, after two weeks' absence, back to MOLLY
SWEENEY.

3 April 1994, Easter Sunday
Finished MOLLY SWEENEY on Good Friday, 1 April. Now I'm
retyping – and reworking – it in a kind of fury.

6 April 1994
The play, MOLLY SWEENEY, goes to the typist this evening. The
only emotion on having finished it is relief: to emerge, blinking,
into the sunlight.

These diary extracts are fascinating, not just because they
reveal the often dispiriting process of questioning, failure and
slow discovery at the heart of creativity, but because they are
shot through with such a clear set of connections between the
writer's material life and his inspiration.

Molly Sweeney is, as Friel realized during the writing, for-
mally related to *Faith Healer*. It has three voices: Molly herself,
blind from very early childhood; her husband Frank; and an
ophthalmic surgeon, the eerily surnamed Mr Rice. Each is
unaware of the others' relationship with the audience. The
dance of death these three characters perform with one another
is always conducted with care, love and the very best of intentions, and yet all three are damaged, perhaps even killed, by
their blundering benevolence and lack of self-knowledge. Frank
is a doer, a characteristically modern Irish figure who has
worked abroad in famine relief as well as in other more arcane
ventures. His world is one where it always seems possible to
achieve with sleeves rolled up and a willingness to learn new
skills, although he is clearly Frank-of-all-trades rather than a
master of one, like Mr Rice, the quondam international super-
star of ophthalmic surgery. Frank's can-do attitude to the world
makes it almost inevitable that he will seize the opportunity to
restore to his wife the sight she lost as a child. Yet it is clear from
the start that Molly has adapted so completely to her disability

that it has become part of her personality. The world of sensuality which she has clawed back from her misfortune has its own integrity and pleasure and is, as the plot reveals, tampered with at great personal risk. Yet Friel is not simply setting the well-meaning amateur Frank against the steely professionalism of Rice. The surgeon has his own life crises, including the elopement of his wife with another surgeon on the jet-set circuit. Above all, insecurity about his professional status numbs him to the dangers of the intervention Frank wants for his wife. Certainly Friel puts on offer a debate about appropriate medical intervention, which touches serious contemporary concerns, but the 'real' play is a passionate contemplation of love and the way love can become possession and control. Both Frank, the obsessive non-specialist, and Rice, the quintessential expert, end up infantilizing Molly, turning themselves into proxy fathers. The journey Molly undergoes at their kindly hands is from darkness into light of a sort, but it also has a rhythm that parodies birth. It's as if the childless Frank and the midwife Rice create a child, when they attempt to give Molly sight, and her descriptions of the experience of sight have something of the disoriented unease of a newborn, as innocent gestures and movement scare and disturb. The birth–life–death rhythm is enacted in the play, but it is accelerated by Molly's jolting exposure to the light she could only dimly see for most of her life. It is one of Friel's achievements in *Molly Sweeney* to create three people, all of whom are decent – even lovable – to have them interact benevolently – even lovingly – and yet for the outcome to be disintegration, despair, emotional and perhaps even physical death as a result. It is a play that sensitizes its audiences to the vulnerability of human destiny even in skilful and benevolent hands; but there may also be an intention to find a parallel for the artist's experience here, in the manner of *Faith Healer*. While it is true that Molly is shepherded into the operating theatre by these two helpful men with their own controlling agendas, it is also the case that she allows herself to embrace the experience. Both Frank and Rice make it clear towards the end of the play that the end result has been a disaster. Molly is apparently in a state of mental collapse and is also unable even to see the simple dark–light gradations she knew before the operation. Yet paradoxically she speaks to us, the audience, of living in a 'borderline country' where she is at ease. In the last lines of the play she seems to be talking to us about the nature of drama itself:

> It certainly doesn't worry me any more that what I think I see may be fantasy or indeed what I take to be imagined may very well be real – what's Frank's term? – external reality. Real – imagined – fact – fiction – fantasy – reality – there it seems to be. And it seems to be all right.
> And why should I question any of it any more?

It's a troubled, paradoxical ending, seeming to return us to the exhausted resolution of *Faith Healer*: *not* to question what is fact and fantasy is to be mad. Friel again seems to be resolving a problem at the same time as he undercuts the resolution, just as he seemed to do at the end of *Dancing at Lughnasa*.

Molly Sweeney was the first play that Friel, notably curmudgeonly about the craft, directed himself. Perhaps in order to signal a change of direction, the play was offered to the Gate Theatre in Dublin, rather than the Abbey. Of its three first actors, two – Catherine Byrne and Mark Lambert – offer their own comments on their work on the play in chapter 3 of this book.

1995–7: *Give Me Your Answer, Do!*

The year after *Molly Sweeney* opened, Friel was again at work, and again the process was anxiety-inducing and initially unproductive. In the last of his 'sporadic diaries' to date, he is again wrestling with the idea of 'the artist'. He uses that word rather than 'writer', suggesting a more theoretical take on his material than the simply professional. In a sense, much of Friel's work is related to problems of art, if only because it is concerned with memory – what happened – and imagination – what might happen – and the fruitful overlap between the two.

That memory and imagination also feed us and nag us in every-day life reflects an underlying Frielian notion that art is central to human living, whether we are 'arty' or not. In the diary entries, comments about bees, trees and dogs rub shoulders with meditations on Wittgenstein and a straining to hear signals from the as yet unwritten play, reinforcing connections between creativity and the material world.

Extracts from a Sporadic Diary: *Give Me Your Answer, Do!*

4 March 1995

Hanging on desperately to the one, wan, casual, insubstantial, unwilling idea. An artist – in a wheelchair? – a birthday (sixti-eth?) party? His wife. Their – his – friends. And the phantom thought that the Husband/Artist and Wife employ a duologue that (a) moves on totally different levels so that there is no apparent exchange between them; (b) consists every so often of interior monologue that sounds as if it were a normal part of their duologue but is in fact emerging from a private depth. (This could be accomplished technically by using a distinctive vocal tone.) Because in life every duologue is composed of the spoken and the unspoken. (When the unspoken is spoken, it is as if the actor puts on a vocal mask.)

4 April 1995

Panic sets in when nothing stirs, when even the wish to sit at the desk has gone. A conviction that it is finally over. And of course that condition will come. And why not now?

I look at the row of Wittgenstein books on the shelf. Nothing. In the past I had notebooks, etc. etc. Now – nothing.

15 April 1995, Easter Saturday

Not working – worse still, the prospect of not working – becomes a kind of malaise that is on the verge of becoming a breakdown. And trying to decide whether (a) to sit it out; (b) face it out; (c) just write – anything; all becomes part of the acute distress. Indeed the act of writing this is an attempt to postpone total atrophy.

And shouldn't this be a day close to resurrection?

16 April 1995

If you just sit and wait – deliberately alert and open – keeping despair and anger at bay – trying not to worry about spent mines and dried wells – will it happen? Why should it?

17 April 1995

Dipping the toe into Wittgenstein again. Especially his belief that the job of the philosopher is to represent the relationship between language and the world. (a) Philosophy cannot answer its traditional questions in meaningful language, i.e. descriptive, scientific language. (b) In imposing the self-discipline of saying only what can be said and thus enjoining silence in the realm of metaphysics, genuine metaphysical impulses are released. The unsayable is not said but it is nevertheless manifest. The very act of taking care to say only what can be said 'shows' another silent realm beyond language (and logic) and so beyond description. And what is beyond description, what is trivialized by the doomed attempt to describe, is what is important in human life . . .

Who said – Engelmann? – that the job of the philosopher is like the job of the cartographer who maps the coastline of an island – not to learn the boundaries of the island but to learn the limits of the ocean?

Much help from J. H. in all this (WITTGENSTEIN).

8 June 1995

Kitezh in Russian folklore is a city that vanishes from sight when marauders approach. As it disappears its bell keeps ringing through the fog.

Rimsky-Korsakov opera (?). Akhmatova poem, 'The Way of all Earth'.

12 June 1995

Went to Monaghan to pick up a (small) swarm of bees from T. B. came over and helped me to put them into the hive. The swarm so small that J. O'H. says it's touch-and-go if they'll survive. And there are only four brood frames intact in the chamber – moths had eaten huge holes in the comb. I put in three damaged sections to feed the new swarm.

28 January 1996
When am I going to look again at the writer/selling-his-papers play? Tomorrow? Need to steel myself for that.

29 January 1996
Exciting discovery today – a God of Silence! Harpocrates.

Lempriere: 'Harpocrates . . . supposed to be the same as Horus, son of Isis, among the Egyptians. He is represented as holding one of his fingers on his mouth, and hence he is called the god of silence and intimates that the mysteries of philosophy and religion ought never to be revealed to the people . . . placed by the Romans at the entrance to their temples.'

Maybe at the entrance to the theatres?

Should I build a shrine to him here? He is represented as a small boy – the child with his finger across his mouth. Imagine those eyes.

1 February 1996
'He carried out the gestures and by doing this he found faith' – Pascal.

Sitting at the desk. Leafing through notes. Hoping to find faith.

18 February 1996
Yesterday and the day before I wrote an opening page; the writer arriving home. The process generated a soft flurry of excitement. But New York tomorrow for casting. Escape!

16 May 1996
Tree men from Ballybofey are here to cut down 160 sitka spruce. 1,300 were planted behind the cottage in 1983. Last month one-third of the alder behind the house were cut down. The alder are stacked opposite the courtyard.

23 May 1996
Put on a second super in the hive.

24 May 1996
The new dog, Molly, is here since last Tuesday, 21 May. The second dog, Daisy, is due tonight with David.

28 May 1996
Both dogs are thriving.

Trying – again – to work. Up early every morning and at the desk. So far to absolutely no avail.

7 June 1996
Still – and so reluctantly! – at the first three pages. And at each attempt the effort to prod it forward just by a line or two is almost too much and can so easily be quenched by indifference or the stuff's worthlessness or by complete disbelief in what is being attempted.

Got a swarm of bees in the walled garden close to Hive 1 and last night put it into Hive 2. Fed it (3 pints/3 lbs) this morning.

12 June 1996
Rewrote the first six pages again yesterday for the hundredth time. I think the purpose of all those rewritings is to get the voice right. At this stage it is more important – well, at least as important – to get the pitch, tone, timbre right than to get what is said right. Maybe what is said can be said only in a certain voice. Or maybe what one says and how one says it constantly adjust one another.

All of which is a tactic to postpone tackling page 7.

24 June 1996
This morning I gathered together the notes and notebooks and pieces of paper and the first ten pages and put them into a cardboard box. The act requires some courage. A formal acknowledgement of failure has to be made.

But the formal putting away of the stuff has two other elements.

By banishing the material (what a dramatic word!) there is a sense of punishing it for disappointing me (and that is more than fleetingly righteous!). And at the back of the mind a suspicion that the material may sneak back, contrite, obedient, perhaps annealed. So in the act of banishing there is a feint [*sic*] cunning. (And the recognition of that cunning is pathetic, too!)

2 July 1996
A signal – weak, distant, but with some assurance – from the play this a.m. that perhaps I should return to it.

What can I do but respond?

I won't drop everything and plunge obediently in. But tomorrow I will call back, 'Yes?'

Meantime I took out the notes and notebooks and looked through them. Sirens.

What a flirtatious game!

30 September 1996
GIVE ME YOUR ANSWER, DO! was left with the typist last night.

Strange feeling of emptiness and disappointment and *tristesse*. But after this play surely I should be able to cope with the Necessary Uncertainty?

The play's central character is faced with a very material professional dilemma. As happens to writers like Friel who have a sufficiently high profile in (usually American) academe, he has been offered money for his original manuscripts. Tom Donnelly, a slightly faded literary figure, needs money. His daughter lives with severe mental illness in a rundown hospital and his wife, the long-suffering Daisy, slipping into a gin-supported old age, shares his genteel poverty without even the consolation of a creative impulse, however atrophied. Yet it is Daisy who offers the answer that Tom seeks, and that is offered up in the title. In defiance of her own needs and those of her daughter, she confirms the idea latent in Tom's mind that he should turn down the offer of dollars. Her justification is in some ways a rebuff to the dead end posited by *Molly Sweeney*, a refusal to question.

Molly, like Tom and Daisy's daughter, lies in hospital, absent from the world. In Daisy's extraordinary speech – '*almost thinking aloud*', in Friel's stage direction – she produces a paean to uncertainty, to risk, to discomfort of spirit:

> a better place for Bridget? But Bridget is beyond knowing, isn't she? And somehow, somehow bills will always be met. And what does a little physical discomfort matter? Really not a lot. But to sell for an affirmation, for an answer, to be free of that grinding uncertainty, that would be so wrong for him and so wrong for his work. Because that uncertainty is necessary. He must live with that uncertainty, that necessary uncertainty. Because there can be no verdicts, no answers. Indeed there must be no verdicts. Because being alive is the postponement of verdicts, isn't it? Because verdicts are provided only when its over, all concluded.

Because *Give Me Your Answer, Do!* is plotted around a writer's problems, it has been too easily dismissed as having a limited set of meanings; but this is only true if *The Master Builder* is only relevant to architects, or *Hamlet* to Danish royalty. Friel's play has little of the deceptive warmth of a *Lughnasa*, but its bleak surface speaks of courage and a survival instinct that may be useful to us all in a world run to the tune of accountants' abstractions.

The *Give Me Your Answer, Do!* writing period concluded with Friel contemplating the necessary uncertainty that plagues him and yet is essential to creative life. It is this acceptance of a kind of chaos that moves his audience away from the death-haunted certainty that Frank Hardy embraced. 'Necessary Uncertainty' was an idea that coloured public life, too, in Ireland at the end of the 1990s. The car bomb that exploded in Omagh, the town Friel knew so well from childhood, killed and maimed people with such cruel inclusiveness and such obscene finality that it created a climate for what became known as the Good Friday Agreement. This accord, based on a kind of wilful surrender of certainty and a rejection of 'terrible beauty' by all sides, offered at last the possibility for Ireland to move on. Christopher Murray has suggested that: 'Ten years after *Making History* was premiered its imaginative impatience with monoliths may be seen as, in Friel's term, metabiologically creating the environment for the Good Friday Agreement of 1998.'

Friel in the twenty-first century

At the time of writing, Friel's latest project is a loose trilogy once more drawing on Chekhov's deep well of poignant failure, rueful tragedy and a peasant society's struggle to come to terms with a modern world careless of its coherence. There is in the characters of Chekhov and Friel a characteristic pattern of knowing self-dramatization. In their wrestling with their social and psychological fates, men and women assume roles that very often serve only to trap them. In these three plays of 2001–2, the reference to drama operates within the very fabric of the plays themselves. Most straightforwardly, *The Bear* is a linguistically vigorous translation of an early Chekhov comedy. Next comes *The Yalta Game*, a version of the Chekhov short story 'Lady with a Lap-Dog'. The clue to Friel's reworking of the original is in the 'game' of the title. A lonely man and a lonely woman enjoy a thrilling flirtation (hardening into a passionate affair) by means of a game of mutual deception, pretence and lying. Both Anna and Gurov, basking in the late-summer sun of the seaside resort of Yalta, address the audience with their perceptions of what is happening to them in a way that makes the audience complicit in this game-playing. Yalta is the resort's name, and also that of a dog that is imaginary. There is a growing sense of uncertainty, in the characters and shared by the audience, about what is real and what unreal, what experienced and what merely intensely desired. What Chekhov cannot know, and Friel does (and surely he assumes his informed audience senses this) is that Yalta has another reality. It is the location of the very real, very unromantic, carve-up of the post-war world by Churchill, Stalin and Roosevelt in 1945. A play about that significant meeting also could well be titled *The Yalta Game*. There is a passionate and sexy charge to the mutual fantasizing of Gurov and Anna, but it has to be compromised by the unmentioned dark cloud of that later meeting on the Crimean seafront.

Friel's profound playfulness finds expression in *Afterplay*, in which two loners meet and share a possibility of human warmth in a tatty Moscow restaurant in 1920. Just as in *The Yalta Game*, a stark historical reality must hang over the piece. It is, after all, four years from the Russian Revolution and in another four years Stalin will be in power. Yet there is no reference to this massive reality. For all the grubby sensuality of the café, we are in a theatre space as much as a Soviet one, for these two disappointed people are characters from two Chekhov plays – Sonya Serebriakova from *Uncle Vanya*, whose desperate hymn to hope and the future concludes that play, and Andrey, the tormented brother of the *Three Sisters*. Certainly one of the simpler pleasures of the play is that 'what if . . .' playfulness which teases us with the significance and nature of drama works we have come to know and love. Sonya still dotes on Astrov; Andrey lives in the shadow of Masha's suicide. Yet *Afterplay* also explores that Frielian theme of self-realization by creative deception. Andrey, a social, marital and professional failure has no resource left other than to lie, to construct an alternative reality. His violin case and evening dress give him temporary cover enough to claim status as a professional orchestral musician, but he cannot sustain the pretence for long. It is only with the removal of the mask that he can hope to open himself to Sonya. Friel's play nearly ends, as *Uncle Vanya* concluded, with more downbeat optimism from Sonya: 'So we stagger on, within an environment of love of sorts, offering each other occasional and elusive sustenance. Not the most satisfactory way to get through your life is it? But it *is* a way.'

However, the very final stage action has Andrey, grasping at the straw of Sonya's address, 'writing furiously', an image with some of the desperate, hugely qualified optimism of Len's chair-mending in Bond's *Saved* (Bond, too, a writer early steeped in Chekhov's unsentimental hope). It is clear that Brian Friel, in 2002, like Andrey in 1920, 'stops to consider what exactly he wants to say. Then he begins writing furiously again.'

The present can often seem deceptively like an ending. 1999 had seen a 'Friel Festival', based largely at the Abbey Theatre, a five-month celebration of the writer's work, with exhibitions and talks supplementing productions and readings. It yielded rich material, including the fascinating discussion included here in chapter 3 on acting and directing. Yet there was a danger, given that it marked Friel's seventieth birthday, that such an event might seem like a premature memorial. Writing in the *Irish Times*, Trinity College Dublin lecturer Brian Singleton questioned the very basis of the Friel Festival. His paradoxical conclusion was that Friel's true legacy might best have been celebrated by the creation of new work rather than a rehashing, however lovingly achieved and well-deserved, of the old:

But is a Frielfest the most sensible format? . . . The independent, poorly or un-subsidised companies that contribute so much to our current cultural well-being and whose work falls outside the parameters of festivalised culture, entertain a youthful and vibrant constituency. Their often deviant visions of the home canon are festivalised also, but contained within the Fringe. We are living at the cusp of heterogeneity, socially and culturally. The cultural practices of our refugees and new immigrants, and the external influences of our new avant-garde, challenge perforce the nature of representation. Can we talk any longer with any certainty of 'our Friel' in terms of solely text-based, realistic representation? Teaching Friel's plays in a racially-mixed classroom in Dublin will never be the same again as our past pains of emigration are our new neighbours' very present sufferings . . . When Friel wrote the dance sequence in *Dancing at Lughnasa* he did more than just permit a paganistic release from social, economic, familial and psychological entrapment for women. He allowed a group of actors to communicate solely through their bodies. Many 20th-century theatre theorists and practitioners such as Artaud and Lecocq have pointed out that the word is the full-stop of communication, coming at the culmination of the idea when the thought has already past.

It may be that, in invoking *Dancing at Lughnasa* in these terms, Singleton does Friel the greatest honour. If we have to consider Friel's 'position' vis-à-vis other writers, then it is clear that he has helped to create a space for Irish drama in the post-war years to rival that of O'Casey and Synge in the earlier part of the twentieth century. Along with a cohort of other writers (Thomas Kilroy, Sebastian Barry and Frank McGuiness perhaps the best-known) Friel's work created a thirst for new Irish playwriting in the 1990s that has persisted into the new millennium.

When Frank McGuiness was presenting his friend with yet another award, in 1999, he eloquently represented the scope of Friel's overall achievement as 'a liberation, a celebration and a censure for the country in which he lives'. In spite of (perhaps because of) his irritated quarrel with politics in theatre, it is the sense of engagement with 'the country in which he lives' that powers Friel's work and will ensure his place in world theatre. When he told his audience that he was not willing, in Dylan Thomas's phrase 'to go gently into that good night', he was cheered and he might well have quoted his Daisy again: 'Because being alive is the postponement of verdicts, isn't it? Because verdicts are provided only when it's over, all concluded.'

She may also be speaking on her creator's behalf to all the critics, commentators and student essayists who have written, or are about to write, about his work. In any case, the temptation to rank and judge without fully engaging with the art and therefore with the ideas and passions that power it is to be resisted. Plays should be, in Arnold Wesker's phrase, 'tools for living', and Friel's plays are, in that most profound sense, useful.

3

Voices and Documents

This chapter offers a selection of documents and interview material by Brian Friel and by his collaborators and fellow-artists. Both Delaney and Murray (for details see 'Select Bibliography' below) have trawled and collected almost all the best published Friel material, and most of the quotation in chapter 2 comes from these books. No one interested in Friel should miss out on these anthologies, even though their material sometimes overlaps. What follows here borrows from and supplements those collections, with an emphasis on the craft and art of performing Friel.

The Director

The author of this first piece is Patrick Mason, a former director of the Abbey Theatre and first director of several Friel plays, including Dancing at Lughnasa. *This tribute was published in the brochure to accompany the 1999 Friel Festival in Dublin that marked his seventieth birthday.*

Dancing at the Abbey

I suspect that he might not like being thought of as an 'Abbey' playwright, but Brian Friel shares the distinguishing marks of the very rarest of that rare literary species. Not only has he had his work produced regularly at the Abbey, and made a huge contribution to the life and work of the national theatre over four decades; but he also had an early play rejected by the board of Directors of the old Abbey – a distinction he shares with Hugh Leonard, John B. Keane, and Tom Murphy.

Falling foul of the 'old men' of the Abbey Board on at least one occasion seems to have been an essential element in the initiation of any talented young Irish playwright in the fifties and early sixties.

Yet although he has sustained a long and fruitful relationship with the Abbey which has outlasted numerous Abbey directors both old and young, Brian Friel has always been his own man, and he has formed links with many theatre companies and their directors not only here in Ireland, but all over the world. However, in one sense he is quintessentially an 'Abbey' play-wright, and that is in the ideal sense of the theatre's founder and chief theorist, W. B. Yeats.

Yeats wrote that his purpose in founding the Abbey was 'to speak the deeper thoughts and emotions of Ireland'. Commenting further on the type of plays that would be suited to this new Irish theatre he continued, 'We do not desire propagandist plays, nor plays written mainly to serve some obvious moral purpose; for art seldom concerns itself with those interests or opinions that can be defended by argument, but with the reali-ties of emotion and character that become self-evident when made vivid to the imagination.'

As a writer true to language, place, the realities of the human heart, and the vivid imagination, Brian Friel is the very ideal of an 'Abbey' playwright. This theatre has been particularly blessed in being able to produce so much of his major work: and not just blessed in having his plays in its repertoire; for his influence on writing, directing, and acting, has been significant, and it is no exaggeration to say that Brian Friel has a decisive influence on the development of the modern Abbey.

Like Yeats before him, Friel is a man of the theatre. For both men it is the art of theatre that animates and shapes, defines and defies, instructs and informs. It is the art of theatre that makes all things vivid to the imagination, and nurtures the imaginative life of the nation and its national theatre.

Directors and Actors

'The Road To Ballybeg'

'The Road to Ballybeg' was a forum held at the Abbey Theatre in 1999 as part of the Friel Festival. It was chaired by Patrick Mason (in italics) and the other participants were the actors Rosaleen Linehan and Niall Buggy, and the directors Conall Morrison and Brian Brady. Mason's remarks about the actor-director relationship in the 1940s and 1950s provide a context for Friel's lingering suspicion of directing as a job. The actors' comments on the demands – technical and personal – of performing Friel's texts are developed by two actors directed by Friel in interviews following this transcription.

PATRICK MASON: *'The Road to Ballybeg' has involved all of us at various points in our careers. We have representation from working on* The Loves of Cass McGuire *to* Aristocrats, Making History, Translations, Dancing at Lughnasa, Philadelphia, Here I Come! *We cover a fair range of plays . . .*

My first involvement came with directing Dancing at Lughnasa *and then subsequently* Philadelphia, Here I Come!, *which I directed here three years ago. I think it's fairly well known that Brian's views on the role of the director in the theatre are not exactly complimentary. Brian is of a generation of playwrights that was and is deeply suspicious of the director as possible usurper of authorship and authority within the theatre. However, I have to say that I found working with Brian on a new play extremely stimulating and extremely demanding at the same time. I think he has an extraordinary precision, not only obviously of language, of expression but also a precision of gesture. And a precision of, if you like, position. A physical sense of positioning on the stage, which might be seen to be more the role of the director than the playwright. But I would argue that all the best playwrights have an acute sense of the physical dimension of theatre as well of course as its music, its power of language.*

He also has this extraordinary capacity, which is very demanding, to nuance a line quite perfectly. By which I mean not just of meaning but of emotion, nuance of character. And these nuances are extremely fine, strangely accurate inflections of emotion and character which are carried in the syntax and vocabulary of a line, in the rhythm of a line, in the placing of a line. One of the things I remember Brian saying to me when we were talking about the script of Lughnasa was that the main thing is that one line provokes the next. It's as simple as that. If you inflect the line slightly wrong it will not provoke the next. Therefore the music of the language is extremely precise and I think that is one of the most demanding aspects, this acuteness of ear to the poise of his language.

Lughnasa was extraordinary because if you read the script there is the most extraordinary stage direction I think I know of, where he describes a dance sequence and he does this entirely from character. I think this was also a great insight for me – he's not a choreographer, he's not a director, but he is an eminent psychologist and drawer of character, and how he describes the dance is purely on the basis of character. He lists in detail the order in which the women dance and he does so because he knows their characters. His calculation is that this character will dance in this place at that time because of who she is. And he will also list in reverse order when the music cuts out, those who will drop out of the dance first, and those whose impetus will carry them beyond the music. And this is all done through an extraordinary insight into character. In other words, language and gesture are all there to carry character, and all rooted in character. And therefore another challenge to the director is to be as acutely aware of the character, the characteristics, as the playwright is.

There's a third thing I'd just like to launch as an idea, which maybe touches on the idea of the relationship between Brian Friel and his work and a director. That is of course the whole aspect of physical presence and of imagery, the whole visual and physical aspect of the theatre event that he describes. His stage directions *for instance in describing settings are very literal. It seems to me he has often in his mind a type of stage design and production that is maybe a little dated to us now. I think one of the most extraordinary things that has happened in the last fifteen or twenty years has been a revolution in our understanding of the whole aspect of representation on stage. The way in which we represent a garden, a house, a factory, a field, bring them to life onstage, has become noticeably less bound by the rules of realism of, say, the theatre of the 1960s or 1970s. There is a tension between the scripts and the interpretative and creative force of the director and the designer, and this is an area where I feel there is a contention between the director and the designer – and rightly so.*

NIALL BUGGY: The interesting thing for me as an actor playing Friel, the wonderful thing, is the realization that he is the great present to the actor. I realized when I was playing Casimir ten years ago (which I think is one of the great creative roles in modern drama) that if I let Casimir play me rather than the other way round, then I was doing it properly. And if there is a secret in any way in the interpretation of Friel, it has something to do with that – he has done it for you. What you are thinking is what you have to say next. And that doesn't always happen in playwriting. Sometimes as actors we have to work very hard to make what we say next what we are thinking. With Friel I don't find that. So, this may seem an odd thing to say, Friel is easier for the actor than a lot of other playwrights. He's a gift. And indeed I think there are similarities between his work and Chekhov's, and that's why I think they work so well together.

ROSALEEN LINEHAN: As the only woman on the stage . . . I don't know which opera it comes from, 'Love and Music, these have I longed for'. This is what for me Brian Friel presents to you as an actor. Music first. The learning of the script, and the text is so vital. Not just the words, his punctuation, and his semicolons and his dots-dots-dots . . . And his dashes! These have to be learned as precisely as the actual words on the page. And this shows you the determination of the writer to present you a score. And you leave that score at your peril. It's a wonderful sort of walking aid to have at any point. Love, because he writes so much beautiful love. He writes magnificently for women, he writes so tremendously for women that sometimes, as a woman, you just suddenly stop and think, 'How did he know that?' I suppose he knew about it because he is surrounded by daughters and a wife and he loves women. But he writes with such grace and such ease about love . . .

But I come back again to the most important thing – the music. At your peril do you move off it. It's like orchestration – there's duets, there's trios, there's quintets, there's solos, and each of these has to be taken on that level and each of these has to be performed as cleanly, as unselfishly really, as possible . . . I don't think his plays attract selfish playing.

The musical analogy keeps on coming back. It's quite definitely, quite literally, music. I remember getting a little prompt about how – this is a hint for any of you going to direct Brian Friel plays – when you see him put three dots, that is a beat, a silence, a beat of time. When you see him write a dash at the end of a line that is not a beat, that is actually a tightening, a closing up, a break of idea. But it is a tightening, not an opening. And when he writes 'pause', it's pause and when he writes 'silence' it's silence . . . There is that precision, absolutely. I think that firm, extraordinary line he gives you, a musical line, is a tremendous support in performance. I remember Catherine Byrne saying when we were rehearsing this about how, even if you didn't quite play into that emotion, if you followed the shape of it and the rhythm of it, it led you to it. It was that strong a thing.

Just turning then to the director's point of view, and with two associates of the Abbey here with me, both of them involved in our current Friel season, Brian [Brady] in preview with Making History, *Conall [Morrison] just about to head off to New York with* The Freedom of the City. *Conall, from a director's point of view, the precision, the shape, the structuring, the music?*

CONALL MORRISON: I've just had my first day of re-rehearsals for *The Freedom of the City* and we read through the play again. A lot of the lines were still in the actors' heads. So what I did was to say, 'Let's just use this as an aide-memoire to see how much is there.' But I wanted the Stage Manager to call them up on every single change, anything they got wrong including any tiny pause, or any kind of ellipsis they'd made. And it was fascinating for them, very rewarding for them. Anything that was not right, that was not consonant with the text, when we went back to what Friel had precisely written, it was better. By their own agreement.

It is a little bit of a cliché about all art aspiring to the condition of music, and Friel has said that he's not interested in the scripts being devised and changed in rehearsal. And he does write them as a musical score. His understanding of the rhythm of a line, of a speech, of an act, of a play is absolutely crystalline, absolutely superb. And indeed the effect on the audience, wonderfully, ironically, is that it just seems effortless. But we know that the man has just created a Swiss clock. Or he has the motor purring away under the Jaguar. So going back into the piece with this company has just been fascinating. A bunch of hard-bitten old Dublin actors illuminate themselves with appreciation of the quality of the work. So it's an absolute delight to work upon.

NIALL BUGGY: The thing is that, with this precision, there is for the actor an enormous liberation and freedom. Enormous. You never get it again. It's incredible that liberation and freedom that he gives you because of his precision. And that's an interesting apparent conflict.

ROSALEEN LINEHAN: He writes such comedy. Love, music and comedy. And it's very important to Brian that you get all his laughs as much as you twist everybody's heart. One doesn't happen without the other. You've got to have them in place. The plays are full of comedy, wild comedy.

[This next point is a useful corrective to the tendency to pigeonhole certain works of Friel as ersatz Chekhov in spite of the writer's obvious involvement with the Chekhov–Turgenev axis and its appropriateness for a peasant society like Ireland, emerging from a period of change. T.C.]

CONALL MORRISON: What I find fascinating about Friel is that – I don't want to be disingenuous because I adore him as a writer – I think he's one of the supreme theatrical intellects and theatrical poets of this century. I find the notion of him being a kind of Irish Chekhov reductive. Because he is his own genre. He has been Chekhov as much as he's been Pirandello or Brecht, with *The Freedom of the City*. Or Shaw, with *Making History*. So it is journalistic laziness to try and pull him down to one particular thing, some encrusted image because we all like *Aristocrats* and *Lughnasa*. That's absolute nonsense and reductive for a man's thirty-year work.

What is personally fascinating for me as a director is that actually he still despises the role of the director. This is a person that I adore personally and revere professionally. So what intrigues me is: 'What is that gap?' He does not acknowledge that it is very fine to write a beautifully precise description of how those six women dance, but actually, what does it take to make them *do* that? There's a slow alchemical process to do that.

One of his acknowledged mentors as a young playwright is one of the great directors of the British theatre, Tyrone Guthrie. So it is a very strange thing that, despite an acknowledged debt to Guthrie's role as a director and a mentor, he has sustained this suspicion of the director.

CONALL MORRISON: A director who knew Friel quite well once told me – and again I'm fascinated by the arc of his creative journey and his parallel with our journey as a society from the early sixties as we drag ourselves into the end of the twentieth century – that actually why there is such precision in the script is partly aesthetic. But it's also about 'I'll control this'. It's because of the theatrical history. The person I was talking to said that the actors were drunk, the directors were drunk, everything was just so bloody lawless, as this theatrical society dragged itself into some kind of maturity. So writers of that kind of calibre tried to imprint a kind of cast-iron blueprint that could not be messed around with. Which is aesthetically rather sad, but it makes perfect sense!

BRIAN BRADY: I've got twenty-five minutes after we've finished here to tell them all downstairs what they've been doing wrong for the last five days! Be lawless, and take a beat on three dots! My God, there's a lot of dots in *Making History* – it'll be a long night! I'm equally intrigued too, but perhaps a little bit less irate than Conall, about this reported disdain that Brian has for directors. I suspect it's a bit of a love-hate relationship because what I've become aware of working as an assistant on Patrick's original production of *Dancing at Lughnasa* – I've previously done a production of *Making History*, and I also worked as an assistant on a production of *Philadelphia, Here I Come!* and I've seen several productions of Friel – what fascinates me is that, like a lot of playwrights, he sort of keeps writing the same play again and again. He keeps coming back to the same themes. Richard Pine in his programme note for *Making History* refers to *The Enemy Within* – how the themes that Friel tries to address in *The Enemy Within* are encapsulated in the character of Hugh O'Neill in *Making History*.

My particular fascination with *Making History* is a whole area about the unwritten story of women in history and how the women's roles have never been celebrated. And then you sit back and think, that's the play he wrote before *Dancing at Lughnasa*. And how the plays speak to each other, I find incredible. And how he refreshes and readdresses those themes by offering extraordinary challenges to directors. But it sort of suggests to me that yes maybe we [directors] piss him off a bit . . .

ROSALEEN LINEHAN: To quote *Oklahoma!*, we'd like to say a word for the actor! I think that possibly Brian's assaults – which was only as far as I know one single particular assault on 'The Director' in the *New York Times* – might have been something that the actor also feels from time to time. That it has all become much more the field of the director and the set designer than the actual actor. And Brian knows that the actor and the text are the two vital elements. You can do it with black curtains – we did it in Glenties with somebody's bedroom blankets pulled across the back because we hadn't got our set. Possibly when he did say that, he may have meant that the two most important items are the text and the actor. [*Applause*]

I think that's true but he actually took time to reprint the same thing in the festival programme! I think there is a truth in what Conall says – the conditions in Irish theatre in the fifties when Brian began writing. Jack Leonard would have the same sort of thing – there was a sort of hand-to-mouth existence and there were occasions where actors and directors misbehaved and there was a certain lawlessness!

It is absolutely true that in, say, contemporary continental theatre, the last twenty years have seen the virtual demise of the playwright in favour of the director. And certainly I would say in German theatre and French theatre the influence of directors has been baneful. Because they have actually taken over a role of authorship and have quite deliberately displaced the playwright. I don't think, though, the equivalent conditions exist really in the Irish theatre.

The interesting thing is that, apart from producing a generation of very talented young directors, we've also produced another generation of very talented young playwrights. And the Irish theatre stands out in Western Europe as being the one theatre that keeps loyal to language and keeps on producing playwrights. And I think that's a lot to with the legacy, if you like, of Friel and Murphy and Leonard. These are career play-

wrights, these are major figures in the cultural and artistic life of the country, and they are playwrights. You can't say that about many European societies but you can say it about Ireland. I think it colours the Irish theatre experience very much.

CONALL MORRISON: I have not come across another playwright bar Shakespeare that actors cling to with such devotion and who is spoken of so fondly. This may sound very pompous but I was in New York auditioning for a musical. There was a guy who was playing the lead in *The Phantom of the Opera* on Broadway. He's on a lot of money, he's quite a name, and I'm trying to reel him in because it would mean him spending a lot of time out of New York. But he's very good. And he auditioned superbly and I thought, 'Listen you know, if I can get you, I'm laughing! I'm going to get a Tony and make a lot of money – this is great!' And I said to him, 'If there's any question, I'm going to be back in New York with *The Freedom of the City*.' He'd been quite cool prior to this and he began jumping up and down shouting, 'Blue Star to Eagle, Blue Star to Eagle.' I was going, 'What?' It's one of the *lowliest* soldiers, one of the smallest parts in the play. And it transpired he'd been in it when he was fifteen! And I thought, 'I've got him!' And he was so in love with the piece and so in love with Friel – all of a sudden all the Broadway nonsense just fell away.

What of this affection? Its very tangible, isn't it? For everyone who works on Brian's plays – there's great affection in the plays, in the characters . . .

ROSALEEN LINEHAN: There's great affection and great love . . . On *Lughnasa*, he would say the odd thing to you. And the nature of my temperament – I suppose there's a large streak of sarcastic wit. But he just wandered over to me one day. 'Just one thing, Rosaleen, I don't write irony.' So that wiped out the performance for that week! But that's very unusual, I think, in Irish playwriting. Certainly he does write some irony but in

Dancing at Lughnasa I don't think there is any irony at all. Its interesting, I think, to find a writer who is not an ironist.

[*In response to an audience question about non-Irish actors being cast in Friel plays:*]

It is difficult. I have rehearsed three British casts [*of* Dancing at Lughnasa] *and an American cast as well. And it was extremely difficult to get those rhythms. Not accent – because Friel himself is always saying, 'God, would they ever stop those dreadful Northern accents! Don't play it with a Donegal accent!' Though you would be more aware of it than, say, an American audience with the American cast, or an English audience with the English cast. It is a thing that is instinctive, obviously, with Irish actors and an Irish cast. You recognize the temperature of the language – what is colloquial, what is ironic, what is affectionate, what is not. There's a recognition factor as well.*

NIALL BUGGY: But I do want to say I have seen some non-Irish actors do his work brilliantly. I want to say that because it's international what he does.

[*In response to an audience question about* Wonderful Tennessee:]

Wonderful Tennessee *remains one of my favourite Friel plays. I think it's one of his most extraordinary plays. Though it's a very austere play in its way, but again you have to remember it came after* Lughnasa. *One of the things – if you look in the order in which he writes things, one thing provokes the other but it also tends to provoke it in an opposite direction. And in many ways there are elements of the darker aspects of* Lughnasa *in* Wonderful Tennessee. *But there are also elements that you can see in* Making History, *that you can see way back in* The Enemy Within, *his first play. So it does resonate throughout and of course that's not to leave out that all-time favourite* Faith Healer, *which is I think perhaps his most astonishing achievement.*

[*In response to an audience question about casting of* Molly Sweeney:]

He specifically said he wanted to direct the première of that play. It would be standard here and in most theatres for any new play that the playwright the director and the producer would be involved in the casting. And very often the playwright would have written the role with a particular actor in mind.

Actors

Catherine Byrne and Mark Lambert were in the first cast of Molly Sweeney. *Lambert and T. P. McKenna were replaced when the play was produced, again under Friel's direction, with names deemed starrier for the US market. Even Friel, it seems, had to fall in with the harsh realpolitik of theatre casting, in spite of his public derision of the Broadway ethos. Their conversations ranged over a wide spectrum of the experience of performing Friel and many of their comments from the rehearsal room and the Green Room echo in very human, pragmatic detail some of the broader perspectives offered elsewhere in this section. I interviewed them at the end of 2000.*

Catherine Byrne

The very first play I did of his was *Aristocrats*. I didn't know him at that point. I was the furthest thing I could imagine from Clair. I had this imprint of what Ingrid Craigie had done in the first production, which was wonderful. She was everything that I wasn't and I couldn't understand why Joe [Dowling] had asked me to do it. We were coming to the last run of the play and he said Brian Friel was coming down to see it. I thought, 'Oh God, tell him she stayed in Ballybeg and she didn't go to finishing school. And what's he going to think of my Dublin accent, and I'm terrible!' All he actually said to me that afternoon was that Clair's just like her mother. And I said, 'Yes . . .', not knowing what he was talking about. That was the kind of relationship I had with Brian then – never quite knowing what he meant and always looking for some mysterious meaning that wasn't there.

I played in *Aristocrats* again just recently – Judith, the elder sister. Brian came to the dressing room after the third preview. I'd told him I wanted to play Alice, which is one of the best parts in the play, and he said, 'Can you just *do* it? Just say the lines, do it.' And I said I didn't know how good this part was. It's only two speeches. He said, 'Yes, there's only two lousy speeches, are you going to screw those up?' I said 'I won't screw them up – but they're very underwritten.' He said, 'They're not underwritten if they're done *properly*!'

Well, I'm just about to go on and I start thinking about what he's said. Bad idea. So out I go, tense, all over the place, not concentrating, try to give him the whole performance in the first line, and blow the whole thing. I walked up to him in the bar after and he laughs and says, 'My God you blew them both! Tried to give us the whole performance in the first line.' And I thought, 'Bastard,' but of course he was right. We went on to have a great night and I began to really enjoy playing Judith.

Doing *Dancing at Lughnasa* I got to know Brian better because he was there all the time. We always got on really well and I always asked him really straight questions. He's quite scary when you meet him first. It's that kind of schoolmaster thing he's got – he'd put red circles all over your compositions!

I was playing Chrissie, mother of the little boy Michael, and after we'd read the play a few times, Patrick [Mason] asked me, 'Catherine, what's this play all about?' I was really naïve and I said, 'It's all about this woman, and her little boy.' And everyone laughed around the table! I was so focused on myself. I thought the whole play was about Chrissie and Michael. And somebody said, 'Oh typical actress!' And then we all went for a cup of tea and Brian came up to me and said, 'You're quite right, that is what it's all about.' That was real Brian. He enjoyed the fact that I was so caught up with Chrissie and the play, but he was also trying to reassure me. He always made me feel he valued my opinions as much as other people's – in fact more than other people's, which I'm afraid I found irresistible, which in turn, of course, pissed a lot of people off.

He started to do an adaptation of *A Month in the Country* for the Gate Theatre, while we were doing *Lughnasa* in New York. So I got it out and read it and thought, 'Nothing in there for me.' Natalya was the lead in it and I thought, 'She's a bit posh,' and threw it aside and thought, 'That's that.' So when he'd finished the adaptation, and Joe Dowling asked me to play Natalya, I was stunned. In the Penguin translation they give you a lot of Natalya's history. In Brian's version we really know nothing about her past. Which is great – it gives you lots of options. But of course it helps if you know which options to take.

I'm afraid I fell between about ten different stools. One rather unkind critic who will remain nameless said I was more Downstairs than Upstairs. So was she right? Maybe, but I liked to think she missed the point. Joe Dowling put it very well, I think, when he said I was a little overwhelmed by the whole event. Anyway, I had a ball and more importantly it didn't put either Brian or Joe off working with me again. A couple of years later Joe and I did a radio version of Brian's *A Month in the Country* which everyone loved. With Joe's help I think I got a better handle on the role the second time around.

I don't have a particular way of doing Friel. Each play you do is different. I suppose *Molly Sweeney* was unique in that I had the script for quite some time before starting rehearsals. When I first read it I could hardly breathe – there were just these pages and pages of words. So I just stopped reading, tried to relax, start again and read it like a story. Of course it was wonderful. My God, what did we have? Thirty-eight monologues, three chairs on an empty stage, one of the characters is blind. And of course Brian is directing for the first time. I mean – you put all those components together, it's amazing we all lived to tell the tale.

I did loads of work on the script before we started. I learned lines, read up on as much as I could. When we started I said to Brian, 'Now Mr Director, what about the blindness?' And he said, 'Now listen here, I wrote the play, you're the actress. You look after the blindness.' Another director would say, 'Where are we going? what are we searching for? what about a blind-fold? let's try this or that.' Brian said, 'That's your job.'

During rehearsals I went to stay with some wonderful blind people, went swimming with them. Twenty people in the pool – I was the only sighted one. I got out and was terrified. They just swam round like lunatics. Never bumped into each other once. *I* kept bumping into them! I came out and *I* felt like the person with the disability. We all went into the dressing room and they all tore off their swimming things and they dried themselves off. And I'm like this nutcase with my towel wrapped round me. What the hell was I afraid of? That they might see me naked?

Brian's great line was always: 'Keep it simple, keep everything simple.' I'm always trying to put loads of business in, loads of subtext. And he'd say, 'Stop, stop. Say the lines, stop moving your hands. Stop jumping around, stop doing anything!' I said 'I can't just sit here and say the lines,' and he said, 'That's exactly what I want you to do.' It was torture for me but I think it worked in the end. He can't always tell you what he *wants* exactly, but he does tell you what he *doesn't* want. Maybe that's more valuable. He hates it if you try to make things more complicated than they are. I think a lot of people tend to do that with Brian's stuff: start reading things into it. You get frightened that you're not doing enough. You tend to get a bit too reverential I suppose – I know I'm guilty of that myself.

I felt I had a go at Molly at the Gate – I thought I was OK. But I don't think we'd climbed the mountain fully. When we went to the Almeida in London we had a different experience there. Mark [Lambert] and TP [McKenna] had played London before. I was kind of an unknown quantity in England. It's sometimes good to go to places where they don't know you . . . In Ireland they were sick of looking at me. I was in my fifth Brian Friel play and he was directing it. I was becoming a bit of a Brian Friel actress. People were beginning to use the word 'muse'. It was all a bit scary. I went with what Brian wanted. I gave them something simple, but they didn't really want that here [in Dublin]. I didn't really know what they wanted. Maybe some kind of Electra, or St Joan. Some big dynamic performance. But by the time we opened I agreed with Brian, I thought low-key was the way to go. Could I have given them a powerhouse Molly? With another director, maybe. If, say, Joe [Dowling] had directed me, it would have been a much more emotional performance, but that would have been a different production. I love Joe Dowling as a director. He pushes me right to the edge and that's great. Patrick Mason's a very patient, gentle director and I like that too. Brian's not like either of them. But isn't that what it's all about – diversity? I loved being directed by him. Yes, maybe he didn't push me hard enough. Maybe I wasn't demanding enough with him as an actress. But we had a wonderful time and his beautiful plays survived us.

I tell you a big, big shock on the opening night at the Gate. The lights go down, and I'm standing there on the stage and they don't know I'm blind. So I start to do this thing with the chair. Touchy-feely-blind acting, Brian used to call it. He hated it – used to go crazy when I tried it. And of course I was trying to slip it in here and there because I suppose I thought it looked good. Within about six sentences Molly makes this little joke about her father. And it just fell flat. So I touched the chair – overtouched the chair. I was saying to them, 'Hey listen! I'm blind!' As soon as I did that, you could hear a pin drop. Christ, it was terrifying. Brian came back at the interval and said, 'What are you doing? All the audience can see is – lights up – disability! That's all the audience can see. They're not listening to a word you're saying – all they're thinking is – blind woman. Poor blind woman. Of course he was right. I need to be told to relax, slow down, trust it. No better man to tell me.

Brian doesn't like to nag too much. He's got enormous respect for actors. He has great respect for everybody. He lets them get on with their job. Our costume designer, Joan Bergen, would say, 'What do you think of this? Do you think it's Molly?' and he'd say, 'Well, I'm the writer, you're the designer.' And I'd say, 'Is it a bit bright?' And he'd say, 'That's for the designer to say.' The only thing Brian is really prickly about is his script. Mess around with that at your peril. If you want to see the dark side of this man, feck around his lines.

The thing people forget about doing a new Brian Friel play is that it's a world event. You try and tell yourself it's just another opening, but the fact is that people are not coming to see your performance at all; they're coming to see the Great Man's new work. It's a privilege, of course it is, but it's also daunting because you know that if you screw up, it's not just your performance you're blowing but two years of Brian's work. This is his latest baby; here you are carrying this beautiful, fragile thing. God help you if you drop it! And there are plenty of people to tell you when you do. Indeed there are many who take pleasure in it. But let's not go there!

When we went to New York to do the play, I was flanked by the legendary American actor Jason Robards and the wonderful Alfred Molina, so I was naturally very nervous. I was glad I'd played the part in front of an audience before. But I needn't have worried. They were both terrific. We relooked at a lot of the play again – didn't change any of the words, needless to say. Jason and Fred liked to explore, play around a bit. I'm not sure Brian was crazy about that, but it was really exciting for me.

There's a bleak side to Brian's plays but he doesn't always like that highlighted. *Dancing at Lughnasa* was all golden corn and poppies, beautiful lighting; the women were colour-coordinated. But there's another production of *Dancing at Lughnasa* we haven't seen yet. We haven't seen how dark it is. Ours was the golden production. He wanted hope at the end of *Molly Sweeney*. I remember sitting in the middle of the rehearsal room saying, 'Hope? But she dies!'

There was a lot of discussion on how to play the last scene. I couldn't just sit there and do it blind. He eventually let me do it sighted. It was an idea I had that the further she's moving away from the world, the more she thinks she can see. But I'm not sure Brian ever really bought into the idea. Let's just say it's open to interpretation. Then all the American critics started analysing how it was to do with the Troubles! And I kept saying, 'Oh Jesus, this is all about the Troubles!' Brian said to me, 'You're playing a woman – just play the woman.' I know what he means; you can overanalyse. You've got to play the people, say the lines on the page. Find the truth, moment by moment.

In *Wonderful Tennessee* [Gate Theatre 1993] we should have played the lines, simply, and not the 'Otherness'. But that's just me. Everyone has an opinion about that play. I'll leave it to the academics to fight over!

With *Give Me Your Answer, Do!* [Abbey Theatre 1997, Byrne as Daisy Connolly] there were too many cooks. People had got greedy. The poor play never really got a chance to breathe. Maybe Brian should have stamped his foot a bit more. I can honestly say that *Molly Sweeney* in New York was without question the high point for me. The American producer said to me, 'You're the leading lady here, you know. When you're up onstage in New York, you've got to come on to the audience and say, "Hey! Hi! I'm the leading lady, OK?" I told him that's not really my style. And he said, 'I haven't brought you all the way from Dublin to be anything less.' I tried my best to rise to the occasion. The critics loved the play, the production and, thankfully, my performance. And I had a hell of a time; what more could I ask for?

After the silly reception we received for *Give Me Your Answer, Do!* he said to me, 'Should I not direct again?' And I said, 'Of course you should.' His plays and characters have touched the world. He's earned the right to direct again. He should do whatever he wants.

Brian puts extraordinary words into very ordinary people's mouths. They might be downtrodden, have ghastly lives, but you know what he does? He gives them this dignity, this humour. He never allows them to be public, whiny. Never allows them to indulge in self-pity.

That wonderful scene in *Lughnasa* when Gerry Evans arrives at the house for the first time – Brian said it should be like a fox coming to the henhouse door. When the women suddenly start dancing to the Marconi, those scenes were incredibly moving to watch. But I tell you this: I did that play for two years and there never was a night that I wasn't moved by those scenes. He loved all those women in *Lughnasa*. I met this nun in New York and she said she remembered his Aunt Kate in school when she was a child in Donegal. His aunt had introduced this little shy boy with dark, curly hair to the class. She said he just stood there with a big red face, staring at the floor, embarrassed by the attention. It wasn't hard to imagine!

Mark Lambert

When we got to *Molly Sweeney*, he's such a blunt man. He might sometimes talk in riddles, but when it comes to the theatre he says, 'I don't know.' I like artists when they admit they don't know, because it frees you. It relaxes you. People who pretend they know – directors, writers or actors – are dangerous because they're frightened. Brian is a writer who's always said, 'I don't know.' He hates answering questions about his writing, and I know that from having directed his plays. He will not answer the questions. I think that's perfectly justifiable.

In terms of actually acting Friel there's a simplicity and integrity about the characters, about the writing. I played Doalty [in *Translations*]. It's very open and artless, though he hides stuff towards the end, Doalty. There's a certain simplicity in the use of the language. As actors we try and work every line – overwork is what we're talking about sometimes. With Friel you just allow them to happen really. His economy, his lack of repetition in the line . . . There's no wastage in any of his work. I think as a performer some of the highlights of my time have been working on it.

One of my favourites was *A Month in the Country*. I think it's his best adaptation. It can be done in any language, although it's set in an Irish context. The character of Arkadi, the husband, has without doubt one of the great speeches I have had the pleasure of speaking, a great opportunity for any actor. Added to that, working with Donal McCann was a great pleasure. Before that I'd also had the opportunity of doing the beautiful Michael monologues in *Dancing at Lughnasa*. Those lines were magnificent, but slightly frustrating in that I wanted to talk to other people on the stage. When you're doing a long run it is difficult.

Brian gives gentle support but he doesn't over-praise, and I actually prefer that – I actually get suspicious with too much praise – but he did say to me, 'Don't go too strongly on the accents.' Maybe he thought my Donegal accent was crap . . . He said the English don't like the accent and I said two things. One is that there's a big difference between a Belfast accent and a Donegal accent. I think the Donegal accent's beautiful – it's a fantastic accent. I think *his* accent's terrific! Secondly, I was quite surprised he was worried. I thought, 'Why are you worried what the English think, as long as they understand it? What does it matter if it's strong?' It's funny that he worried about that . . .

It's true that he wanted to be professional and accessible to people. What is wonderful about his characters is their depth. They're three-dimensional, those characters; you can dig deep in them. One thing about some of his male creations is the female dimension of them. Brian is very much of a lad, very much of the boy that you meet socially to have a drink with. He calls a spade a spade – he comes across as a man's man. But his characters have got really sensitive sides to them. And a comic side to them as well.

Frank in *Molly Sweeney* is a bit of a dangerous man, a bit of an eejit. Obviously an actor sometimes has to have an empathy with a character – even sometimes sympathy. Sometimes even further – he falls in love with the character. But one of the things that's very easy with Brian's characters is that he always has a compassion for them. And what I clung on to was

Frank's enthusiasm – the man who creates projects. A kind of life force. He's full of life, but he is, in the end, unattractive. He was foolish, impetuous and in the end quite dangerous in the way he plunged into things sometimes. But in the end there was no malice behind any of it. That's why Brian's clever. He never allows the audience – and it was the actors' fault if they drove them that way – to make someone completely foolish.

I've tried to avoid the word 'Chekhov' in this conversation because it's often alluded to about Brian, and he must be fed up with it. But with Chekhov's characters there is always a compassion and depth to them. Even the dull and boring characters are somehow intriguing.

And of course, in the case of Frank, he's quite funny in his foolishness. I found a huge pleasure acting Frank. He has twelve monologues in the play. They were fabulous, and when we started doing *Molly Sweeney*, I read it and thought this was a fantastic read. But I really did doubt that it could translate to stage. I thought there was no seeming interreaction between the characters. I was just worried about the dramatic quality of it. I thought maybe it could work on radio but how's it going to work onstage? But because of the experience of seeing *Faith Healer*, where there are four massive monologues, I realized you've got to trust it. There were some people who argued that it wasn't good. There was a drama within each of the monologues

He actually cut twenty minutes out of *Molly Sweeney*. He cut across the board. I don't recall him cutting any one character more than another. He felt that the play was too long, that there was wastage in it (he may not have used that word 'wastage', but he thought it was too long).

This is what fascinates me. Apart from *A Month in the Country*, which I wouldn't think any production would need to cut – but I think in one or two of his other plays, possibly, snips here and there . . .? Either people are afraid to ask because they are in awe of him, or because he won't – I don't know. I've heard he's reluctant to change things. Certainly in this he literally cut swathes out of it, which was a shock to us and to anybody we told. And it was a good and brave thing to do. You could have performed the extra twenty minutes, because he's such a good writer. People would have accepted it. He obviously felt instinctively that it could sustain – particularly as they're monologues as well.

I don't feel any material went that was really important. I remember at the time we argued the toss on a couple of points. Because sometimes an actor will have an instinct about some piece of writing, and say, 'Actually, you shouldn't lose this, I know I can use this.' But other times, actors will say, like Eliot says, you've got to kill your darlings. Sometimes you've got to kill the things you love. It may be good but it's repetitious, say. But he balanced it very well.

Very early on he allowed us to know what the other characters were doing. I don't think we worked in isolation. I don't know whether he worked with Catherine individually – I'm pretty sure he didn't. My first experience of him directing was him saying he didn't know how to stage it. I liked that honesty. For the first couple of days we talked about ways of doing it, where the characters stand – beside each other or apart, in isolated spots, whatever.

In rehearsal, I always encourage people to give me notes. I make it very plain early on that I have no ego in terms of being directed and criticized. And I thought Brian reacted to that, because he was feeling vulnerable and shy as a director. Despite the fact that he's sat for years throughout rehearsals, watching. And being critical of directors at times. But it's one matter, as I know, being a third eye and another actually doing it. And I think he was quite nervous, but his saving grace was his honesty. And I responded to any suggestions he made, because directors *do* feel threatened by actors. I'm not saying I'm an established actor, but I do see all over Dublin really good actors standing still, because they don't like being criticized. Then directors get frightened of them. And then they stop learning. Everybody stops learning. Even a bad director can sometimes give you a good note. That's my theory. You can reject bad notes there and then or later on, but just get them – get those bloody ideas. And Brian was very, very helpful to me. Obviously his strong point was the text – no question of that – but he was also quite truthful, because the character I was playing was very exuberant and very extrovert and I made him quite physical. Brian was quite honest when he thought I was doing too much and when I was doing too little. There's no point in saying 'inspirational', because it wasn't that kind of play – I don't know what he'd be like in another context. He *was* inspirational about the text. He wasn't taking you into dark corners and saying, 'I've got this amazing acting method for you to follow.' It wasn't like that. I don't think anybody would approach the play in that way. But he was extraordinarily helpful, which is more than I can say for many directors . . .

About the play, I thought afterwards rather than during that, like a lot of writing, it's about him. The thing that intrigued me – apart from my basic actor's instinct to enjoy playing this character because he's got such vitality – was the style of passing on the narrative. Unlike *Faith Healer*, where you knew each section in a sense was an entity on its own, this was a rolling narrative which you were part of, and your contribution to it was almost symphonic. You keep coming back to a musical analogy to describe it. The pleasure in it was your part in playing that orchestral piece. And there was definitely an awareness – which you could argue happens in any good play by anybody and by BF – that there are sections – slow, slow, quick quick, slow. And here's the dark piece followed by the light piece. But in this you were much more 'hands on', because you were passing back and forth from one to the other and back again as part of the narrative. And that was quite exciting and became more apparent as one got into rehearsals.

At first your focus is on what you're doing with a character and just your own musicality of the lines. Maybe that's true of an orchestra – I've not played in one – your concentration is always at first exactly on your own part and then after that you start to listen to the whole and there's a vague awareness of taking part in the whole symphony, the whole piece . . .

My character, Frank, wasn't that aware of himself. So he wasn't that tragic and certainly he was important to lighten a lot of the factual and emotional stuff. That was very much his contribution – to lighten with his madcap ideas and to lighten just simply with the energy of the character. Brian is very good with characters of energy. Casimir's got huge energy. I saw *Translations* the other day – those Doalty characters, those people who come bursting in with massive energy. That's very exciting to watch, and exciting to play. They're not self-aware characters. There's a naïvety about them as well, which is also a point of Brian's greatness as well. He can write naïve characters, which for a sophisticated intelligent man is actually not that easy. He can do both – create the articulation of an intelligence like *Faith Healer* and yet create those characters who aren't aware of themselves. Or they show only touches of awareness, which is very poignant. Even with Frank there's the odd moment where he says, 'Maybe – maybe I should have done this . . .' There's always that slight thing of regret, that lament for things they should have done.

Concerning Frank and playing the part, I enjoyed it, but I have to say I did it for six months, and when I suffered the slight indignity (and I don't mind that word being used . . .) of promises to go to New York and then not being used, I didn't suffer the loss of not playing the character. I loved doing it at the time, but doing a monologue to the audience week after week, month after month . . . I suffered the same slight problem with playing Michael [in *Dancing at Lughnasa*] nine months in the West End: that as an actor you desperately want to talk to somebody else onstage. You do talk to the audience as a person but it's not the same. It's not in the end as satisfying as being *in* a Brian Friel play.

I would have loved that play – and of course it wouldn't have been that play – if suddenly the characters turned and started talking to each other.

We had seven producers come to see the play and our management chose the one who was the most commercial. And the play was never going to be a Broadway hit. I can't imagine even Brian would think that. It was too much of a chamber piece and it wasn't a 'feelgood' play. It was sad, sad. And those kind of plays don't really work in a commercial context. Brian doesn't write plays to be commercial – I really don't believe he's ever done that. But then there's another side to him that's a fox that goes, 'Well, if the thing's going places, I'd like the thing to be as successful as possible.'

I directed *Translations* at the Royal Lyceum in Edinburgh and I decided to cast across the border – used Scottish and Irish actors. I was amazed the play hadn't been done in Scotland because I thought it was so apt. It is a universal play, one could argue, but particularly pertinent to Scotland in terms of cultural identity. I was thrilled to be able to do the play because, apart from having played Doalty at the Bristol Old Vic, I had used the central love scene in teaching at drama schools. I think it's one of the great love scenes. When you're casting for *Translations*, one of the central things you've got to crack first – and probably with a lot of his plays – is who you cast as the heavyweight. You've got to get the lead heavyweight right. In the Abbey Theatre there were always the lead actors, it's true – the ones that played Captain Boyle – because they had a permanent company. (I'm sure that's why Brian didn't always give his plays to the Abbey. He didn't always want the same actors playing the parts. Brian is always very good at choosing who directed and where his plays went. You could argue that Field Day didn't help some of his plays. The original production of *Translations* wasn't necessarily the best production. I thought *Making History* was undercast. So I thought it was understandable that he wanted to break out and take *Dancing at Lughnasa* to the Abbey. And since then he's been very careful whether he gives the play to the Gate, the Abbey, the [Royal] National Theatre. He's quite picky and choosy and he's right to be, I think.

Casting the central role – who do you cast in *Faith Healer*, you know? Those three huge roles. Obviously in terms of leading Irish actors, you had Ray McAnally, Donal McCann as prime people. One hopes that one will be the next generation that Brian keeps writing for! Hugh in *Translations*, though in size, oddly enough, he isn't that big, is a central character. I would call it the 'lead' character and yet Owen and Manus have more to say than he does. But you need that weight of authority and charisma. It's a hard part to cast. I found a great guy in Tom Watson, a small, old, Scottish actor, who you've probably seen in loads of things. And he was fantastic in it. I was just very lucky – he was put forward at the last moment and he helped galvanize the whole cast. I'd got a very good young company of top Irish actors – Pat Kinevan, Stephen Kennedy, Fionulla Murphy – along with some very good Scottish actors as well. I did it very traditionally. I'd be very interested to know, rather like *Juno and the Paycock*, if anyone ever tries to do some kind of expressionist set or anything like that.

I was pleased because before I did it people said it's 'dangerously mythical' now. But it's bollocks; it still works fantastically well. It works on a theatrical level – it's funny and entertaining, intriguing and moving, all those things – whatever the political context of it.

Thinking about Brian's influence now, someone like Conor Macpherson [author of *The Weir*] is more influenced by someone like Billy Roche. I remember before I'd actually met Brian doing a workshop for which they'd found six writers, six actors, and [playwright] Tom Kilroy overseeing it with Patrick Mason. It was a fantastic idea developing first-draft plays of young writers. Brian Friel came up and was rather pithy and almost useless actually, in that he just said, 'You've just got to get out there and do it.' He has influenced a lot of writers, but I remember him saying, 'Look don't admire me – I wrote out of a sense of rebellion, attacking and all that sort of thing, in a period of drama that I thought was dull and boring.' But his mentors are some of the international playwrights like Ibsen and Chekhov – playwrights that he'd seen.

So now this generation have seen Friel plays and I think he has been vital, putting Irish playwriting back on the map, there's no question of that. He's been a huge influence – also in the fact that he's experimented with the form. And in a sad way he's experimented *more* than a lot of contemporary playwrights. You could argue that he *hasn't* influenced that many in that particular way. But it is a TV generation, absolutely. And they may have reacted against some of the naïvety. Some of his theatrical form is fantastically naïve. Using the two characters in *Philadelphia, Here I Come!* talking to each other is just magnificent. You can't just copy that. But it's the idea of playing around with the form that doesn't happen much now.

He never took writers' workshops himself. He never preached to other writers. Actually I think he'd be terrible at it. I remember the actors in the Lyceum *Translations* asking him, what does this mean, this last speech? Would you ask Brian this or that? I said, 'OK, I'll ask him, but there's no point.' I got two 'Could be's', a 'Might be', a 'Do what the fuck you like', and one 'I don't know' – or something. Literally that. And I knew I'd get that, and I was amused by that response. Some of it's honest and some of it isn't quite, I think. But I think he's in a position as a writer not to answer those questions.

Talking about writers' workshops – we were workshopping a play at the Abbey – he said something I found very exciting. He was saying the play's the play and that's it; you just give the play, you don't see his drafts. And then he said, 'What you've got to understand is where I came from. I came from the base where I as a writer would hand my script over to actors who ripped out the pages and only kept the pages they were speaking.'

So as a writer you didn't welcome changes in the script – even though it was for the better. There was no way he was going to do that. I now realize that's where he was coming from. So I don't think he spurns the idea of workshops or anything like that – he just couldn't do that himself.

So he's given Irish theatre prestige and an international name again, and he's given actors huge opportunities. At one point single-handedly. Nobody else was doing that. And also the fact that he's been prolific has been a great bonus, even if one could argue the last couple of plays haven't been . . . maybe they've got too poetic or something. Too metaphorical maybe? There's not the bluntness of the other plays, I don't know. *Wonderful Tennessee*? It's got a bit mystical and nostalgic for me.

But he's so clever it wouldn't surprise me if he came up with a cracker. And I'd certainly want to be in it and be part of it. Direct it . . . act it . . . read it!

This next piece was written for a brochure to accompany the 1999 Friel Festival. Between April and August, productions, readings, discussions and events celebrated Friel's achievement on his seventieth birthday. Donal McCann is an actor invoked by both Byrne and Lambert – with good reason. He was the best-known interpreter of Frank Hardy in Faith Healer, *and was cast in the Abbey Theatre production of* Wonderful Tennessee. *His early death in 1999 ended the career of one of Ireland's most admired actors.*

Brian Friel and an actor

In 1980 I was given *Faith Healer* to read, with a view to playing the part of Frank in the Abbey Theatre. I accepted, of course, because I had never read anything like it. Then I became sweatily petrified as it dawned on me that I had never seen anything like it. I had nothing to measure it against; nothing in my experience had prepared me for it.

After maybe a week's rehearsal it became very clear that there was only one way to do it and that was, as simply as possible. Who told me that? The play itself told me – demanding that it be performed without flourishes. Friel had informed it so. I took the play at its word and asked it more. It suggested to me that I was wrong to think that nothing had prepared me for it. Twenty-five years an actor, it whispered, a quarter of a century making mistakes, and you say you have no experience! You're right, I said – thanks. Don't thank me, said the play, the Fantastic Francis Hardy asked me to pass it on.

I grew pleasantly confused but let it pass. Of course an actor does not become a character in a play, but a beautifully written character can become an actor and I began to find Frank very becoming indeed. I also found him great company, though occasionally the pair of us seemed to me like sad people in an early house before a funeral. At such times, I could do nothing for him because he was written, but I would emerge from these depressions feeling I had gained a bit more as an actor. And a bit more, and a bit more, and by the end of the first run of that production a lot more than I ever thought I might know. *Faith Healer* influenced everything good I have done since in the theatre.

I have tried to suggest the sense of privileged responsibility that attaches to the playing of the work of Brian Friel, and I hope I have made obvious the feeling of gratitude that I, an actor, have for the author of so much of my good fortune.

The Friel Festival brochure included a series of meditations by Friel on different aspects of his craft.

Brian Friel On . . .

. . . Great actors

I have worked with many great actors over the years and the experience of working with them in the rehearsal room is one of the great joys and satisfactions of the theatre.

A great actor mustn't be confused with a star. He or she may be a star. But that isn't central to what he is, nor is it something he aspires to. What is it then that makes an actor great? And for convenience I'll refer to him as he.

First of all his theatrical instincts are so finely tuned that he moves into those plays that offer his particular physical and intellectual capacities their full reach. And he makes those choices mostly intuitively. So that the plays he chooses to do challenge him but they also affirm him.

When he reads a play, in a sense he reads it with his ears. And what he sees on the page isn't necessarily the character so carefully described by the author but a version of himself, himself assuming those characteristics and making them his characteristics; sees himself penetrating that character and being suffused by it; so that what finally emerges will be neither quite what the author wrote, nor what the actor is, but a new identity that draws from the essences of both. That is why we call it 'creating a part'.

But there is another way in which great actors manifest themselves: they are wonderful singers of the written line – perfect pitch, perfect rhythm. And they can do that because they know intuitively the exact meaning of that line; and not only the exact meaning but how that line was composed and why those words and only those words were used. So that not only does he understand the precise composition of a line but he knows that this line is inevitable now because of what was said in the preceding line; and the line that follows will be inevitable because of what is said now. So each of these lines, following necessarily on one another, generates the necessary propulsion of the text. And the great actor knows all that – intuitively. So that once he understands the engine of the play, he can transform the text into an opera that is indeed greater than the writing and greater than its enactment. That is why great actors are scrupulous with the text. That is why great actors don't improvise. And that is why writers owe so much to them. We aren't mute any more.

They bestow eloquence on us.

This next piece by Friel, ostensibly about amateur theatre, continues his preoccupation with acting and actors. In effect, it praises the Caesar of amateurism in order to bury it! It was published in the Friel Festival brochure.

... Amateurs

One of the vigours of our theatre has been its roots in the amateur movement.

Yeats acknowledged that vigour and tapped into its untutored energy. Indeed the Abbey Theatre used that source until the sixties; and it nurtured the uncertain institution satisfactorily.

What did the amateur movement offer? It offered energy – mental energy, physical energy. It supplied a quick and intuitive imagination. It brought to the theatre a great enthusiasm and an eagerness to show off. Come and look at us because we have a natural talent for performance and it's all going to be the best of fun and it gives ourselves and our friends a great laugh. And indeed all this was a useful antidote to the vanity and self-regard of the gathering of fifty in the drawing room and their starchy hostess.

But the days of the amateur having anything to contribute to the theatre are long gone. Because over the years the theatre, like every profession, has become more and more specialized. The amateur's high spirits are now applauded only in the parish hall. Because now we want our actors to have the finely tuned bodies of athletes. We insist that they have the same control over their breathing and their voices as the trained singer. We ask that they can dance and ride horses and swim and fence and speak a couple of languages – as well of course as being able to analyse a text closely and then interpret it with consummate skill.

And do we have these magnificent creatures? I think they are beginning to emerge. There is still a residue of the amateur traces in our theatre today – groups who had fun putting on plays when they were in college and who stayed together and worked together after college. But the brio and high spirits of the old days is no substitute for training. And today that training is vital. But we have efficient drama courses being taught all over the country. And more and more highly trained actors are available. And I now believe that a great theatre – which is possible only with great actors – is more and more possible here. If these great actors aren't seduced into film. Which they will be if we don't recompense them adequately. But that's another story . . .

The Director

Given Friel's gentle cynicism about directors, discussed above in 'The Road to Ballybeg', it is as well to preface Friel's own views with a rich discussion, both practical and wide-ranging, of working on Friel's plays from Joe Dowling. Now director at the Guthrie Theater in Minneapolis, where coincidentally Friel learned so much so fast in 1962, Joe Dowling wrote this piece for the anthology The Achievement of Brian Friel, *edited by Alan Peacock.*

Staging Friel

'Words are signals, counters . . .' Hugh Mor O'Donnell reminds us in one of Friel's most accomplished plays, *Translations*. This is a useful starting point in looking at the staging of any writer, particularly a playwright for whom language has always been used to convey the emotional landscape of the play. For the actor working in Friel, language is a vital consideration and the most important way for signals to be conveyed to the audience. In discussing any dramatist, it is important to remember how incomplete the work is until it is performed onstage by actors. The value of any piece for the theatre cannot be assessed fully until the skill of the actor is used to explore the sub-text and reveal the emotional truth behind the surface dialogue.

Themes and ideas may be analysed and dissected by an academic study of the text, but the essence of all drama lies in whatever emotional response can be created by the interaction between actor and audience in the theatre. Some texts, which on the page can seem trite and superficial, in the hands of skilled actors have a depth and meaning which even the writer only hints at. For the actor to realize the full value of a character, it is essential to go beyond the language of the text and delve into the sub-text. Guided by the director's overall vision of the production, the actor must explore aspects of the characters' life which do not appear as part of the text. Together, the actor and director can uncover the unspoken thoughts which help to identify the imaginative life of the role. Exploration of this kind can take the actor into difficult areas of his own personality and psyche. Through the work of rehearsal, the actor must find parallels with his own experience which provide a common thread of understanding with the character he is playing.

The work of rehearsal is devoted to the careful piecing together of the text and the world behind the play. Essentially, whatever the complexities of form and theatrical style, the function of the writer in the theatre is to tell a story, to weave the imaginative narrative fabric which actors can then stitch together into a multi-coloured quilt. A writer without interpreters can only tell half the story. Great theatre is created from a lively combination of the author's imaginative world and the actor's emotional discovery. Very often, plays which on first reading seem uninspiring can, in the hands of good actors and a sensitive director, turn into vibrant and exciting theatrical events.

Similarly, a fine play can be destroyed by the failure to convey its real quality in performance. The history of the theatre is littered with plays which needed to be rescued from their first disastrous productions.

Brian Friel is a writer whose work always demands a particular quality of acting and direction. With each new Friel play, the director and actor are presented with major challenges of staging, of characterization and often of language and its theatrical possibilities. The staging difficulties usually relate to a correct balance between realism and an instinctive theatricality which is part of each play, no matter how naturalistic the basic story. The characterization must always be based on a sense of reality and truth. The language is often heightened to a point where the actor must find a way of making the poetic vocabulary seem real without losing the rhythm.

A typical example of this stylistic and linguistic balancing act occurs in *Translations*, perhaps Friel's most complex play. There is a real challenge of interpretation for the actor playing the character of Yolland, the young British soldier whose enchantment with Ireland and with the local girl Maire leads to such tragic results. He speaks of his first impression of Ballybeg and the society which the Hedge School represents:

> It wasn't an awareness of a *direction* being changed but of experience being of a totally different order. I had moved into a consciousness that wasn't striving nor agitated, but at its ease and with its own conviction and assurance.

The language used here is more literary than conversational and the actor must find the correct way to present it so that the enthusiasm of the young man and his fascination with the place and the people is palpable and at the same time not lose the structures of the sentences and the stylistic integrity of the language.

The great value of Friel's language is that it is always possible for the actor to find the correct imagery behind the line. In this case, there is a sharp contrast with the world which Yolland's father expected for him. A world of exciting possibilities, a new world. His father was born on the day the Bastille fell:

> I've often thought maybe that gave his whole life its character. Do you think it could? He inherited a new world the day he was born – The Year One. Ancient time was at an end. The world had cast off its old skin. There were no longer any frontiers to man's potential. Possibilities were endless and exciting . . . I'm afraid I'm a great disappointment to him.

Taking this expectation of dynamic achievement with Yolland's own desire for a quieter energy, one can immediately see how the archaic world of Ballybeg would appeal to him and make him feel at ease with himself and with his surroundings. The clear contrast between the forceful language of this speech and the fluidity and poetic flow of the description of Ballybeg gives the actor the clue to the delivery. There is always a subtext to be found and a context for the attitudes in each scene.

No matter how formal the language, there will always be a psychological root to the character and the situation which allows the actor a clear direction as to its meaning.

Friel is an exceptionally fine story-teller who uses the characters and their place in his carefully structured image of society to advance his narrative. The world of his plays unfolds gradually and without obvious force. Where violent actions occur, as they do often in his work, they are used as an indication of the brutality of the world surrounding the play. The savagery and almost inevitable violence of *The Gentle Island* comes as a shock and is used in ironic counterpoint to the physical beauty of the island. The same effect is used in *Translations*, where a stranger becomes enchanted with the atmosphere of the Donegal countryside without ever realizing the depth and the intensity of his isolation from the community. The death of Frank Hardy in *Faith Healer* is a similar shock and happens at the hands of people who are strangers to him and who seem at first glance to be unlikely murderers. Frank describes their first appearance:

> When we came downstairs to the lounge in the pub we got caught up in the remnants of a wedding party – four young men, locals, small farmers, whose friend had just gone off on his honeymoon a few hours earlier. Good suits. White carnations. Dark, angular faces. Thick fingers and black nails.

Within a few lines, Friel creates a whole picture of the men who later demand Frank's life in return for the inevitable failure of his healing gift. This counterpoint between the simplicity of the situation, the ordinary nature of the people and the effects of extreme violence, gives *Faith Healer* a heightened theatricality which makes it attractive to audiences and triumphs over the unconventional nature of the monologue structure. In the majority of the plays, however, it is the unspoken things, the silences, the misunderstandings, the deliberate confusions and the tricks of memory which tell us the stories and maintain the narrative drive.

For the actor and the director, it is the minutiae of the work which provide its most important exploration. The actor must always delve behind the line, examine the sub-text and then accurately reproduce the sound of the character as Friel has written it. His ear for dialogue is uncannily accurate and the actor will find that the speech of the character will always feel right on the tongue. Witness the girlish chatter of Mags in *Lovers*, with her references to nuns ('screams if you don't take them seriously') and the other details of her crowded young life such as the concern for the baby she is carrying:

> I think now, Joe, it's going to be nineteen days overdue. And in desperation they'll bring me into the hospital and put me on the treadmill – that's a new yoke they have to bring on labour; Joan told me about it. An aunt of a second cousin of hers was on it non-stop for thirteen hours. They keep you climbing up this big wheel that keeps giving away under you. Just like the slaves in olden times. And after the baby's born they'll keep it in an oxygen tent for a fortnight. And when we get it home it'll have to be fed with an eye dropper every forty-nine minutes and we'll get no sleep at all and . . .

This breathless and fervent imagination contrasts with the formality of language and the bleakness of imagery in the final monologue of *Faith Healer* where Frank Hardy goes out to a willing death:

> And although I knew that nothing was going to happen, nothing at all, I walked across the yard towards them. And as I walked I became possessed of a strange and trembling intimation: that the whole corporeal world – the cobbles, the trees, the sky, those four malign implements – somehow they had shed their physical reality and had become mere imaginings, and that in all existence there was only myself and the wedding guests. And that intimation in turn gave way to a stronger sense: that even we had ceased to be

physical and existed only in spirit, only in the need we had
for each other.

Friel has a remarkable capacity to convey dialogue which
actors can speak with ease and which yet provides a sense of
beauty and roundness. The rhythms of speech are not only created to carefully indicate the meaning of the speech but also to
convey the essence of the character. Each character is given the
right level of articulateness and just the right vocabulary to
illustrate social and educational background.

Lily in *The Freedom of the City* speaks with a different
flow and a different vocabulary to Hugh O'Neill in *Making
History*. Lily's world is described with a colloquial ease
which immediately sets her social status for both actor and
audience:

> D'you see our place? At this minute Mickey Teague, the
> milkman, is shouting up from the road, 'I know you're
> there, Lily Doherty. Come down and pay me for the six
> weeks you owe me.' And the chairman's sitting at the fire
> like a wee thin saint with his finger in his mouth and the
> comics up to his nose and hoping to God I'll remember to
> bring him home five fags. And below us Celia
> Cunningham's about half-full now and crying about the
> sweepstake ticket she bought and lost when she was fifteen.
> And above us Dickie Devine's groping under the bed for his
> trombone and he doesn't know yet that Annie pawned it on
> Wednesday for the wanes' bus fares and he's going to beat
> the tar out of her when she tells him.

The world of the Earl of Tyrone is somewhat different and is
expressed in a language so far removed from Lily's patois:

> O'NEILL . . . Do I grasp the Queen's Marshal's hand? –
> using Our Henry as a symbol of the new order which
> every aristocratic instinct in my body disdains but which
> my intelligence comprehends and indeed grudgingly
> respects – because as a boy I spent nine years in England

where I was nursed at the very wellspring of that new order
– think of all those formative years in the splendid homes of
Leicester and Sidney and indeed at the Court itself – hence
the grand accent, Mary –

MABEL Hugh, I think –

O'NEILL No – allow me – or – or do I grip the hand of the
Fermanagh rebel and thereby bear public and imprudent
witness to a way of life that my blood comprehends and
indeed loves and that is as old as the Book of Ruth. My
dilemma. Help me, Mary. Which hand do I grasp? Because
either way I make an enemy . . .

Yet both characters speak with conversational ease and in a
way which at once provides the exact context for the character.
By following both the intelligence of the speech and the traits
of language, of phraseology, and even the punctuation, the
actor and director can easily find the character. The next step is
to reproduce it with the same accuracy as it appears on the
page. In Friel's work, there is never a word astray and if the
actor finds the line hard to say, it is usually because he has not
analysed the sub-text of the speech. Such examination must be
conducted with a fine-tooth comb as clues to the character can
be found throughout the text.

There is no consistency of theatrical style or a defined
approach to language and characterization which a director
and actors can fall back on. From the device of the two Gars in
Philadelphia, Here I Come!, where both actors must be aware
of the thinking of the other if the performances are to have a
necessary unity of character, through to the equally innovative
monologues in *Faith Healer*, where the actors must believe
diametrically opposed accounts of the same events, Friel
always makes enormous demands of the actor. The stylistic
devices force him to find new ways of expressing the character
and frequently demand a detailed offstage life which must be
understood and imaginatively explored. Essentially, Friel is a
master story-teller and the role of the director and actors is to

convey that narrative in as direct a way as possible for the audience. Any deviations from what is implicit in the text can do great harm to the intentions of the author.

Directors who see Friel's work as a way of making their own theatrical statements without taking very careful note of the nuances of the text will inevitably do considerable damage to the concise and accurate theatrical imagination which is always evident. It is vital for the director to approach the text of any Friel play with scrupulous attention to detail. The way of producing the play is always to be found within the work itself. It rarely requires extraneous production ideas.

The director has to listen to the music of the text. The actor can often find the clues to the characterization in the dialogue, not only of his own character but that of others. Friel's characters are always rooted in a detailed psychological reality, and however heightened the language may be, it is ultimately in that area of emotional truth that the impact will be made on an audience.

Actors can sometimes find this textual orthodoxy constricting as they must restrain their own creativity and become interpreters of the music of the text rather than the inventors of fresh new ideas. The role of an actor in a Friel play is analogous to the members of an orchestra who respond to the music of a symphony. The director is the conductor and is responsible for the accuracy of the sound on the stage. In Friel's work, there is no room for sloppy intentions on the director's part. If the whole piece is to have an accurate resonance, the value of each line must be understood and realized as the author intended.

The main thing the actor can rely on is that Friel will have a particular sound in his head in writing the line and if that is found, the line will be correct.

In *Philadelphia, Here I Come!* we find out the details of Gar O'Donnell's life largely from the information given by his private self. On the surface, he seems a quiet, almost reticent man of 'average' intelligence, as his old schoolmaster reminds him. However, if we listen to the cynical, sensitive and at times bitter commentary of the private persona, we can appreciate a depth of feeling which the public man cannot express. This must affect the way the actor approaches the character of the Public Gar. While we focus particularly on the evidence of the private self, another witness who can indicate his personality is Madge the faithful housekeeper who has been a mother substitute for the young Gar in that house of silence, of things unspoken. If the actor playing Public only listens to the evidence of his more extroverted Private self, he will miss out on a whole aspect of the character which Madge reveals.

> When the boss was his age, he was the very same as him: leppin, and eejitin' about and actin' the clown; as like as two peas. And when he's the age the boss is now, he'll turn out just the same.

With this information, the actor now knows that the silent and unloving father, whom Gar thinks of as 'Screwballs', once had the same energy and vitality which his character displays. He must now seek points of similarity with the character of the father and areas of the text where the truth of Madge's words can be conveyed. Similarly, the actor playing S. B. O'Donnell also has a sub-text which informs his actions. While the body may be old and the memories different, there still exists somewhere inside him, the young man so lovingly described by Madge. All the way through the play, there are similar hints for the actor and it is only by listening carefully to the text that they can be found and applied.

In *Aristocrats*, the character of Casimir is revealed to us slowly and carefully and his real eccentricities are not obvious from the start. Friel is quite emphatic about this in the stage directions when he first appears:

(One immediately gets a sense that there is something different about him – as he says himself, 'peculiar'. But what it is, is elusive: partly his shyness, partly his physical movements, particularly the way he walks – rapid, jerky, without ease or

grace – partly his erratic enthusiasm, partly his habit of sud-
denly grinning and giving a mirthless 'ha-ha' at unlikely times,
usually when he is distressed. But he is not a buffoon, nor is he
'disturbed'. He is a perfectly normal man with distinctive and
perhaps slightly exaggerated mannerisms . . .)

Casimir is not an idiot and the temptation for the actor to play
the obvious comedy in the opening scene must be very carefully avoided. The director must maintain a discipline in that first
scene and allow the details to emerge slowly and effortlessly.
Often, an inexperienced director will want to rush the pace and
get to the heart of the action quickly. That is a terrible mistake
and completely unbalances the play.

For the first twenty minutes he is onstage, we know that something is astray but we are not sure what it is. Casimir talks of the
delights of Ballybeg Hall where, for him, the sun always shines,
the doors and windows are always open and music is a constant
companion. It is essential that the actor does not play the complete character in the opening scene. He must persuade us that
his memories are accurate and that his recollection of the many
distinguished visitors to the Hall is also true. Friel destroys our
first impressions of the character when he introduces the father's
voice on the baby alarm. This gives us a more telling image of the
damage caused to Casimir's confidence and personality than all
the enthusiastic protestations of an idyllic childhood.

Finally, it is Alice who reveals the truth behind Casimir's
present bleak situation:

Began law in the family tradition but always hated books.
So he left home – went to England – worked at various
'genteel' jobs. Then he met Helga and she took him off to
Germany. I think he works part-time in a food-processing
factory – I don't want to ask him. Helga's the real breadwinner: she's a cashier in a bowling alley . . .

Eamon casts further doubt on Casimir's veracity when he
questions even the existence of Helga and the children: '– all

a fiction, all a game'. Suddenly the audience's perception of Casimir changes significantly and gradually the actor can present the whole figure. The actor knows all the strands of the character in advance but can only allow them to emerge piecemeal so that the author's intention in the stage direction is realized. The first real indication of the depth of the childhood trauma is given at the end of Act One when he reacts so desperately to the voice of the father on the baby alarm. The dramatic effect of that moment will be destroyed if the character seems eccentric or persecuted. The skill of the actor and the responsibility of the director is to allow that frightened, damaged personality to slowly emerge so that the impact of his 'great discovery' in Act Three can be as significant for the audience as for Eamon.

In Friel's work, for an actor, there must be more than what Stanislavski describes as 'the shallow physical life of the role'. An inner life which takes us behind the language and into the soul of the character must be created and sustained throughout the performance. The actor and director must find that life within the text and then work outwards. Friel's work, which has so often been compared with Chekhov, demands an application of the artistic principles of the great Russian teacher and director, Constantin Stanislavski, whose collaborations with Chekhov created a new awareness of the strength of emotional naturalism in the theatre. It was he who first identified the need for an actor to work from the inside of a character out to the external details.

He demanded that actors should find an inner life for the characters, a sense of a life separate from the immediate world of the play. Performances should not start simply at the moment the actor walks on the stage. The actor must be familiar with the daily routine of the character's life as much as with his deeper psychological realities.

With a new approach to the reality behind the character's life, Stanislavski swept away the whole artificiality of 19th-century acting where gesture and attitude were used as a substitute for truth and emotional directness in the actor's repertoire. He laid the foundation for the theatrical realism which we have come to take for granted in modern theatre and which also influenced the development of the cinema. This search for honesty demanded a sense of the spiritual meaning which motivated the characters as well as the more obvious material functions which affected the surface of the text. For Stanislavski, the aim of acting was the creation of the human spirit in artistic terms. This the actor could do only if he fully absorbed the inner life of the character and, in imaginative terms, understood the internal drives and motivations which dictate the action of the play. To this end he created a series of exercises and games which allow the actor to explore his own attitudes and reactions and to apply them to the character he is playing. This use of an emotional memory allows the actor to find parallel feelings and emotional responses in his own personal experience which can then be made to apply to the work of the writer.

As Stanislavski outlines in his seminal work *An Actor Prepares*:

> Our whole creative experiences are vivid and full in direct proportion to the power, keenness and exactness of our memory . . . Sometimes impressions once received continue to live in us, grow and become deeper. They even stimulate new processes and either fill out unfinished details or else suggest altogether new ones.

Memory is often a theme in Friel's work, whether the false memories which trick the mind and shape present bitterness, or the shared memories which bind families in an endless repetition of the past. Gar O'Donnell remembers the blue boat with its paint peeling and the simple gesture of fatherly concern in placing a coat around his shoulders as protection against the rain. S.B. has no such recollection and can only piece together the bare facts of the boat colour and the pleasure of the fishing. Similarly, he can remember the sailor suit worn by a chatty child on his way to school, hand in hand with an adoring father. Madge, the centre of their lives and their emotional go-between, knows that no such suit existed.

Memory is used here to serve the particular emotional recall. If the actor wishes to fully realize the character of Gar or the father, he must decide on a particular memory from his own experience, a parallel situation which may not link directly with the play but will be sufficiently strong to allow a similar emotional response. By such a juxtaposition of emotional memory, the actor can convey the depth of feeling implicit in the scene. So often the memories of the characters in the plays are presented in graphic detail or have an ambiguity which leaves the audience unsure of the exact truth behind them. To play that ambiguity, the actor needs to believe the text fully and allow it to speak directly to the audience without frills and intrusions. The plays demand a discipline and a honing of the emotional truth to fully engage an audience's attention.

Technical problems rarely occur in Friel's work. With the exception of *The Freedom of the City*, his plays usually demand only one setting or a composite set which allows for few scene changes. In *Translations*, where the famous 'love scene' takes place in a field near the school, he suggests in the stage directions that it 'may be played in the schoolroom, but it would be preferable to lose – by lighting – as much of the schoolroom as possible, and to play the scene down front in a vaguely "outside" area.'

This lack of concern for the visual environment is typical of a writer who creates mainly through the language and the characterization rather than through extraneous theatrical effects.

In spite of his early apprenticeship with Tyrone Guthrie, one of the most innovative and visually exciting directors of this century, Friel never really developed a sense of the possibilities of stage design as a way of expressing the imagery of his plays. He is usually very literal in his demands for the physical environment, describing in detail exactly the type of setting he requires. This rarely allows for an imaginative approach from the designer and demands a clear naturalism – even in plays which have a more expressionistic possibility. His most recent play, *Dancing at Lughnasa*, is an example of the potential of modern stage design to illuminate a script and to provide an audience with a range of signals which can add to the pleasure of the evening in the theatre. The play contains some of the most exciting visual and theatrical possibilities in the frenzied dancing of the sisters and the continual hints of pagan ritual and African customs. However, the stage directions demand a detailed realism against which the domestic ordinariness of the sisters' lives and the exotic activity described by Fr. Jack's memories are seen in contrast.

Essentially, the plays demand productions which concentrate on the performances without much emphasis on the externals. Directors who ignore this reality about Friel can do untold damage to the integrity of the work without adding anything substantial in its place. On the other hand, modern theatre demands a visual awareness and a sense of the set as more than a mere backdrop to the actors. Striking the balance between Friel's demands and the expectations of the audience in contemporary theatre creates the biggest challenge to the director and the designer. Without making statements, they must reflect the essence of the piece and widen the possibilities for the audience.

Friel is not only one of the most significant voices in contemporary Irish theatre, he is also one of the most important writers on the world's stage. With his constant exploration of both form and theme, he is one of the most innovative theatrical writers in the speaking theatre without ever falling into the murky territory of the 'experimental'. While many contemporary writers eschew the use of narrative and find contact with their audience by use of disconnected images and intense physical activity, Friel has never abandoned the central role as storyteller. His methods of telling the story may change with each new work, but the starting point is always rooted in a naturalistic reality.

While many lesser writers make obfuscation a virtue and confuse their audiences with contradictory signals, Friel is always clear in both meaning and form. He writes to communicate with the audience rather than alienating them and holding them at bay. Few playwrights working in the contemporary theatre can match the elegance of his language, the breadth of his vision and the remarkable understanding of the emotional power of the theatre which he brings to each character he creates. It is this capacity to create such wonderful, rounded and complete characters which makes his work so popular with actors. In theatrical terms, he is an 'actor's writer' rather than one who can be manipulated by a director's vision. This means that his writing does not fit into a modern concept of Director's Theatre where the director sees himself as co-creator of the dramatic piece. With so much of the modern theatre, critics place as much emphasis on the 'concept' behind the production as on the value of the text. With the majority of Friel's work, such a conceptual approach in the production would seriously affect the integrity of the author's intentions.

This is not to suggest that a director is not an essential ingredient in every production. Rather it affirms the crucial and delicate nature of the relationship between writer and director. Without a strong director shaping each scene, finding the correct pace and rhythm for each character, dictating a sense of momentum which the play requires, the plays may not realize their potential. Actors cannot find that objective realization of a scene without the careful and intelligent reading of the text by a director who respects the text. It is not always essential to see the hand of the director in an obvious way in a production, but it must always be there and it must have a strong influence on each element of the performance. The directorial function is to draw the best from all the elements – actors, designers, technical crew – in order to fully realize the intentions of the text. To play the music of the text as clearly as the writer has composed it must always be the overriding objective of any production of a Friel play. Extraneous production ideas, novel and unnecessary bits of theatrical 'business', bizarre settings and costumes have no place in the performance. Just as the writing is always disciplined and controlled, so the production must be solidly based on the evidence of the text and the imaginative power of the actors.

As Friel's work develops, the demands on the directors and actors will change. The evidence of his most recent play, *Dancing at Lughnasa*, suggests a more theatrically expansive framework which must be filled with a non-naturalistic detail. However, the essence of the work remains emotional and human and these features will continue to be the strengths of this unique Irish writer.

This is the document referred to in 'The Road to Ballybeg' discussion in which Friel raises a quizzical eyebrow at directors and their craft. It was first published in the New York Times, *and reprinted in the Friel Festival brochure.*

... Directors

Over the years I have worked with dozens of directors and with a few exceptions they have been very agreeable to work with. Why is it then that I have never quite come to terms with the idea of a director? I think it must be because after all these years I'm still not at all sure what this person contributes. For 2500 years, since the time of Aeschylus, there was no such thing as a theatre director. And then they appear – suddenly – about 150 years ago and infiltrate the process and make themselves central to the making of theatre; so central that the production of a play today without a director is unthinkable. But let's look at this again. Why is the entire putting together of a play – choosing the actors, set designer, lighting designer, costume designer, understanding the text, realising that text – why are all these responsibilities entrusted to one man or woman who has no training whatever in any of these jobs, who can't design sets, who can't write plays, who can't act? – although he or she probably tried to be an actor once. Why? And why do actors place themselves so docilely in the hands of this person? And why is the playwright asked to entrust the realisation of his play in the hands of this interloper who has no demonstrable skills?

And how they crept into the process is not at all clear. Probably by accident. Just as we once thought that a bus must have a conductor. Until one day we realised that the conductor was altogether superfluous. Of course directors are convenient. Actor-managers who used to do the job could now concentrate on acting or managing. Theatrical producers who may be juggling four or five plays at the same time were happy to hand over some of that burden to the director who would carry out his subcontract obediently. Actors weren't unhappy: here was an authoritative figure who makes sure that rehearsals are structured and the play is put together in a workmanlike way. And more importantly from the actors' point of view, isn't the whole process being overseen by somebody who – out of all the actors available – who chose me? So mustn't he or she be a very perceptive person? Who wouldn't want to trust that person, to serve that person?

But none of this tells us what the director does. Efficient management of a process? Yes that's useful; but scarcely enough, is it? A unique interpretation of the text? I have never experienced that. A rare gift to draw out the full creative potential of the actors? I've never seen that either. So I'm puzzled. But what I do know about directors is this – because I have witnessed it: that the creativity and intelligence of actors, even great actors, can be sapped by placing their talents unquestioningly into those hands. And what I know, too – because I have witnessed it – is that directors attempt to usurp the intrinsic power of the play itself. Of course they insist their role is to serve the text, to ensure the play is given space and air to sing out. But in their hearts the song they want heard is their song, because this is their interpretation, this is their vision. It is a sorry pass.

Of course there have been a handful of magnificent directors in the short time of their existence – people like Stanislavsky,

Guthrie, Grotowski, Brook. But their talent lay not in offering personal interpretation of a text but in exploding a whole calcified tradition, in turning upside down the whole practice of theatrical presentation so that we saw it all anew. They didn't offer us deep personal revelations about an entirely new kind of experience in the theatre. But innovators like that come round all too seldom. So let's not wait. And let's not be bamboozled by the bus conductors. I'll happily settle for a stage manager – if he can manage competently and especially if he or she never wanted to be an actor.

The stage manager

Bo Barton, quoted below, is a leading production and stage manager, now teaching at RADA in London. In 1980 she was approached to manage the first Field Day tour and also managed the tours of Friel's Three Sisters *translation and* The Communication Cord. *I interviewed her in 1999. Her insights and anecdotes give a sense of Friel's working relationship with members of the company. Lest there be lingering doubts whether stage managers are true creative collaborators, remember that Brian Friel himself (see 'Friel on . . . Directors', above) ranks the role as highly as that of director!*

BARTON: I'm almost certain a friend of mine Alison Ritchie [then a production manager at the Royal Court] was going to do it [*Translations*] and she couldn't and asked me. I know she suggested me to Stephen Rea. It just sounded really exciting. He said it was a new play, a Brian Friel play, it was touring all over Ireland, it was a company run by poets. And it sounded fabulous and I really wanted to do it!

Stephen had worked in England for a number of years and said quite clearly that at that point in 1980 there was nobody in Ireland that he could trust. He very definitely wanted an English stage manager. Because he'd worked with them for years and years and he trusted them. I think it's probably different now.

I wasn't in on all the rehearsals because I wasn't on the book. So I don't know if it was what Brian would consider a normal rehearsal process. Brian was there all the time.

There was a certain amount of friction between the director and Ray McAnally [the late actor who played Hugh O'Donnell], which made the director's job very difficult. I think Brian had to do quite a lot of mediating there. And a lot of supporting the director but supporting the actor too.

I think Brian and Stephen weren't always happy with the choices that they'd made. Perhaps that's because they expected more of people than people could deliver? They worked on perhaps not enough info – I don't know. There were two or three instances of them being not happy with either directors or cast or creative people that they'd chosen – I don't think they had that wider view. I think that they're both geniuses. And I loved working with both of them and I won't have a word said against either of them. But they're both good haters and they're not awfully tolerant people. They have standards and if you don't come up to those standards, they're not going to make excuses for you. They're going to let you go – or speed you on the way, I think.

Stephen's not a democratic actor. Brian's not a democratic director. What Brian said and what Stephen said went – there wasn't any pretence of being democratic, thank you very much! They had ambitions and visions and they wanted to achieve them. I saw nothing wrong with that at all.

To be honest, when I went to Derry I didn't even know that Derry and Londonderry were the same place! I was completely ignorant. I didn't know anything about Irish history. I didn't know anything about the Troubles. I'm ashamed to say how ignorant I was. People said to me, 'You can't go to Derry, you'll get bombed!' I didn't think I'd get bombed or shot or anything. But I just thought, because I'm English people might not be friendly to me. And everybody in Derry couldn't have been friendlier. Every shop we went into, every bar – 'Ah you're from the Play, the Play.' And they were just fabulous. I had a great time there, I absolutely loved it. But I wouldn't have known who was Protestant and who was Catholic.

My ASM was a woman called Margo Harkin who had very little experience but was very, very talented. She talked to me in the Guildhall one Saturday afternoon. About Bloody Sunday and her family – she lives there. And I just sat there for about two hours going [*expression of amazement*] . . . because I had no idea. And I was quite careful not to be offensive, if you know what I mean. I didn't go into the Bogside into the pubs and say, 'What side are you?' I never met with anything other than friendliness and a desire to explain what was happening, really. It was extraordinary, I know – the Guildhall superintendent Miles' son had been shot. He was a Protestant and he never let that show. He was so pleased and proud to have Brian's play there . . .

It was one of the first things back in the Belfast Opera House after it had been bombed. We did the Gate in Dublin and we also did a week of one-night stands around Northern Ireland. From Belfast Opera House to Dungannon Academy and Magharafeld School hall! The get-ins – some of them were up fire escapes, through tiny doors. All these schools we went to where you had to get someone to unlock the Ladies' toilet! It was a lunatic tour. But it was friendly . . .

Seamus our lorry driver was just brilliant, but when we got to Carrickmoor he walked down the main street with me saying, 'She's a Brit, kneecap her!' Carrickmoor were fabulous, very very welcoming. As we were walking down the street people were saying, 'Have a glass of whiskey!' Especially as it was not long after that Panorama programme which said effectively that Carrickmoor was the hotseat of the IRA . . .

People's reactions were much more immediate, much better than working in England. People really thought it was real! The soldier that gets killed – 'He was there for the curtain-call – I'm glad to see you're all right.' They can meet you in the street next day and talk about it as if it's real. I don't think anyone came out with a literary criticism of it the same night, but

I'm sure they did appreciate the subtleties of the script. You may not be able to describe what you've seen and heard, but it works. You don't always want to know how it works or want to get into why it works like it has done. And that's why people are passionate about having seen it.

For Brian this was a real learning experience. He wouldn't trust anybody until you'd proved you could do it. And then he just trusted you completely – that was my experience. He was constantly checking up on what I was doing. Because he was frightened – God knows I was frightened as well. But once he knew I could do it he almost trusted me too much. He was fabulous to work with. It was an enormous learning curve to be involved in the production side of it. I do remember the sense of achievement when I managed to explain that to have one sound cue costs as much really as to have thirty-five, because you still have to have all the equipment to play it through, to record it . . . I think he thought that if we cut thirty-four of them it would be a lot cheaper!

As far as I remember, everybody was completely committed to the play and to Field Day – the fact that it was the first time anything like that had ever been done. I think the Irish actors – they were all Irish apart from David Heap and Shaun Scott – obviously were much more politically aware than I was. They just thought it was a very, very exciting project to do. Certainly I'd never worked with a company like that either before or since. You'd think it was a recipe for disaster but it wasn't. It was just fabulous. We just thought we could do anything. Anything!

What surprised me when we went to Dublin after being sunk in the North and learning a lot, very fast, was how uninterested a lot of people in the South were in what was going on in the North. They really didn't want to know – thought it was a problem they didn't want to know about. It's up there and it can stay up there, thank you very much. That's not true of everybody, of course, but I was very surprised, being then a fairly recent convert to it . . .

The Communication Cord wasn't as good a play. I got a feeling he might have written it as it were on demand. And perhaps his heart wasn't in it, I don't know. It wasn't that funny, no.

The tours were good, though they could be a nightmare. You finish getting out of one place at three o'clock in the morning and drive to the next one and you're in there at seven o'clock in the morning. Absolutely lunatic. But Field Day was the best time in my life. I couldn't do it now.

What I feel about Field Day now is that what Brian and Stephen did was, they invited me into a country and they made me aware of it and they welcomed me into it. Field Day was the best job I've ever had. I stopped doing it because I was pregnant and I think possibly it was winding down a bit by then. And the passionate involvement of the poets wasn't as strong. In some ways I think they'd done it. How long can you sustain that passionate commitment? They both put their full-time commitment into Field Day for three years probably. And Brian had other plays he wanted to write, I'm sure. And he wasn't a natural administrator to start with.

What drove it was that two people wanted the same thing. I think they might just have got together at the right time for an idea for which the time was right and everybody would go to it. And it worked because of the passion – everybody who worked on those shows was just completely passionate about it. To work on something that nobody's cynical about is really quite rare. But I don't know how long you can keep up that level of passion because people have other lives . . .

I'm very glad I wasn't there for the falling out because it would have upset me very much. It wasn't visible when I was there. Not at all.

The choreographer
I interviewed Terry John Bates in 2000. He was the choreographer of Dancing at Lughnasa under Patrick Mason's direction. As well as dealing with dance, the interview also sheds light on the central place of music in most of Friel's work.

I had worked with Patrick Mason before on about three or four productions at the Wexford Festival. And so as I was in Wexford he asked me if I would be interested. And that's how I became involved.

For me the most exciting thing about *Lughnasa* was actually working with the playwright. He was working *through* the characters. I'd choreograph something and he'd say, 'Oh, what about this?' – he had little inputs all the time.

I work very much about people in dance. To me it's more important how people move in dance from their characters. He was very specific about Agnes – she was a very nice dancer. She was the *best* dancer. I think he had a soft spot for Agnes. In the rehearsals, with Brian sitting next to me, you learnt who these people were. So they weren't just doing a dance and they all go mad. He was very specific. He knew exactly who these people were, and he used to talk about the character and how they moved. He was very specific about all that.

Most actresses have a freak-out, really, when they've got to dance. You had to channel their energies and also keep each woman in their character as they dance. Most people look at the dance and think, 'Oh, it was just improvised.' And I always have that problem going into rehearsal. The actors said, 'Well I think I'll do this and do that.' And I said, 'Well you can't because actually there's a traffic problem . . .' You have to have that feeling of claustrophobia. If they all start to prance around the stage, you've lost that claustrophobia in the kitchen. I think you've got to keep the frustration of these women. There's only Kate who goes out into the garden and dances because she doesn't want to be seen to be dancing inside houses.

You have to explain to the dancer or the actresses that this is done for a reason. Its not this arty-farty choreographer in a sort of 'Oh, let's do one of these.' I was in the Irish Ballet Company and I knew a bit about Irish dancing, but it was very intimidating for me to work with these five actresses. These five Irish actresses were talking about their history, their life. And for me there's, 'What's this Englishman doing?' I'm sure even Brian Friel thought, 'What's this Englishman up there doing?' and I suppose it's like everything – you have to prove yourself. I think what was so nice about it was that I actually think that I created exactly what he saw when he wrote it.

It's creating an emotion, the dance. I wasn't there to do another sort of step-dancing competition. I was there to actually create a piece of drama. Especially that one moment. And each time now I'm choreographing it I have to put more into it because people are waiting for that moment. Then they're looking more *into* that moment. So each time you do it, it's getting more and more technical. Whereas before that first moment you could actually get away with far more.

The first performance I was very lucky because Frances Tomelty [Kate] had been a champion Irish step-dancer. And she was brilliant. She has the sort of energy which is very, very scary. I was very lucky there for choreography, to come in and this girl to do the Irish step-dancing. It was wonderful. And you just shaped it.

Everyone underestimates this. If it looks free, it actually takes longer to rehearse. I get annoyed with some directors. Luckily Patrick [Mason] was very understanding because he's actually done classes. He's done movement. But some directors say, 'Oh well, you know, we'll have a bit of something in the middle . . .' They spend hours studying text and I think actually most people aren't trained to move. You know you have to actually train them and then untrain them.

This is where actors and actresses feel very vulnerable. And singers as well. You think, well, you don't start from down there, you don't actually start with the feet. You slowly start with the brain. That's how I work, that's how we achieve unison. And the boys – I mean, they get very nervous because they have to be able to lead. Gerry Evans is a born dancer. And Brian was always very specific about that.

I always have problems with the boys. I always have to say look, listen to the music. Listen, listen, listen. Don't count,

count – you will not dance if you count. I mean dancers count, but people don't count when they dance. It's a feeling. It's an actual feeling. It's actually necessary to stop people counting, you know. Luckily the boys were brilliant but, you know, the first few rehearsals they always get edgy because I don't go in doing one-two-three. If you start counting they'll never ever listen to the music.

Every movement Gerry does is actually telling a story. All through that dance there's a physical relationship going on. There's no sort of waste. Its not a Fred Astaire/Ginger Rogers number. Because every move *means* something. Its just one of those things that the only way they can talk is through dance and that's where they're happiest. It mustn't turn into a routine. As soon as it starts into routine you've lost it.

[*Terry John Bates choreographed both the première production of* Dancing at Lughnasa *and the 1999 revival*]

In the first production, the Ceilidh was about shaping the energies. Also the technique of the girls. I didn't have enough time to choreograph the technique – I'm talking about the Irish steps and things – one had to go with the energy of the five women. Which was amazing because they went five hundred per cent each rehearsal! And they just energized, shaping the energy, creating the energy. They physically, visibly built up as much as the energy was, but then you had to stop it, had to know when to stop. Because if you went too long it just gets boring, five screaming women! They all had to sort of let go in their own personal way that first time. The second time I did it, I went into rehearsal and I had to put in more steps. There were far more steps the second time because people were *expecting* the energy then. You had to satisfy the audience.

I do work quickly and I'm very much an ideas man. I know when I go in there I always have two or three ideas with me. But this play, because it was all set, and also the way Brian writes, it's all very specific. I mean the directors are handcuffed really. I was working with [Michael] Bogdanov [Director of *Dancing at Lughnasa* in Hamburg] and you know he kept swearing about Brian, because he said he's just got our hands tied! I don't think he actually really liked the play, you know. Someone like Bogdanov feels he has to try to do something different, but can't. You know it is so well written as long as you actually trust the play. Funny, I've worked with two directors recently who don't really like the play because, well, it's a 'woman's play'.

Lughnasa was the start of the Irish success story, really. After that you got *River Dance* [dance and music spectacular based on Irish styles that became a massive theatre hit in the 1990s] and then you've got these other shows and just suddenly the dancing took off. I had to redo it after *River Dance* again, you know. The audiences were conscious of *River Dance* – totally.

There's also the problem that actresses come into it thinking they're coming into this great big sort of history of Irish theatre. Its so daunting for them. Even the Irish girls. They want to carry on the success of the play. One of the actresses did say to me once, 'You know, Terry, you must let it go, you must let it go.' But, you know, if in rehearsal people are going against their character, you can't let go. I know who these people are, and I do *direct* dance because I'm not going to let anybody do a movement unless there's a reason for it. I get bored just watching people dance. I thought, 'What are these people trying to *say*?' There's nothing pretty. This is the problem – they're all locked into this. And when they do go wild, it is, I mean, 'The Child'. I'm sure they have a dance every so often, but it's like it's this one moment where it all comes to the boil. That's the turning point of the play, really. They are doing extreme things. I mean Kate would *never* dance in that kitchen, but maybe she's been driven to do it. She has to get out of the house, and it is a very awful moment, really. They're all letting off steam. And also you have the Agnes and Kate needling, needling, needling and Agnes' dance is 'in spite of', you know?

It's total frustration. It's not a celebration at all. It's pure frustration. It's just like, you know, what the hell am I doing? It sort of echoes Africa and Father Jack. There are little moments where it's all picked up from Africa. It's awful really because she knows she'll never get married. And that's the awful moment. It's just suddenly that the one boy she really likes lives in Australia.

I think the reason this play works so well is that people everywhere relate to it. You know everywhere I've been abroad, every family has a Kate and a Rosie and an Agnes. I mean they all relate to it. It's quite extraordinary!

[*Asked if the style of Irish step-dancing signified emotional repression*:]

I don't think of it as repression at all. If you see a lot of the old videos of step dances, they're quite free. Kate would actually learn it at school, where it's like, 'Put your arms down! Don't use your arms!' I think it's a Catholic thing, being taught by nuns, you know. But while I was looking at these old videos, the arms are quite free. There was only one person who does an Irish dance there, really, and that's Kate. Nobody else does an Irish dance there. Maggie is almost primitive. She's stomp, stomp, stomp! There's no dance, there's no Irish dance there at all. And Rosie couldn't even coordinate Irish dance steps actually – it's all gangling. And Agnes loves dancing, but the obvious type of dancing. She is very dainty, elegant and sort of, you know, skipping round and lightness. But the more I do it, the more I give Agnes step-dancing because I think it gives more of a flavour. And also I don't want to give away what comes up later.

I always think how much feeling Brian has for dance, although he has never danced! And this is what's amazing. No, it is actually incredible. He hasn't danced socially. I think it wasn't till the first night that I had to dance for the party that I danced with his wife, and I think it's the first time that they'd gone out dancing socially, after *Lughnasa*. It's strange because he had such an affinity for dancing, Brian. I think it sort of opened up something in him. That last speech, it's just amazing! You know it just sums up every dancer's life. There's something about dance, it's such an emotional thing – he just hits it right on the head. He's quite amazing and every time I hear it I still think it's incredible how somebody who has never danced has written that!

The sound designer

In recent years, the craft of sound production in the theatre has greatly expanded. New technologies have developed to match the ambitions of directors, and those technologies have themselves suggested new possibilities. The new specialism of sound designer is as likely now to be found in bigger producing theatres, as set or costume designer. David Nolan, whom I interviewed at the Abbey Theatre in March 2000, started as an electrician in the building trade and a DJ at night. When the building trade slumped, in 1983, he got involved in the Abbey operating sound, and was, until his untimely death in February 2002, one of Ireland's most respected sound designers.

Dancing at Lughnasa

In *Lughnasa* the majority of the sound was the material coming from the radio but there were also a few small scene-change pieces. Patrick wanted something that would have echoes of Father Jack. So we went looking for Ethiopian – Ryangan – music. And we ended up using a great chant piece called the 'Celebration Dance'. That was used once or twice as scene links.

Brian came in with clear ideas for the radio music. We often get phone calls at the Abbey from people doing Friel plays, particularly *Dancing at Lughnasa*, from all over the world. I now have a standard e-mail which gives as much information as I can about the music we used. For example, 'Dancing in the Dark' is Ambrose and his Orchestra with Sam Browne as the vocalist, though we used just the instrumental bit. In the thirties a big-band would be led by a vocalist or musician of some description, but inevitably there would be one instrumental verse, a vocal verse, another instrumental verse with a featured soloist, and so on. So we were able to chop it. In a lot of cases there's usually two different bridges, so you're able to make it sound unrepetitive, which is the main thing. 'Anything Goes' was by Henry Hall and the BBC Dance Orchestra. Again we got a couple of versions and we picked one of them.

But the major bone of contention for the show was the big dance number, which was done to a traditional reel called 'The Mason's Apron'. I remember working through seventeen versions of 'The Mason's Apron', when we thought we were never going to find a magical version!

The first version we got was for Terry John Bates, the choreographer, to rehearse with. It was a speeded-up instrumental for military brass band. Then we arrived in the rehearsal room with live musicians. We watched them do it once or twice and then realized that the whole dance takes about four, four-and-a-half minutes. But it's quite a short tune and would've been very, very repetitive. So one of the musicians suggested a reel which is in the same key, called 'Miss Macleod's Reel', just to get into the whole excitement of 'The Mason's Apron'. And then we just run it through.

We recorded the music in a studio in town – we hadn't got multi-track facilities at the Abbey at the time – with Dublin session musicians. Another part of the brief was that Patrick Mason wanted to give it a kind of African ethnic vibe. Brian quite liked that idea. We did it by doing a lot of bodhrán over dubs, making it very, very heavy and percussive.

When we recorded it, there seemed to be more producers in the studio than actual musicians. The producer, Noel Pearson, was there, his assistant, somebody from Gael Linn, the Irish record label, as well as Brian and Patrick. The problem was then that it ended up being a production with the mix done by committee. When we brought it back to the Abbey it wasn't quite what we were looking for. So I went back the following day and remixed it. And that's the version that we have now.

Some shows are heavily sound-influenced, but with *Lughnasa* most of the atmosphere is created by the play itself. When we were rehearsing we tried a few atmosphere bits and pieces. But as we got more and more into the piece itself, the need for them just wasn't there. The atmosphere was really being created by the characters themselves.

It was great to come back nine or ten years later [*Nolan worked on the original production and the revival*] when the technology had moved on, because it was cartridge paper and razor blades the first time around. I was really, really happy with the edits and then ten years later I thought, 'We can do a lot better now. We can run it through the computer.' We used what we'd done the last time as a sort of template to put the music together again. It worked really, really well and as good as I thought the edits were on tape, they're nothing in comparison to the edits we got when we had them sampled on the computer. It was really good to get the chance to redo.

Wonderful Tennessee

We decided there'd be an ambience running right the way through, in real time, from before the audience come in to after they leave. It was basically sea wash. But we also had some wave samples which we slowed down, very, very slow, so there was this sort of movement in it, sort of windlike but within the waves. It was a series of loops recorded on to two-hour DAT running at slow speed. We had four hours of material so we were able to start it at half seven and run it right through. We set it up so it was coming from up high behind the cast from where they were on the pier. And we set a sound level that you didn't really notice until everyone went quiet. So it really punctuated in the pauses.

The music was all live and there were two or three other bits which we did just for scene changes – some wave atmospherics, but with dolphins larking about. You'd get the dolphin cries round the auditorium behind you and left and right to get a nice little sound picture, while the time change or whatever would happen.

The opening starts with a Toyota Hi-Ace van full of people driving down a mountain singing 'Happy Days Are Here Again'. So we spent some time driving round the country roads at the back of Dublin airport. We had quite a few speakers placed at different levels, and different heights. We'd start off up at the back, up at the flies, and end up down at the deck at the front of the stage. And then as it came closer you could hear a bit more, the voices being muffled until the van stops and opens the doors. At that point you can hear a little bit of the cast onstage. Joining in. So they manage to walk onstage singing the song you heard them sing as they came down the mountain. That was fun!

The Freedom of the City

And then there's a show like the Conall Morrison production of *The Freedom of the City* which was very heavily atmospherically underscored. There wasn't an awful lot of music, bar 'The Man Who Broke the Bank at Monte Carlo'. Conall went for showing you things that were described or spoken, so, with Brian's permission, we essentially had a full-scale riot onstage to cover a scene change. As people were firing rubber bullets and throwing missiles, they also had to put furniture into place as the whole thing happened round them! Soldiers were baton-charging with all kinds of things going on. Then all of a sudden they've transformed the streets of Derry into the Lord Mayor's Parlour! And again there was quite a lot of atmospherics running throughout that, from choppers flying overhead of the audience, ambulances and bits and pieces in the background to the riots and disturbances outside. For the baton charges, we had radio mikes on each soldier. They came on and started beating on the shields and we fed this through a lot of processing to give it a sort of very ominous and percussive feel – the sound of impending doom. It was probably one of the more sound-heavy of his plays and all the incidental stuff and technical jiggery-pokery really lent itself to the piece, gave a little edge to scenes.

When Brian writes a play, it works. And it works on so many levels. He knows, he's been listening to this music in his head as he's been writing it. It just really works so well. Brian is very specific as regards the music and that kind of stuff. To the point in some cases where he arrives with it. This is what he's been listening to when he was writing. It's written to the score. It's almost opera!

In a lot of his plays Brian is very specific music-wise, but then there are some that he gives you a completely blank canvas. He tends more to be involved with new works than revivals. He will obviously spend a lot more time on new work that he's actually directing. But I still think, when he's writing, he has a very clear idea of a musical score and a pace at which a play will work. You really can't fault him on that.

Little pieces just become sort of gems – moments of just pure theatre. I love *Lughnasa*. But there are others – I've worked on *Philadelphia* two or three times and whenever I watch that, as soon as the whole Gar Public, Gar Private starts and you're looking at one and listening to the other, you think, 'Oh my God this is going on inside this guy's head!' And it's one of those hairs-up-the-back-of-your-neck types of experience. It was written before I was born. But it's an experience that we all – young Irishmen – sort of grew up with. Even if we didn't have to go through it ourselves – we've all got cousins and uncles and brothers who did. I last worked on it about three years ago now, and *Philadelphia* is as fresh a play now as it ever was.

Dave Nolan makes it clear that working on Sound for a Friel play inevitably means working on Music. Whether it is classical music in Philadelphia, Here I Come!, *or dance music in* Dancing at Lughnasa, *or popular song in* Wonderful Tennessee, *musical pieces act as potent signifiers of meaning and emotion. It is not intented to be used simply to add a wash of emotion that is absent in the script. Here are Friel's own thoughts on the subject.*

. . . Music

I have used a lot of music in the plays over the years – nocturnes, jazz, symphonies, ceilli bands, piano accordion.

In some plays the music I chose was in part a gesture to people I loved. For example, I used Tom Moore's 'Oft in the Stilly Night' in two plays because sixty years ago my father taught that song to his school choir that I was in and we won a cup at the Omagh Feis and he was inordinately proud of us – and of himself. And for months afterwards he would line us up and start us off singing that Moore song. Then he would leave the classroom and cross the school yard and go to the far side of the country road and just stand there – listening to us singing in harmony in the distance. And although I couldn't see him standing there, I knew that we transported him. And I imagine that that may have been my earliest intimation of the power of music to move an audience.

In a play called *Give Me Your Answer, Do!* I used Mendelssohn's 'On Wings of Song' because my two sisters sang that duet when they were about nine or ten. And even though the piece is clichéd I suppose it evokes for me a time of simpler pleasures and imagined innocence. So that even now I hear their voices, wavering and uncertain, 'On wings of song I'll wander / With thee, my sister, I'll glide.' And I tell myself fancifully it is their unease before their difficult years ahead, just like the difficulties that confront Daisy in the play. But maybe these linkings between fact and fiction are too fanciful.

And I used a song called 'Down by the Cane-Break' in a play called *Wonderful Tennessee* because it was a song my mother sang; and because the words of the song – the promise of happiness in the Eden of Tennessee – those words echo the theme of the play.

And in *Philadelphia, Here I Come!* I used a piece of ceilli music – or what one of the characters calls a 'piece of aul thumpety-thump'. And a similar piece – only more anguished and manic – in *Dancing at Lughnasa*. And in both plays the

purpose was to explode theatrically the stifling rituals and dis-
cretions of family life. And since words didn't seem to be up to
the job it was necessary to supply the characters with a new
language. Because at that specific point in both plays when the
ceilli music is used, words offer neither an adequate means of
expression nor a valve for emotional release. Because at that
specific point emotion has staggered into inarticulacy beyond
the boundaries of language. And that is what music can provide in the theatre: another way of talking, a language without
words. And because it is wordless it can hit straight and
unmediated into the vein of deep emotion . . .

The designer

*Friel's roots may have been in the literary drama of the Abbey
Theatre, but his early willingness to engage with less naturalistic twentieth-century forms has made him a stage poet of the
visual. Undoubtedly his 'apprenticeship' with Tyrone Guthrie
also sensitized him to the way meaning is conveyed visually in
the theatre. One of Friel's most important collaborators is the
Dublin-based designer Joe Vanek, designer of* Dancing at
Lughnasa *and* Wonderful Tennessee. *Echoing some of Friel's
own steely confidence in his craft, he has written that he
believes 'in the complete control of the visual side . . . I don't
believe that two people, unless they're absolutely clued in, can
really have the subtlety and cross-reference of one person,
because so much of it is instinct.'*

*Vanek and Patrick Mason have collaborated on over twenty
productions since 1984, but it is their collaboration on* Dancing
at Lughnasa *for which they are best known. In the first piece,
published in the January 1991 journal* Sightline, *Vanek offers
his own perspective on that famous production. Its detail ideal-
ly requires to be read with production photos to hand, but
what communicates strongly is the wholly practical creative
energy dedicated to the play's realization by the designer. This
piece can be read alongside Joe Dowling's comments (above)
about Friel's fairly literal, albeit strongly felt, idea of the visual.*

Vanek lays out the process whereby the writer's elaborate detail becomes transformed into a concrete stage metaphor.

Brian Friel's quite extraordinary play *Dancing at Lughnasa* first surfaced in script form in October 1989 while Patrick Mason and I were working at the Wexford Festival. On learning that it concerned the day-to-day lives of five sisters in thirties County Donegal, despite Brian's distinguished record as a dramatist, I have to admit to being less than enthusiastic. I was, however, little prepared for the tenacious hold the script was to exert from first page to last as I was drawn into his uniquely observed world of ritual, dance, humour and, inevitably, heartbreak.

It soon became apparent, as we approached the design process, that there were several key aspects of the play to be considered. It is first of all a 'memory' play. Michael, the seven-year-old child in the Mundy household in 1936, is now a grown man and remembers with warmth and irony the last golden days of summer before the family was to disintegrate. It is a world recalled more for its 'atmosphere' than as 'fact' and a time when communal escape from an impoverished life was through the release brought about by various forms of dancing, social and primitive. It is also a play about the clash of Catholicism and a wilder pagan world still abroad in Ireland at that time. Complications arise with the return of the older, missionary priest brother, gone native in Africa and extolling the virtues of sacred rites and communal living. It is also (and here perhaps, the major chord was struck) a play about harvest (La Lughnasa being the ancient Celtic festival), about unfulfilled passions and faded dreams.

Brian's imagined home for the Mundy girls is one bound by conventional stage imagery: the traditional, small stone country house with its loft and almost Shavian details of windows, doors, furniture and domestic utensils. Around the house, a neat but uncultivated garden, home to a few hens and a symbolic rooster, and a lone tree which houses the aerial to the radio which from time to time dominates the action. But to us, grappling with this imagined world, it seemed at once much greater and more enigmatic than this realistically described stage picture. The spirit of the old pagan god, Lugh, and its subtle and not so subtle manifestations, coupled with a certain emphasis on nostalgia, that golden haze of memory, the word 'atmosphere' and the overwhelming significance of the harvest, seemed to us the springboard to a world that encompassed the scale of Brian's vision.

We quickly reduced the basics of the house as described in the text to a single, diagonal wall that contained all the necessary physical elements: a stove, a press, and a door off to the rest of the house. As we developed the floorplan of the kitchen and its arrangement of furniture, the walls and the windows gradually vanished and the main flagstone floor floated free as three open sides anchored by the fourth main wall with its gigantic angled beam and massive sill. The overall framing of the set developed simultaneously, from a harsh, angled granite walled box in a wash of naturalistic greens and browns of the mountainside to a more neutral, simply textured white box, hazed with a wash of amber pollen or dust. That we wanted a field of wheat to figure in some respect was an early decision, although there was no mention of one in the script nor did we consider the possible complexities of achieving such a 'real' image on stage. After various experiments with angles across the box behind the house and angles rising up through the box, we conceived the field as the rear wall of the house itself, rising in an improbable but dramatic wedge. Through the wheat we chose to carve a path, cutting diagonally and opening out into the scrubby garden, now reduced to little more than an undulating arm of dried grass and dusty topsoil. Visitors to the house would be viewed approaching.

At an early stage in rehearsals it became apparent, so delicate is Brian's dramatic balance, that a shift of focus not indicated in the script would damage the effects immeasurably. The pathway into the garden was sealed with wheat and the path became suspended behind the house, with plain doorway openings set into the walls on either side of the stage. The tree was to vanish also. This starker and more suggestive world clearly could not support the huge naturalism of the tree as depicted, especially on the fringe of the set. In Dublin we had a handy perch, so Gerry Evans, the boy's father, could be seen aloft, scattering leaves and playing devil-may-care. At the National, a similar perch used was too far up and hidden in the auditorium walls to work; he simply became a tantalising voice, and possibly more effective for that.

The field of wheat with its path served as several visual metaphors which changed subtly with the intensity of the russet-hued, softly focused break-up gobos that Trevor Dawson used to light it. At times it seemed like the smouldering Lughnasa fires that are referred to in the script; whilst at the end of Act One, to the accompaniment of distant jungle drums, it resembles an expanse of veld, baking in the sun. Would the path through the wheat ever be used? Having sealed its garden entrance and relegated it to 'the path not taken', it suddenly re-asserted itself during a final run in the rehearsal room. Father Jack, still in thrall to the spell of Africa, takes a walk with Kate, his eldest sister, at the end of the first act. As the lights fade and the principal characters become silhouettes, the field flares up and to the beat of drums they traverse the field. Jack tries to woo the sisters to his unconventional ways and the image of them waist-deep in the golden wheat serves to reinforce an idea: who is taking who for the walk and where exactly?

The Abbey Theatre in Dublin has a very wide and unfocused stage and auditorium. Curved walls give up to an impossibly wide, gaping hole of a stage with limited depth. The immediacy of the characters seemed to necessitate as close a contact with the audience as possible. The Abbey design extended out on a thrust into the auditorium which supported most of the garden area and about a quarter of the kitchen floor. Entrances downstage were through wings where the auditorium walls meet the stage.

For the Lyttelton transfer, there was clearly no chance of achieving a similar intimacy. The repertory system and the fixed position of seats almost on top of the stage put paid to that. But I endeavoured to keep a sense of that thrust by stopping the walls six feet short of the stage edge and extending the floor only between black, textured slabs that connected with similarly textured side flats housing the downstage entrances. The final effect was of a sharper frame than had been the case in Dublin.

The plastering of the basic box was a fairly awesome task and we had some problems at the National getting a finish that avoided a 'theme-pub ceiling'. The texture, in fact, is only really apparent in several pre-set states when it is lit predominantly from above, and otherwise appears as a vaguely scumbled background that was more vigorously painted as the box emerges towards the audience.

From the photographs it is evident that the design entailed a dedication beyond the call of duty for a lot of work that was repetitive – little more than an assembly line, in fact. But the painstaking concern for detail shows in the impact of the final design and I am grateful to all those who worked so hard in both theatres to achieve what I'd hoped for. In Dublin also, particular thanks go to Trevor Dawson and the paintshop team led by Angie Benner, and Barbara Lavery. At the time of writing, what looks like a sell-out run in London finishes on January 1st and then returns to the Abbey for a further seven weeks from mid-January. Broadway beckons for later in the year, though as yet dates are unconfirmed, but it is unlikely that the set will be rebuilt in its entirety in the USA!

This excerpt from an assessment by critic Derek West focuses on the design of that famous production of Dancing at Lughnasa. *It was published in the Spring 1992 issue of* Theatre Ireland.

Brian Friel's work sets a series of verbal echoes and resonances but in *Dancing at Lughnasa*, in exploring the nature of memory

and the life of the family, he has called upon the resources of
theatre in a more comprehensive manner than he has ever done
before – particularly through visual images, tableaux, light,
sound and movement. At the Abbey, Joe Vanek's design brings
to the stage a striking image of the late summer that encom-
passes the major themes of the play. The set is dominated by a
field of barley climbing steeply above the kitchen and farm-
yard, where most of the action occurs. This superbly executed
field, apparently the designer's invention, is commanding, mes-
merising – verging on the obtrusive – as if Vanek had an urge to
translate a Monet painting on to the stage. The published text
makes no mention of it and yet the barley forms more than a
three-dimensional backdrop – it is a constant visual presence,
an attendant image of fertility, growth and, most poignantly,
the promise of a fulfilment that is elusive and at best fitting for
the main characters.

Vanek's setting seems to draw its colouring from Africa, life-
time home of the missionary priest, Jack, rather than from
Donegal (Friel returning to a corner of Ballybeg, the locale for
Philadelphia, Here I Come and other of his plays). This
involves the audience in two juxtaposed worlds: that of tribal
Uganda (with its own rhythms and ceremonies) and a rural
Ireland clinging in folk memory to the vestiges of the pagan
rites which are being stifled by the conventions of a thirties
Catholic society.

The pastel shades with which Vanek has painted the farm-
house serve to underline the memory framework of the play –
Michael, who narrates, casts his mind back to that summer of
1936. 'In that memory, atmosphere is more real than incident
and everything is simultaneously actual and illusory.'

The setting, albeit firmly naturalistic in much of its detail
(the turf stack, the range, the iron, enamel jugs and buckets) is
frequently bathed in a summer light, in a largely successful
attempt to render atmosphere rather than fact. Each object
assumes the importance of Synge's description of household
utensils in the Aran Islands.

Yet, within the design, Vanek has interposed elements that unsettle the spectator – the field is boxed in by high, plain flats; the path through the barley is reached by an odd, clearly defined doorway. Combined with Michael's somewhat sardonic view of his past, this creates a detachment. It places nostalgia at arm's length, but also, for me, distracts from the full tragic impact of the sisters' lives. Whatever Friel's intentions, the major achievement of Patrick Mason's production lies in the powerful representation of the women. If they owe something to Chekhov, Friel has triumphantly subsumed the influence into his own creation. Joe Vanek's contribution to this has been to dress each of them precisely, appropriately – from the rarely unbending rectitude of Kate (Frances Tomelty), conveyed by her spinsterly neatness, to the sensuality of Catherine Byrne's Chris, the only one among them to bear a child. Trevor Dawson's lighting serves to illuminate them in moments of repose or when they go about the fundamental rituals of domestic life – bringing in turf, baking bread, ironing, sewing, knitting, scrubbing – as dignified and profoundly moving. The casting of Brid Brennan (Agnes), who can express so well this serenity and sadness, of Brid Ni Neachtain (Rose) with a shining morning face, of Anita Reeves (Maggie) holding off despair with bubbling vitality, is masterful. The three male figures are more enigmatic, at odds with the household. Michael (Gerard McSorley) looks back from the distance of time and unspecified experience. Jack (Barry McGovern) has lived his life abroad 'and is seen in the shreds of his earlier existence'. None fits the setting as well as the sisters. Vanek's touch is less assured here, as if reflecting the sense of alienation.[. . .]

This next article by Denise Tilles is from Theatre Craft International *journal (January 1994) and describes Vanek's work on* Wonderful Tennessee. *The BBC Northern Ireland documentary 'From Ballybeg to Broadway' documents the rehearsal and opening of this show and offers useful insights into the design process and the sometimes dispiriting business and experience of a Broadway run.*

The moment that the set is in sight it's plain to see where we are. Once again, set and costume designer Joe Vanek has transported the audience into another locale in the mindframe of Irish playwright Brian Friel. This latest outing, *Wonderful Tennessee*, probes the suppressed emotions of a group of middle-aged Irish couples stranded at a pier waiting to get to an island far off in the distance (a trip which never occurs). As in much of Friel's work, the oftentimes superficial conversations of his characters belie issues far more spiritual underneath that surface.

Wonderful Tennessee opened to rave reviews at Dublin's Abbey Theatre last May, followed by an unfortunately brief New York run at the Plymouth Theater on Broadway in October. Vanek took time from his busy schedule this past August, between the opening of *The Matchmaker* at the Chichester Festival Theatre and the readying of *Wonderful Tennessee* for its Broadway run, to discuss the Friel play, and his twenty-two years as a designer.

Even Vanek, a tough self-critic, concedes that the opening scene of *Wonderful Tennessee* was 'pretty impressive. I think I actually prefer it to that of *Dancing at Lughnasa*' [his last work with Friel]. The effect is stunning. When the audience enters the theatre only a mysteriously shrouded pier is visible. Then an 18m x 15m silk sheet blows off in a wind to reveal a pier. A crew of stagehands, and grilles built into the set which house fans underneath, remove the large silk, to give the effect of 'mist pervading the island; the silk looks as if it's blowing off like a huge wave.'

The pier, located in County Donegal, is in a state of disuse. It is framed in a huge, speckled, grayish-colored proscenium box, much like a picture frame. The bottom part of the frame is deeper than the rest of the vertical top area, making the structure tilt down towards the audience. The frame continues at the side of the pier in a series of recurring picture frame bases going higher and higher up the set. A vivid purple, turquoise, and gray sky is painted behind, which fuses with a grayish-green, gauze-covered hillside stage right, balanced onstage left by an almost bleached wall which fuses into the frozen picture-frame sea against the back.

Making a strong contrast to the set are Vanek's costumes, which tell a story of their own. 'The clothes are modern, fairly straightforward,' he describes, 'but they have to clearly indicate the character the moment someone comes on. Nobody's [i.e. the characters] really considered what it means to stay out all night on this island. They're there to please the man who's organized it.' One character, a barrister, comes spruced up in a smart dress, and another woman wears her best outfit, which she might have worn to a country wedding some years before. These improbably dressed people highlight the very real-looking pier on which they're stranded.

The pier set was conceived after many weeks of visual research in Ireland. Vanek drove about 300 miles up and down every inlet in Donegal, and photographed approximately eleven different piers. 'This is a very unusual play to research, given that you've got a very physical setting that is quite specific in the script. It needs to provide certain things. You need to see what these things look like, and then work them in different sorts of ways according to the dramaturgy.

'The way it's designed,' Vanek continues, 'the pier is lateral across the stage, and the people appear as if on a Greek frieze, reinforced by the use of a low proscenium. With the emphasis on the horizontal, and the pier set behind this huge picture frame, the characters appear stranded on this long, very thin, multi-levelled wedge. As they move up and down on them in various groupings, the aura of a classical world emerges. Director Patrick (Mason) has been very clever in the way he has staged it.'

. . . Indeed, the Gate has earned the reputation of being a difficult space to manage. It does not have great depth, and, Mason says, 'There's a no-man's land between the proscenium and the front of the stage. I thought Joe was the ideal man to kind of cope with them creatively, and, fortunately, I was right.'

Both Mason and Vanek say that it is the respect and value for the play's text that is a binding force of their collaboration. 'We both start from the text,' Mason emphasizes, 'which is something we both share a kind of value for, and what the play itself says, rather than coming to the play with a particular viewpoint or ideology.' [. . .] 'We think the same about everything from a theatrical point of view,' says Vanek. We believe in essential simplicity in the visual statement that you put on a stage, making things eloquent. We both feel that it's important to tell a story clearly, not to bog it down in too much obscure visual distraction.' [. . .]

It was the work dramatizing Fathers and Sons *that saw Friel through a period of fallow preparation in the 1980s. Effectively what he talks about here is translating and dramatizing Russian literature, marking the particular affinity that he feels with that country's nineteenth- and early twentieth-century history, and the way it finds echoes in Irish experience. Friel's occasional translating/transforming projects are part homages to favourite writers, part dramaturgical self-education, and part immersion in Russian culture. Only* The London Vertigo, *Friel's updating of his theatrical antecedent Charles Macklin's play, is non-Russian. Here are Friel's own thoughts on the craft, from the Friel Festival brochure.*

. . . Translating

I have done four translations from the Russian – Chekhov's *Three Sisters* and *Uncle Vanya*, and two versions of Turgenev, his play *A Month in the Country* and a stage version of his novel, *Fathers and Sons*. And over the years I have circled around Gorky and Gogol and Ostrovsky but for some reason haven't attempted them.

I'm not sure why I find the late nineteenth-century Russians so sympathetic. Maybe because the characters in the plays behave as if their old certainties were as sustaining as ever – even though they know in their hearts that their society is in melt-down and the future has neither a welcome nor even an accommodation for them. Maybe a bit like people of my own generation in Ireland today. Or maybe I find those Russians sympathetic because they have no expectations whatever from love but still invest everything in it. Or maybe they attract me because they seem to expect that their problems will disappear if they talk about them – endlessly.

Anyhow, when I looked closely at those texts the experience of those people seemed very much at odds with the experience as offered in most of the English translations. For example, the received wisdom was that Chekhov was wistful and elusive and sweetly melancholy, and the English translations of the past sixty years have compounded that misreading. And the received wisdom was that Turgenev was a dilettante caught between his Slavophile and his Europhile leanings and finally was faithful to neither.

I think these readings are unfaithful to both men. But then the notion of faithfulness – of fidelity – to an original text is a complex one. How possible is translation at all? I have written myself about being faithful to the spirit of a text. But now I'm not at all sure I know what that means. Borges has elegantly turned the whole notion on its head. He says that originals have a way of being unfaithful to their translation – and in his heart every translator knows the truth of that. On the other hand Nabokov has said that a translation should read like a translation and should keep reminding the reader of its artificiality; it must insist – this is counterfeit. I find this difficult. The various disbeliefs that the theatre asks us to suspend cannot be added to by demanding that we keep acknowledging that we are watching a counterfeit. Because we know that already; and the moment the curtain goes up we agree to enter into a make-believe and connive with it.

But maybe the pleasure I got from doing those four Russian plays had to do with the actors I had in all four. *Three Sisters* was an early Field Day production in the days when we were brash with assurance. *A Month in the Country* and *Vanya* were done beautifully at The Gate. And *Fathers and Sons* in the National Theatre in London with a cast that was collectively thrilling. And with actors like those I had in Derry, Dublin and in London any half-decent translation must be exciting.

Friel's theatre is literate, in that words are important (but not the only) carriers of rich meaning, but it is not literary in the sometimes derogatory sense of the word. The language his characters speak is part of the event of theatre, to be experienced as action and gesture. Here, again for the Festival brochure, Friel muses on the essential raw material of his drama.

... Words

The tools that are available to the playwright to tell his story are few enough – words, action, silence. In the theatre that has engaged me words are at the very core of it all. The same words that are available to the novelist, to the poet; and used with the same precision and with the same scrupulous attention not only to the exact kernel meaning but to all those allusive meanings that every word hoards. But there is a difference. The playwright's words aren't written for solitary engagement – they are written for public utterance. They are used as the storyteller uses them, to hold an audience in his embrace and within that vocal sound. So unlike the words of the novelist or poet, the playwright's words are scored for a very different context. And for that reason they are scored in altogether different keys and in altogether different tempi. And it is with this score that the playwright and the actor privately plot to work their public spell.

But even though these written words aren't fully empowered until an actor liberates them and fulfils them, when that happens – and if the playwright is in full mastery of his craft – then that theatrical language acquires its own special joy and delight; because what is written to be sung is now being sung. So that the language in its meticulous use and in its accomplished utterance finally and fully realises itself. So that what the playwright wrote – and even as he wrote listened closely to and actually heard – that has now been transferred to the stage, and those words, written in privacy and out of privacy but for public utterance, they are now fulfilling themselves completely. A private wisdom is being proclaimed from the rooftops.

There is no contradiction in this. It is a contrived miracle – well, a trick of the trade. Because the public utterance must still retain that private intimacy where it has its origins. And even though the audience hears what it calls speeches, it hears too the author's private voice, that intimate language, that personal utterance. And that composite, that duet – the private and intimate set free into public canticle where both voices are distinctly audible – that is what makes the experience of theatre unique. And every time that happens the theatre fulfils itself again.

The penultimate voice in this collection rightly in my view goes to another playwright, Friel's contemporary and one-time Field Day comrade, Thomas Kilroy. Published in the Alan Peacock anthology The Achievement of Brian Friel *(see 'Select Bibliography'), the piece observes Friel's working from another part of the writer's workshop floor. This is a most revealing essay because it understands more than most commentary what drives a writer like Friel. It also uses two of what he calls 'the more literary plays' to make his points, ending on a consideration of* Faith Healer – *'a sublime work of the imagination' – and a play Kilroy hugely admires.*
Theatrical text and literary text

The playwright

We write plays, I feel, in order to populate a stage. It is this curious desire to move about actual living bodies, to give them voice and the mantle of character in a conspiracy of play, which distinguishes playwriting from all other kinds of writing. It is also the element which makes the place of Drama in Literature so problematical. This is a form of writing which employs a physical medium, that of the human body and its physical environment, to communicate with others. The very surrender of creativity to a third party runs counter to the whole principle of literary method which is based upon the strict control of a single authority.

Yet there have always been playwrights who have insisted by their practice that their plays be accepted as literary as well as theatrical texts. Brian Friel is one such. His plays arrive in the theatre scrupulously finished. He would have little patience, I think, with the notion that improvisation, workshops or extended rehearsal discussion could contribute very much to the actual business of writing a play. Certainly any treatment of his extraordinary technical skills should be framed by this acknowledgement: his is a sophisticated literary intelligence. Many of his effects are close to those of the novelist and short story writer. His plays consistently test the histrionic adaptability of these techniques, whether or not they can be made to work on stage. I want to look at two of the more 'literary' of Friel's plays, *Living Quarters* and *Aristocrats* and end with the play *Faith Healer* in which Friel challenges the very nature of conventional dramatic action itself.

There is nothing as desolate as an empty stage. It is an intense model of all desert places unwarmed by human presence. But the intensity derives from artifice, not nature, from the eye of the voyeur, the ear of the eavesdropper, the expectant imagination of the bystander. Somewhere within this nexus is the dynamic of playwriting and it is removed from the territory in which most literary works are plotted and executed. Dramatic technique is simply anything which serves to excite the expectancy of a theatre audience and then proceeds to satisfy it.

All dramatic technique begins with the first image that is imposed upon the empty stage. As playwrights we are defined by that first image. We are what we are by where we choose to make things happen.

In particular, this helps to place us in relation to our tradition. The more audiences are consoled by the familiar on the rise of the curtain, the more traditional the playwright. In the Western European tradition the most familiar of these first images foisted upon the stage is that of the domus, the house, home, room, palace or cabin, at any rate some version of the human domestic. This is merely a concession (again given the nature of our European tradition) to the fact that the human drama has been seen to exist in its most vital form within the cell of the family. Those playwrights, particularly in this century, who have radically departed from this in a bewildering display of different settings, have been attesting to the displacement of the family from its traditional place of eminence in the human story.

Brian Friel is not radical in this way. Most of his plays are firmly set within the family and in the community which radiates out from it, his Ballybeg, an imaginative portion of Ireland which has attained a ripe identity so extensively has he employed and developed it over the years. Kitchen in the home of County Councillor S. B. O'Donnell. Commandant Frank Butler's living-quarters. Ballybeg Hall, the home of District Justice O'Donnell. The hedge-school, old byre, habitation of Hugh Mor O'Donnell. These are solid properties precisely because they come to the stage already carrying the weight and ramification of fully imagined families.

Actors love playing Friel for the same reason that they love playing Chekhov. They can feel the immersion into a world which is fully in place and fully knowable. Actors crave security and here they can sink into the embrace of kinship and neighbourliness. Stephen Rea, in conversation with me, has talked of this 'sense of people who are well used to living together' in the work of his friend.

But there is something else. Although an intensely private writer whose plays are a gentle lifting of the veil on inviolable privacies, Friel nevertheless presses these images into images of Ireland itself. Obviously there are variations in the degree of political urgency between one play and another. But the general tone of the plays is referential in this way; it has a kind of loving attentiveness to the broader fate of the people of Ireland and their culture. Pre-eminently in the theatre of our time, Friel is a custodian of certain public values, those of tradition and place, of kinship and tribe, of all those necessary pieties which allow people to live with some decency in close proximity to one another. I can recognize this the more clearly because I have none of it myself in my own work.

Part of the excitement in September 1964 for someone of my generation watching the first production of *Philadelphia, Here I Come!* was in the recognition that a staple Irish formula was being reinvented before our eyes. There had been meticulously observed plays set in Irish country kitchens before this. There had been Irish plays of non-comprehending fathers and dreamy sons, of comic house-keepers, lonely school-masters, big-shot neighbours and prudent, arid priests. There was even a characteristic Irish style of naturalism (which so infuriated Yeats) matched by, perhaps engendering, a whole school of naturalistic Irish acting. All of this was based upon a close attention to surface character and a usable stage speech which accurately mimicked the vernacular. It was a style badly in need of infusion.

Friel was heir to all this in the sixties. What marked him apart from the best of his predecessors, T. C. Murray, say, or Paul Vincent Carroll, was not so much his material (since it arose in the first instance out of a similar background) but what distinguishes all first-rate writers: the range of his sensibility. Yet, with some exceptions, he was to remain loyal to this inherited tradition: that branch of naturalistic Irish drama which originated in and took its inspiration from rural Catholic Ireland and which had dominated Irish theatre, not always happily, throughout the late twenties, the thirties, forties and fifties. It is a measure of Friel's integrity that one is always assured of the value of tradition even when he is pressing it into change or registering its obsolescence.

Historically (as opposed to the individual reputation) I believe that Friel's importance will be seen in the way he received this youthful tradition (scarcely four decades old when he began writing for the stage) and opened it up to the enquiry of a mind schooled in modern theatre and literature. In this way he exhausted some received forms or, perhaps more accurately, his writing coincided with their demise and he has given them a fitting departure. Certainly it would be difficult to conceive of anyone writing another peasant play, without irony or distancing, after *Translations*.

It is now commonplace to talk about *Living Quarters* (1977) as a not entirely successful trial-run for the later, more popular *Aristocrats* (1979). To do so is to distract attention from Friel's remarkable application of literary narrative technique to the stage. One play, it is true, leads into the other. Both plays are built upon family reunions. Each reunion is the occasion of the death of a father; in each the mother is already dead before the rise of the curtain. Each father is authoritarian in a family of three sisters and a brow-beaten, errant son. Each play ends with the dispersal of the family. Even the attendant figures duplicate one another. There is the comic male neighbour husband-suitor.

And, finally, there is the narrating or choric outsider whose viewpoint of events is Friel's principal distancing device, perhaps his most contentious use of a fictional device in his plays. Sir, in *Living Quarters*, the stern ring-master of events with his ledger of completed but endlessly repetitive actions, is the more obtrusive of these choric figures and the one who has met with most resistance from audiences. Tom, the American researcher in *Aristocrats*, because he is integrated into the action rather than left as a cold observer of it, is generally understood to be an improvement. I cannot see it like that.

The first (and only) production of *Living Quarters* failed to find a place, a style for the figure of Sir in what was offered as a surround of naturalism. The chilling mechanics of the play failed to lock and whirr and run out to full, terrifying effect.

But what appears to be cosy naturalism in the family scenes is, in fact, high stylization in need of a studied, highly theatricalized presentation. Among his other roles Sir is a projection of the imagination of that group of people assembled on a May day in a remote corner of Donegal to act out, again and again, that brief, dire collision of the Butler family. It is one of the points of the play that once the imagination has called up a record, a register, a ledger of events past the results take on an implacable momentum. It is as if the imagination were a way of freezing time or of generating that force which the ancients called Fate. For imagination here read theatrical imagination. Nowhere in Friel is the potential impersonality of theatre, its bending of human will to serve action, to serve effect, so beautifully imbricated, so clinically impaled.

SIR And in their imagination, out of some deep psychic necessity, they have conceived this (*ledger*) – a complete and detailed record of everything that was said and done that day, as if its very existence must afford them their justification, as if in some tiny, forgotten detail buried here – a smile, a hesitation, a tentative gesture – if only it could be found and recalled – in it must lie the key to an understanding of *all* that happened. And in their imagination, out of some deep psychic necessity, they have conceived me – the ultimate arbiter, the powerful and impartial referee, the final adjudicator, a kind of human Hansard who knows those tiny little details and interprets them accurately. And yet no sooner do they conceive me with my authority and my knowledge than they begin flirting with the idea of circumventing me, of foxing me, of outwitting me. Curious, isn't it? . . .

There are two passages at the beginning of *Living Quarters* which illustrate Friel's handling of fictional narrative on the stage. The text is a cool modernist one in which the narrative, over such a short span, has the density and pith of complex prose fiction. There is information here, terse, complete but there are also multiple shifts in perspective as well as a testing of character. There is also that element, so rare in drama, so essential to first-rate novels, the presence of a formidable auctorial mind which is a constituent of the writing itself. This is the element that James understood, in *The Art of Fiction*, to be the ultimate criterion of literary art, 'the quality of the mind of the producer'.

These two passages are rather like prologues to the play proper since they involve minor characters, a kind of sharp sketching of the strict geometry of what is to happen, a precise notation of tone. The first has to do with Father Tom, the pathetic alcoholic priest, friend and honorary uncle of the Butler family. In the early part of his plays, Synge removed the priest as a figure of irrelevance, the irrelevance of established Christianity, in order to clear space for the bare moral action which was to follow. Friel does something similar here. The space in which the Butler family re-enact their tragedy, for all its Donegal sign-posting, is elemental, secular, devoid of conventional consolations. In short, it is the pure space of the stage. Indeed the text might be further sharpened by the excision of some of its realistic labels and references.

Father Tom belongs to the world of weak Irish half-truths, evasiveness, easy feeling, the inability to face the truth. It is a world that Friel understands as few other writers and one for which he has compassion. Here, however, he is pitiless. Father Tom stalks Sir and tries to see into his ledger. Like any weak man the priest believes or hopes or blusters that moral transformation can be simple. Sir strips him to the core.

TOM Sir

SIR (*Busy*) What is it, Father?

TOM I don't suppose it would be a breach of secrecy or etiquette if I – if you were to let me know how I'm described there, would it? You know – something to hang the cap on – 'good guy', 'funny guy', 'bit of a gossip'. Which of my many fascinating personas should I portray?

SIR (*Still busy*) You'll be yourself, Father.

The persistence of the priest is that of the man who itches at his own petty foibles until they swell into profound failure. In a very true, Faustian sense he is the creator of his own tormentor. To this scene Friel adds the mute presence of Anna, the young wife whose adultery is the instrument of the play's action, a strangely immune presence in the play who alone, with Sir, is allowed to be an observer. Sir is reading from his ledger.

SIR 'The children used to call him Uncle – Uncle Tom.'

TOM (*Delighted*) Tina still does – occasionally.

SIR '"Is Uncle Tom coming with us?" they'd say. And he did. Always. Everywhere. Himself and the batman – in attendance.'

TOM That's one way of –

SIR '– and that pathetic dependence on the Butler family, together with his excessive drinking make him a cliché, a stereotype. He knows this himself –'

TOM Cliché? For God's sake –!

SIR '– but he is not a fool. He recognizes that this definition allows him to be witness to their pain but absolves him from experiencing it; appoints him confidant but acquits him of the responsibility of conscience –'

TOM That's not how –! O my God . . .

SIR 'As the tale unfolds they may go to him for advice, not because they respect him, consider him wise –'

TOM (*Sudden revolt*) Because they love me, that's why! They love me!

SIR '– but because he is the outsider who represents the society they'll begin to feel alienated from, slipping away from them.'

TOM (*Beaten*) Outsider?

(ANNA *goes to* TOM *and puts her arm around him.*)

SIR 'And what he says won't make the slightest difference because at that point – the point of no return – they'll be past listening to anybody. At that point all they'll hear is their own persistent inner voices –' And so on and so forth.

TOM (*On the point of tears*) O my God – O my God –
SIR It's your role.
TOM No, it's not. No, no, no, it's not.
SIR And to have any role is always something.
(ANNA *begins to lead* TOM *away.*)

The second passage replicates this one but in the different mode of comedy. Sir's antagonist this time is Charlie, one of those Friel clowns, bumbling and honest and attractive, who light up the edges of even the bleakest scene. Ever-reliable, handyman, bit of a gaum, simple, loyal lover, Charlie is the eternal spear-carrier and scene-shifter in the everyday drama. As befitting a play in which theatre itself is a controlling metaphor, his scene with Sir is based upon the old acting game of shifting about for the high ground, the brightest spot, manoeuvring for centre-stage. Charlie desperately wants to be a player in the action but, like Tom, he is insulated from some layer of knowledge, some fundamental implication of what is happening, that protects him, in turn, from the suffering:

CHARLIE Tell you what: suppose I just sat about, you know, and looked on, I'd –
SIR There are no spectators, Charlie. Only participants.
CHARLIE Promise you – wouldn't open my mouth –
SIR If your turn comes, I'll call you.
CHARLIE Could keep an eye on the ledger for you.
SIR Charlie.
CHARLIE Oh, well – see you later – good luck.

To speak, then, of this play as some kind of exercise in preparation for *Aristocrats* is to confuse, so to speak, chalk and cheese. Passing from one to the other is like moving from hard-edge to impressionism, from a cold metallic surface to a rush of warmth and colour. It is relatively easy to account for the greater popularity of *Aristocrats* in this way. For all its charting of disintegration, *Aristocrats* is written with all the considerable charm of Brian Friel. *Living Quarters*, in contrast, is one of the harshest plays that he has written. It looks forward, not so much to *Aristocrats*, as to the masterpiece *Faith Healer*. It is arguable that Friel discovered the extraordinary narrative tone of the later work – grievous and elegiac but also lyrical and marmoreal – in the narratives of *Living Quarters*. The narratives of *Living Quarters* are multiplex; in *Faith Healer* the narratives have been soldered into monologue.

There is a further point about *Living Quarters*. Friel effects something quite unsettling with the old formulaic material of the Irish family (if this is a version of *Hippolytus* it is also a version of *Autumn Fire*). He puts it under scrutiny which painfully exposes its inefficiency when faced with the utter isolation of the tragic individual. By fixing it within a narrative that is as discriminating as anything in prose fiction Friel creates a distance between us and the family. This forces us to look upon the happenings through the impersonal, comfortless eye of Sir, a viewpoint which the modern theatre does not often tolerate but which would have been entirely acceptable in the theatre of the Greek fifth century. The disintegration of this family is beyond condolence; it can only be attended on like a clean ritual. By contrast, the denouement of *Aristocrats*, with its running-down of plot into the natural dispersal of people, is consolatory.

The question is: why should novelistic narrative with its information, its reliability or unreliability, its pressing of opinion, its lapel-tugging insistence, be such a problem in the contemporary theatre? In the past theatre has always found ways of admitting editorializing or commentary whether by way of soliloquy, aside, chorus or choric character. Is it that modern audiences feel manipulated? Is it a matter of entertainment? Or laziness? Assuredly a theatre which seeks to make its audience think has a better chance with people who read than with people who don't. The pleasures of such drama, in other words, are literary as well as theatrical. I am not suggesting that Brian Friel has suffered through a resistance to his more literary writing but aspects of his work have been neglected for this reason. *Living Quarters* is a case in point. It is a seriously neglected work. On the other hand, there has been far less difficulty with that other literary feature of his plays: the use of stories or story-telling as a form of dramatic action.

I have tried to write elsewhere (*TLS*, March 1972) of the way in which the anecdote resides at the centre of Irish fiction giving a vocal rhythm to the Irish novel which has at least partially displaced the deep social preoccupation in classical fiction elsewhere. The fiction of Joyce, Flann O'Brien and Beckett is like a vast anthology of anecdotes, of voices constantly talking and telling, even to the point of dementia. And while our culture may have had no indigenous, native theatre prior to the eighteen-nineties it did have the seanchai, a distinctively histrionic artist with his repertoire, his own audience. It was inevitable with such an oral tradition that the told-tale should be subsumed not only into the literary short story (see Walter Benjamin on Leskov) but into the novel and emerging drama as well. Our classic play, *The Playboy of the Western World*, is not just a comedy about a story-teller and his story. It is also about the awesome effects upon his listeners when his story fails to pass the test of authenticity. It is a parable of the limitation of theatrical illusion. It is about that strange curtain which separates performance from actuality.

Brian Friel is a superb creator of story-tellers. They are not only expert in delivery, in all the skills of an actor in full-flight, mimicry, timing, playing upon the audience as upon an instrument – even their body language is enlisted in the way Friel has written the parts. Story-telling in Friel's plays may offer succour, consolation, relief, renewal but it can just as easily offer deception of the self, of others. Like every substantial writer of fiction, Friel has a healthy scepticism about the nature of fiction itself or at least the uses to which it can be put. Frequently the virtuoso story-teller in a Friel play is an outsider, his or her gift a kind of scar or wound, a misfortunate or fatal gift. More subtly than any other Irish playwright Friel has transcribed this national skill into the theatrical medium. That is why we often have to enlist a literary or quasi-literary vocabulary in talking about some of the plays.

Friel's complex attitude to his own culture, his celebration of it as well as his critique, may be seen to good effect here in his use of the patterns and cross-patterns of story-telling. Ours is a culture of gossip. It may partly account for our exceptional population of fiction readers and our splendid theatre audiences, particularly in rural Ireland. But such an appetite for the imaginative representation of life brings with it its own recoil. There is, for instance, the escape from the ugly factuality of life. The widening of this gap between the hyperbolic, the fanciful and the prosaic or earthbound may be comic or tragic. It is one of Brian Friel's main themes and the authority of the story-teller one of his main devices in the pursuit of it. Whole sections of dialogue in the plays appear to be composed of compacted story-telling, speaker vying with speaker, the dramatic conflict in the competitiveness between the different tellings. It is as if what is, is partial, incomplete, dissatisfying until refracted or filtered through this verbal athleticism.

Because both plays are plays of reunion, *Living Quarters* and *Aristocrats* are both made up of this story-telling grist. Each stage of present action has to be bolstered up or tempered by versions of what has happened in the past. When people come home they have stories to tell and stories to listen to. It is the process by which a family re-establishes its codes, a way of recovering intimacy. But this linkage provided by stories is extremely tenuous and can never get around the testing of feeling in the here and now. This is the hard bone running through both plays, the way in which Friel subjects stories and story-tellers to the strict demands of immediate plot.

Some items so recalled have a spectral, numinous or epiphanic quality like the picnic at Portnoo in *Living Quarters* or the mother's song in *Aristocrats*. Other recountings are more robust in the sense that they generate direct, even brutal conflict. There are, for example, the competing versions of the house's history in *Aristocrats*: the official history of patient

Tom's research, the funny, hysterical ramblings of Casimir, the hurt, angry, street subversiveness of Eamon. The much admired dying-fall at the end of this play is based upon the exhaustion of story-telling. There are no more stories to be told. Or the capacity to listen to them has gone. Willie, the comic outsider, attempts one and it stands like an interrogation mark in the air. The others drift into song, the song of a dead mother who cannot be recalled with sufficient clarity to make up an anecdote. Singing is like an aftertaste of feeling. But the song is a ballad; it, too, tells a story. Like Willie's anecdote it is a story which floats away on the air in diminuendo, a matter of inconsequence in the light of everything that has happened except that it catches perfectly the unwinding of the bonds between those people on the stage.

Faith Healer, in my view, is the one theatrical text of our time which unmistakably takes its place with the best of Beckett or Synge or the Yeats of *The Herne's Egg* and *Purgatory*. That is to say, it is a sublime work of the imagination in which the distinction between theatrical text and literary artefact ceases to be of account. It is profoundly affecting and intellectually satisfying both in the theatre and within the individual mind of the reader. This is but another way of remarking upon the play's formal perfection, the perfect congruence of passionate feeling and the controlling mind of a first-rate artist. Very few plays are written with this high degree of literary skill. Even the very best of them too often show their stage effects, marvellously effective, indeed, within the sounding chamber of the theatre but contrived and rhetorical on the cold page. In part, the consummate writing in *Faith Healer* is the more evident because Friel has consciously eschewed the usual notion of what dramatic action should be, the direct inter-play between characters. Instead he offers four monologues that are allowed to stand in austere, frontal engagement with the audience.

There has been a persistent tendency in modernist literature towards the monologue, the elimination, the erasure of others, of the Other. Speech pruned of answers. A retreat into privacy, that most valued, most sought after and most threatened condition in our century. *A Portrait of the Artist as a Young Man* ends in the privacy of Stephen's journal. *Dubliners* ends within the dwindling and yet rapidly expanding consciousness of Gabriel Conroy. *Ulysses* ends with the monologue of Molly Bloom. *Finnegans Wake* is the total monologue which has subsumed all other voices into itself, a great mastication and/or regurgitation of words. This retreating in Joyce is a paradigm of one important strand of twentieth-century fiction and an equally important one of its drama.

Finnegans Wake, in its histrionics, exemplifies two recurrent features of the theatrical monologue: its self-containment and its obsessiveness. Both present severe technical problems to the playwright. The hermetic, excluding nature of monologue is inherently nondramatic. Friel deals with this by making his three witnesses give conflicting evidence on the same events. It is like a serial Chinese puzzle. If you believe one witness of the three you cannot believe the other two. All are given to omission, partial truths or downright lying. The important thing is not whether the statements are true or false but the degree of falsehood and its motivation, whether the deceits are self-serving or other-serving, black, white or grey. The creation of this nest of evasion and concealment is critical to Friel's purpose in the play.

A monologue is a worrying of hidden or half-hidden obsessions into conscious life, that is to say, into speech. In Friel's play, not unexpectedly, these obsessions are those of the story-teller. In an earlier draft the play consisted of a single monologue, more or less that first monologue as it now exists in the finished, published play. That early monologue, however, did include a shortened version of the end of the present play, the dawn encounter in the yard with McGarvey and the wedding guests. In the further writing, Friel detached this from the opening monologue, postponing it for effect to the end of the play.

What are missing from that first draft, however, are the two nuggets, the two haunting stories of the completed play: the miracle, if such it was, in the old Methodist Hall at Llanbethian and the bloody miscarriage at Kinlochbervie. In discovering these through the process of writing, Friel broke through the fixity of the single monologue into a form of engagement between the three characters, even if that engagement or sharing is the source of contradiction. There are differing versions of these incidents offered by Frank, Grace and Teddy. The versions contradict or modify one another. Yet the play in its totality is an assurance of an essential truth in each monologue: the transcendent heights to which Hardy's art can aspire and the squalid shit to which he can descend as a man.

To be theatrical a monologue has to possess its audience as a confidant. The literary analogy is the Browning dramatic monologue where meaning, if it is to exist, is a product of shared consciousness between the speaker and reader and the hidden, ventriloquial poet. In the theatre persuasion must come not only through the voice but also through the scene. What scene does a single speaking voice inhabit? Where can it achieve greatest credibility but where the stage is a stage, no more, no less? This autonomous space, reflecting nothing beyond itself, this Nowhere Land dressed with a few props is where the monologue . . . is best situated as it is, with differing levels of artistry, in Beckett, Shepard and Pinter. Here are the *Faith Healer* stage-directions:

The stage is in darkness. Brief pause.
Then out of this darkness comes FRANK'S *incantation,* '*Aberarder, Aberayron . . .*' *At the end of the second line bring up lights very slowly . . .*

Three rows of chairs – not more than fifteen seats in all . . .
Note: Stage directions have been kept to a minimum.

We discover GRACE HARDY *on stage, the same set as Part One, with the rows of seats removed. She is sitting on a wooden chair beside a small table . . .*

We discover TEDDY *on stage . . . sitting beside the table – the same table as in Part Two; but* TEDDY's *chair is more comfortable than* GRACE's *. . .*

The poster is gone. The set is empty except for the single chair across which lies Frank's coat exactly as he left it in Part One. We discover Frank standing down stage left, where we left him.

Friel's scenes are set, respectively, in one of the Faith Healer's drab halls, in Grace's digs on Limewood Grove, in Teddy's equally awful digs on some other Grove or Crescent just around the corner in London. The Hardy poster presides over the first three scenes, Grace and Teddy share the same table and there is a general melting of particulars one into other the way reality bleeds into fiction, fiction bleeds into reality. In the end one has to concede that all the scenes simply happen upon a stage, that the naturalistic props are like remnants from another life beyond, deposited upon a stage to facilitate an enactment before an audience. In this way Friel elevates *Faith Healer* above conventional naturalism. He also lifts it out of conventional time and lodges it in artificial stage time where the improbable is possible and where credibility can be created without corroboration. This accounts for one of the more poignant details of this play. Two of these voices are from beyond the grave. One conducts us with icy style towards his own horrible destruction. The other makes it perfectly clear why her suicide was inevitable. The MC who survives to preside over all this, the work's stage-manager, another of Friel's choric presences, is a tatty, vulgar man of quite extraordinary fidelity, in other words a fit-up Prospero, the spirit of Theatre itself.

Finally, to the nub of the play. This is a play about one of the most disturbing paradoxes in art, one which has bothered people throughout the history of civilization. It may be best stated interrogatively: how is it that persons of ugly, sordid even depraved character, persons with apparently no redeeming features in their personal lives are capable of creating great redeeming beauty in art, works of sustaining spiritual resource? Or, more temperately, why is it virtually impossible to connect the integrity of the work to the deviousness and pettiness of its creator? The whole style of *Faith Healer*, in particular its use of the ambiguities of story-telling, is based upon this crux. Art is, indeed, created out of concealment, illusion, fictiveness, a conscious reinvention of the self. If it is spun out of the common dross of the individual the web has such a finished, tensile and beautiful distancing from its source that its source is completely hidden. *Faith Healer*, in its bleak fashion, will not allow this forgetfulness. The bloodied, abandoned woman, the black foetus on the side of the road and the white healing hands are offered as part of the same ferment. From an entirely different angle the play is nevertheless a gloss on that great question in Herbert's poem 'Jordan (I)' on the mysterious deceit, the mysterious art, of false hair and painted chair.

The 1999 Friel Festival brochure ended with the following brief fable. Its quiet lyricism, and his own pertinent comment upon it, distil both the ambition and the achievement of Brian Friel's work.

Kitezh, by Brian Friel

There is a Russian folk-tale about a mythical town called Kitezh.

The story goes that when Kitezh sensed that marauders were approaching, it encased itself in a mist and shrank into it and vanished from sight. But even as it disappeared, even after it had disappeared, the church bell never stopped ringing and could be heard through the mist and over the whole country-side.

I suppose like all folk-tales this story can be interpreted in whatever way your needs require. But for me the true gift of theatre, the real benediction of all art, is the ringing bell which reverberates quietly and persistently in the head long after the curtain has come down and the audience has gone home. Because until the marauders withdraw and the fog lifts, that sacred song is the only momentary stay we have against confusion.

Select Bibliography

Critical studies

Andrews, Elmer, *The Art of Brian Friel – Neither Reality nor Dreams*, Macmillan, 1995.

Dantanus, Ulf, *Brian Friel – A Study*, Faber and Faber, 1987.

Dymoke, Sue, and Maurice Quirke, *Translations – Critical Reading at post-16*, National Association for the Teaching of English and York Publishing Services, 2000 (a stimulating book, devised and written by teachers for teachers, but full of insights for anybody interested in the play, and offering a model of how to approach any Friel play).

Grene, Nicholas, *The Politics of Irish Drama: Plays in Context from Boucicault to Friel*, Cambridge University Press, 2000.

Jones, N., *Brian Friel – Philadelphia, Here I Come!, Translations, Making History, Dancing at Lughnasa*, Faber Critical Guides, 2000 (an excellent starting point for anybody familiar with any of her four chosen plays).

Maxwell, D. E. S., *Brian Friel*, Bucknell University Press, Lewisburg, PA, 1973.

Pine, Richard, *Brian Friel and Ireland's Drama*, Routledge, 1990.

Anthologies

The narrative of chapter 2 of this book is peppered with material trawled from these two indispensable anthologies of interviews with, and other material about, Brian Friel. There is some overlap between the material offered in these two collections.

Brian Friel – Essays, Diaries, Interviews 1964–1996, ed. Christopher Murray, Faber and Faber, 1999.
Brian Friel In Conversation, ed. Paul Delaney, University of Michigan Press, 1999.

The following are rather more esoteric collections of essays about particular aspects of Friel and Irish literature, but full of fascinating material, including the Kilroy and Dowling essays reprinted above.
Brian Friel – A Casebook, ed. William Kerwin, Garland Publishing, New York, 1997.
Irish University Review, special edition on Brian Friel, 1999.
The Achievement of Brian Friel, ed. Alan Peacock, Colin Smythe, Gerrard's Cross, 1993.

Bibliographies

O'Brien, George, *Brian Friel – A Bibliography*, Gill amd Macmillan, Dublin, 1995 (an essential sourcebook for the dedicated Friel student).

Irish history, culture, literature and drama

Deane, Seamus, *A Short History of Irish Literature*, Hutchinson, 1986.
Deane, Seamus (ed.), *The Field Day Anthology of Irish Writing*, 1991.
Fitz-Symon, Christopher, *Irish Theatre*, Thames & Hudson, 1983.
Hederman and Kearney (eds.), *The Crane Bag – Book of Irish Studies*, Blackwater Press, Dublin.
Hogan, Robert, *After the Irish Renaissance*, Macmillan, 1968.
Kee, Robert, *Ireland – A History*, Abacus, 1980 (the book of the major BBC/RTE series).
Kenneally, Michael (ed.), *Cultural Contexts and Literary*

Idioms in Contemporary Irish Literature, Colin Smythe, Gerrard's Cross, 1988.

Lee, Josephine, 'Linguistic Imperialism, the Early Abbey Theatre and the Translations of Brian Friel', in *Imperialism and Theatre: Essays on World Theatre Drama and Performance*, ed. J. Ellen Gainor, Routledge 1995.

McHugh and Harmon, *A Short History of Anglo-Irish Literature*, Wolfhound Press, Dublin, 1982.

Richtarik, Marilynn J., *Acting Between the Lines: The Field Day Theatre Company and Irish Cultural Politics 1980–1984*, Oxford English Monographs, 1995 (the essential book for studying Field Day).

Worth, Katherine, 'Translations of History: Story-Telling in Brian Friel's Theatre', in *British and Irish Drama Since 1960*, ed. James Acheson, Macmillan, 1993.

Broadcasts

Arena: 'Field Day', BBC2, dir. Andrew Eaton, TX: 16/12/88.

'Brian Friel', Ferndale Films for BBC Northern Ireland and RTE, dir. Sinead O'Brien, TX (Ireland): 21/12/01; TX (UK): 20/4/01.

'From Ballybeg to Broadway', Ferndale Films for BBC and RTE, dir. Donald Taylor Black, TX: 1993

'Profile of A Playwright', BBC Northern Ireland, dir. G. P. McCrudden, TX: 12/8/84.

Acknowledgements

I would like to thank the following for their help: John Collis, librarian at Rose Bruford College, Alan Lambert at BBC Education, Judy Friel at the Abbey Theatre Dublin, and Friel's artistic collaborators whose contributions are in this book. My apologies to others of his collaborators who gave me their time but whose no less interesting contributions did not make it into the book for reasons of space.

For permission to reprint copyright material the publishers gratefully acknowledge the following:

BYRNE, CATHERINE: pp. 151–8, 1999 interview transcribed with the permission of Catherine Byrne. DELANEY, PAUL ed.: *Brian Friel in Conversation*, extracts published with the permission of the University of Michigan Press. DOWLING, JOE: 'Staging Friel' © Joe Dowling, 1992 published in *The Achievement of Brian Friel*, ed. Alan Peacock, reproduced here by permission of the author and Colin Smythe Ltd. EATON, ANDREW dir. *Arena*: Field Day, BBC2, first transmitted 16 December 1988. KILROY, THOMAS: 'Theatrical Text and Literary Text' © Thomas Kilroy 1992, published in *The Achievement of Brian Friel* ed. Alan Peacock, reproduced by permission of the author and Colin Smythe Ltd. LAMBERT, MARK: pp. 158–67, 1999 interview transcribed with the permission of Mark Lambert. MASON, PATRICK: *Dancing at the Abbey* © Patrick Mason, 1999, *The Road to Ballybeg*, reprinted with the permission of Rosaleen Linehan, Niall Buggy, Conall Morrison and Brian Brady, 1999. MCCANN, DONAL: pp. 167–8, 1999 interview reproduced with the permission of Donal McCann. MURRAY, CHRISTOPHER ed.

Essays, Diaries, Interviews 1964–1996, Faber and Faber 1999.
STEINER, GEORGE: *After Babel: Aspects of Language and Translation*, Oxford University Press, 1976,

Faber and Faber Limited apologize for any errors or omissions in the above list and would be grateful to be notified of any corrections that should be incorporated in the next edition or reprint of this volume.

Index